The Spirit Transcendent

The Spirit Transcendent

*Exploring the Extraordinary
in Human Experience*

Mark F. Yama

Jefferson, North Carolina

Everything in this book is based on the experiences of real individuals. Indeed, everything stated here is as true to my sources as my abilities allowed. However, for the sake of anonymity, all of the names have been changed, save those belonging to famous persons.

ISBN (print) 978-1-4766-8050-7
ISBN (ebook) 978-1-4766-3918-5

LIBRARY OF CONGRESS AND BRITISH LIBRARY
CATALOGUING DATA ARE AVAILABLE

Library of Congress Control Number 2020007230

© 2020 Mark F. Yama. All rights reserved

No part of this book may be reproduced or transmitted in any form or by any means, electronic or mechanical, including photocopying or recording, or by any information storage and retrieval system, without permission in writing from the publisher.

Front cover image © 2020 Kichigin/Shutterstock

Printed in the United States of America

Toplight is an imprint of McFarland & Company, Inc., Publishers

*Box 611, Jefferson, North Carolina 28640
www.toplightbooks.com*

To those who have the need—
and the courage—
to find the truth for themselves

Acknowledgments

As you might imagine, the writing of a book like this has been quite the journey, and I myself would never have guessed it would take about nine years from inception to completion. I am indebted to many, first and foremost to my spiritual clients and friends who were my real educators. I apologize to them for the use of pseudonyms because, almost without exception, they would have preferred me to use their actual names. A second apology is due to all of those who trusted me with important spiritual experience but did not appear in the final draft. They should know that every story told to me did make an important contribution, although often in ways invisible. I'm grateful for the help of my students who were at work making transcriptions of the clinical material. Two, Emeric Thorpe and Alexandra Wilson, deserve special mention, for contributions that went far beyond. Then there were the readers at various stages of this work: I would like to mention Prof. Stephen Banks, early on; Fr. Joseph Schmidt, both at the beginning and toward the end; and Dean Andrew Kersten, somewhere in the middle. I thank Dr. Kersten especially for lending a supportive ear. Suzanne Ryan gave valuable advice from the perspective of a professional academic editor at a critical juncture. I would be remiss not to mention important editorial advice from my daughter, Danielle, who is on her own journey toward becoming a novelist. Through it all, my wife, Shelley, kept everything together and gave me the freedom to pursue this project, even through the long hours and what must have seemed, at times, to be an obsession.

Table of Contents

Acknowledgments	vi
Preface	1
ONE—The Witch of Orofino	5
TWO—Hallucinations of the Angelic Variety	20
THREE—Death and Transcendence	41
FOUR—At the Bottom Rung of the Ladder	57
FIVE—Theory of the Soul	69
SIX—Travels to the Collective Unconscious	81
SEVEN—The Gates of Heaven	93
EIGHT—The Christian God Meets the Great Spirit	110
NINE—Hallucinations of the Demonic Variety	127
TEN—Through a Glass Darkly	147
ELEVEN—Science and Spirituality	169
Chapter Notes	177
References	191
Index	197

"A little philosophy inclineth man's mind to atheism, but depth in philosophy bringeth men's minds about to religion."—Francis Bacon (1625)

Preface

What are we to make of firsthand reports of spiritual experience? The easiest answer is that there is nothing real about them and that they are merely examples of hallucination or delusion. As a clinical psychologist steeped in materialist scientific culture, I at first did not question this traditional explanation. However, either by chance or by fortune, I found myself in a setting where I was presented with story after story, none of which made sense given what we think we know about the workings of the material world. This book describes a personal journey where I ended up believing that materialism describes only a portion of reality. I was a most reluctant convert to this view, and I certainly did not begin with any set of religious beliefs, nor did I set out with the intention of proclaiming some message about spirituality.

It was about nine years ago that I began to receive stories of spiritual experience in my clinical practice. It began with one individual, Betty, whom I came to know deeply. She had a lifetime of visions, conversed with God as a personal friend, and constantly told me about miracles that had occurred during her life. A few months after meeting Betty, I had a religious experience of my own, modest by Betty's standards, but significant nonetheless. Then, perhaps because now I had ears to hear, it was as if a floodgate had opened and there were so many others who had to tell me about *their* experiences.

I did not seek these people out, and no one knew of my newfound interests in spirituality. There were no cues in the clinic where I worked, and the setting was pretty sterile: there were no religious pictures on the wall, no quotes about spiritual life, nothing at all that would prompt the patient. Yet I would arrive at work in the morning with no particular expectation, and then first off I would have a client tell me about the appearance of an angel; then another client, that same day, was excited to tell me all about a message they had received direct from God; another, about being attacked

Preface

by something evil; and later that week I would be told about a near-death experience, where it seemed as if a window had truly opened onto the transcendent.

All of it was completely unexpected. Once I realized what was happening around me, I began to record these stories. Pretty soon, I began recording spiritual material whenever it arose. I began with an interest that was mostly intellectual: what I was hearing went against everything I had been taught and it interested and intrigued me. With time, as I became more involved, it began to seem that there truly were cracks in the foundation of accepted science, mystery upon mystery that only made sense if our material view of the world was incomplete. Once I owned up to the implications of what I was hearing, I felt as if I had turned into a kind of modern-day heretic, where, unlike the heretics of old, my particular sin was to disbelieve scientific dogma.

This book bears upon metaphysical questions, yet the tools that I use to try to provide answers to those questions are more scientific than they are philosophical. In other words, I am in the curious position of using data, albeit the data of individual experience, to try to answer questions that are not yet in the domain of psychology. However, questions like these—whether materialism defines all of reality; questions of the existence and nature of the spirit; and the problem of survival after death—have not always been the sole concern of theology and philosophy. In the late 1800s there was the hope that a scientific approach could give definitive answers to these age-old problems. Those days witnessed the formation of the Society for Psychic Research, composed not of cranks or crackpots, but of highly respected academics and scientists, William James among them, who committed themselves to the pursuit of scientific understanding of spiritual matters regardless of the risks to their personal reputations. Some of the results of the Society's research did seem to powerfully challenge the material view. Most often those observations were in the form of individual case examples concerning events of great salience to the person involved—death of a loved one; threat to one's being; personal crisis—and it was here where the typical rules that guide the world seemed to break down.[1]

The similarity between the patients I have worked with and some of the subjects interviewed by members of the Society may not be coincidental. Many of my patients have faced personal tragedy of one kind or another; many have faced death. Some have had their heart stop, were resuscitated, and returned to life with a profoundly spiritual experience that

Preface

they had to tell. It was as if I was granted my very own laboratory for the investigation of extreme experience. However, the real surprise is not simply in the similarity in settings or in the kinds of subjects I interviewed: it is that my observations *replicate* many of the findings of the Society, most surprising among these being evidence for survival of the personality after death.[2] Other of my cases provide evidence for precognition, telepathy, and spiritual presence.

Because this book is about spirituality, it is important to be absolutely clear about the meaning of the term as it is used here. Often the term "spiritual" is used merely to denote some form of religious belief. In this manner of speaking, reading the Bible is a spiritual practice because people read Bibles to learn about or to worship God. However, thinking about or even worshiping God is not incompatible with our material understanding of the world. Obviously, it is our material brain and the (presumably materially-based) human cognitive system that is doing the thinking, the understanding, and the worshiping. In contrast, the second use of the term "spiritual," and the way it is used here, implies something that is real but that is apart from, and possibly in conflict with, the material world. Grace itself, if it be something real, is spiritual in the second sense.

I believe that science can be done in this difficult area, but clearly spirituality (and by that I mean the *core* of spirituality) is not something that can be brought into the laboratory to be measured and quantified. At the turn of the century, William James was able to illuminate the nature of this core aspect in his great work, *The Varieties of Religious Experience*.[3] James' approach was one where he gave priority to a collection of individual experiences, presented free of preconceived notions, and only later used those reports to abstract general principles. Nothing written since has yielded as deep an understanding as the *Varieties*, but I do not believe James' approach has been exhausted. An examination of cases, presented without bias and then later used in the service of theory, still has much to offer. This is the general approach used in this book.[4]

It is just because of the very radical (or even unbelievable) nature of the stories told here that I felt it extremely important to represent what was said to me as exactly as possible. I recorded almost all of my interviews, and typically the dialogue in the book is transcribed from those audio files. I did rearrange the order of the material for the sake of readability, and sometimes conversations gathered across several sessions appear in a single place. However, everything important is presented in my

Preface

patients' own words, using their own grammar and mode of expression. Everything you read is as faithful to the source as I could make it.

For good or ill relative to the ideal of scientific perspective, I have not been a neutral observer in what I am about to relate. I worked with the main persons that appear in this book for years, basically in a co-investigation of ultimate questions, and often we became great friends. As time went on, instead of meeting one on one in the traditional way common to clinical practice, I brought many of us together. The results were surprising to say the least. To my amazement, the natural sequence of events as they happened to me made up a story. A story which I will now attempt to tell.

One

The Witch of Orofino

For more than a dozen years, I consulted in a pain clinic about an hour's drive from the university where I teach. The clinic is in a small town in Northern Idaho; patients come from all walks of life, and many of the clientele are drawn from surrounding rural areas.[1] My role was to provide the psychological side of pain management. Most of my clients were not seriously disturbed in any way, but often they had reacted in understandable ways to the challenge of chronic pain and disability, and I tried my best to help them whenever I could.

On one particular day in October, several years ago, Betty was on my schedule. Before I actually sat down with Betty, I reviewed what was in the chart: 73 years old, survivor of three serious cancers. The first was colon cancer, successfully treated surgically 18 years ago, but requiring a colostomy. She was diagnosed with cancer a second time about eight years ago, an "infiltrating adenocarcinoma in the pelvic region," and was successfully treated with radiation. Then, about a year and a half ago, she was diagnosed with cancer for a third time—"metastatic rectal cancer spreading to the right iliac bone." She had radiation treatment and an extensive resection. Understandably, pain management continued to be a problem.

When Betty met with one of our physicians, she asked whether the clinic had someone who might treat her with biofeedback or some form of psychological treatment. This was how she was referred to me.

I greeted Betty in our waiting room. She had a caretaker with her, and I led the way to my office which is on one side of the clinic. Betty was a petite woman, right at about five feet tall. Everything about her spoke poverty. Her clothing looked like that of a homeless person: she was wearing several layers—a worn men's plaid shirt and a threadbare coat she never took off. Instead of a cane she used a crooked tree branch as a walking stick. She had the use of just one eye, the other having been closed since birth. Her choice of words was simple, and you could hear from the quality

The Spirit Transcendent

of her speech that she had no teeth and was not wearing dentures. And, as if she had just wandered out of the backcountry, there was a weathered black felt hat with a broad brim atop her head.

Betty's caretaker helped adjust a pillow beneath her, so she could sit in my chair more comfortably, and after some small talk, Betty began by telling me about how she was having a difficult time coping with pain. I was prepared for this, and we began by talking about how pain was a problem in Betty's life, how she coped with it, and if there were any other approaches that might be tried.

All of this was a fairly ordinary beginning. But it was not long into the session when Betty told me that where she lived, a little town by the name of Orofino,[2] people thought she was a witch. I don't remember, word for word, what she said to me in that first session, but a few sessions later I became so fascinated with Betty that I began making recordings. In one of our later meetings I had her go back and tell me the story again.

"So let's go back to what you told me about being called a witch. This was in Orofino, right?"

"Yeah, Orofino."

"Well, when was it?"

"I'd say sometime early '70s or thereabouts. I changed the old cabinet shop and made it into apartments. So this fella and his girlfriend wanted an apartment, so they rented one of the apartments. I told them when I saw this dog … they would have to take care of the dog; if they wanted to take it outside, they would have to do it on a leash, because I didn't have a fence up and I had some chickens running around." Betty explained that the dog continued to be a problem: "I had a little swing bridge that went across the crick, and the dog was very frightened of going across the bridge. So the guy would just let his dog out when he wanted to go out and do 'his job' … and on the way [back to the apartment] the dog would run down my chickens because it was a great big bird dog."

"Well, after the third day he let the dog out—I had a little Banta [Bantam] hen with six little baby chicks—and that last day he had gone out and had killed my Banta hen, and I couldn't find any of the baby chicks…. I knocked on the guy's door and I said he needed to take care of his dog that just killed my hen with the baby chicks—I was very upset about it. I wasn't going to charge him or anything like that; I just wanted to talk to him about it. And he came to the door, seeing I was upset—he's this big logger guy. And he started laughing at me, and I told him—I said, 'You better take care of your dog,' and I told him if he didn't, '*God would take care*

One—The Witch of Orofino

of his dog for him.' And then he laughed even more. And [the next thing that happened], because the door was open, the dog ran out of the house between his legs, and crossed in front of the building there. And I thought he would call his dog back. Well, he didn't. And the dog just went on a beeline right to the bridge, crossed the bridge, and out on to the highway on the other side of the creek. And lo and behold at the same time a great big logging truck come down, a big semi-kind of truck. And it hit that dog, just smashed it onto the highway, killed it deader than a doornail. And that guy was still laughing [until he saw what happened, and then] he broke down, he got this wild stare in his eyes and he took off running across the bridge to go check on his dog. Well, the guy on the truck had stopped his truck, but the dog was dead. He picked up his dog in his arms and brought him back across the bridge and laid it down in one of the flower beds. And he looked up at me. And by then I thought, 'Oh boy, I'd better get out of here,' and I took off up the hill. The next thing I knew I saw the guy go back across the bridge in his car on the other side of the bridge and he took off."

It seemed to me to be quite a stretch that this event alone could give Betty the reputation of being a witch. There had to be more to the story. And in this I was correct.

With a chuckle (or perhaps more like a toothless cackle), Betty continued: "Well, the next thing is, he [the renter] went down to the sheriff's office and reported me as a witch. And the sheriff came out to see me and asked me about what happened and so I told him just exactly what happened."

I was amazed and not a little entertained. I know Orofino might be a bit behind the times, but to think that even in the 1970s, a renter could report that his landlady was a witch and be taken *seriously* or at least seriously enough by this particular sheriff—well, this takes the term "backwards" to a whole new level.

"Well, did you actually curse the dog?" I asked, thinking that there might be a simple reason for being accused of witchcraft.

"No, I didn't have no time for no cursing of the dog," Betty replied, "I just told him, 'God would take care of it.' And I believed God would take care of it. And I know God, and the guy of course didn't know I know God like I do. And so the sheriff came out and talked to me about it. And I told him what happened, and he got the story from the other guy, you see. But you know, that guy never, never came back, not for anything in the apartment, or anything. He never showed his face again. And the story started going around town that I was a witch."

The Spirit Transcendent

"Well, had you done *anything else* that would get you that reputation?" I asked.

It turned out there *was* something else. "About a week later," Betty said, "I was walking down the street and the prosecuting attorney pulled over and said, 'Come on down, I want to talk to you in my office.' So I went to his office and went in there. And he started telling me I shouldn't practice witchcraft. And I couldn't put two and two together, why he was talking about witchcraft. I tried to tell him, 'I'm not a witch,' but he was not taking it, or not letting it sink in his head, the fact that I wasn't a witch. And he ran it on there for about an hour and a half telling me I shouldn't [practice witchcraft]. So, about then, I got tired of all his jangling on about witchcraft and about how I should obey the law, you know, yah yah yah, all such tales—but it all centered on to the fact that I shouldn't practice witchcraft. So I looked at him finally, when I got tired of listening to him, I looked right at him, I remember, and I told him, 'If you don't leave me alone,' I said, 'if you don't leave me alone, *I'm going to turn you into a toad.*' And he was sitting in the chair, and he put his hands on the desk in front of him and he looked me right in the eye, and his eyes started bulging out just like a frog, and then his hair started standing on end. And he pushed himself away from the desk and run out of that office just as fast as he could."

I was as interested as I was entertained. I remember, in that first session as I watched Betty tell her story, that I had the growing impression that she *really did* look like a witch, what with her one eye peering at me, her short stature, her crooked staff, and her arthritic fingers that seemed a match for the kinks in her walking stick. On top of this, what really completed the image was that black hat of hers with the broad brim. The only thing missing was a pointy top. I was charmed.

I suppose, in that first meeting with Betty, I was mostly humored. I did not yet take her seriously. At the time I assumed that when Betty said, "God took care of the dog" that there could be nothing behind it, certainly nothing having to do with God—that it was just a religious interpretation of chance events, even if the likelihood that this particular dog, at that particular moment, would choose to die by 18-wheeler seemed vanishingly small. But soon Betty began to give me other examples of God's intervention, and there were many.

When I met with her, it was the third time Betty was diagnosed with cancer. Each time, there was a different diagnosis, so each illness was independent of the other. Not only had Betty survived the cancer twice before,

One—The Witch of Orofino

each time she was pronounced terminally ill, and each time she was given a very low chance of survival. Betty told me, also in that first session of ours, that she was "healed by God." At the time, I expected she would tell me about some variety of "faith healing," but the story of how she came to be healed proved to be even more interesting.

Betty told me that she was cured because God sent messages to her on a continual basis about what she could and could not eat. In one phase of her illness she was told to eat "lots of broccoli"; during another, she was on a diet of watermelon; and for long stretches of time she existed pretty much on just peanut butter and some crackers. The cancer had "nothing to feed on," Betty told me. "It just stayed there like a lump on a log." Betty's messages from God were in the form of something she called the "telepathy language." She would receive a strong feeling of what she was allowed or was forbidden to do. It was a kind of prompting from outside of herself, exactly as if she was contending with another person's will, in this case, the will of God.

Here is an example of how it worked: Betty told me she used to enjoy ice cream and she had the habit, every time she got off work, of stopping at Dairy Queen to have either an ice cream cone or a Blizzard.

"Each time I went to get the ice cream," Betty explained, "God told me, 'No.'"

"Come on, God, let me have my ice cream."

"No, you can't." Betty folded her arms, like a parent might, in imitation of God.

"*Please—*"

After God had enough of Betty's nagging, He answered her in another way—not with another direct message, but with an event: Betty was at one of her medical appointments when "God led me to a magazine in the doctor's office, and there it was [in front of me] talking about a connection between cows given antibiotics and cancer." Soon after, Betty told me, "God is looking over my shoulder telling me 'no milk, no cheese,' and after that 'no, no, no pudding either.'" Then cookies were off the list, "because God told me I could not have my cookies," and when she pleaded again with Him to know why she had to give this up too, God directed Betty to yet another article, again in the doctor's office.

"It showed me refined sugar causes the T-cells in the body to go to sleep [so they cannot fight the cancer]. So I learned my lesson right there," Betty summed it up, "so I cut out eating sugar. I might use molasses or honey because it does not affect the T-cells."

The Spirit Transcendent

Within a few months, Betty, who was supposedly terminally ill, had no trace of cancer.

The coincidences were multiplying. I had no real explanation, at least not one that fit my bias that everything could be explained by material laws, without recourse to God or to spirituality. It was at the end of our second meeting, filled with as many surprises as the first, that Betty was to say something to me that would lead me to seriously reevaluate what I thought I knew.

Just as she was walking out the door, Betty picked up her cane, stabbed it in the air, pointing and poking in several directions, and said, darkly, "I can poke, poke, poke, and feel the future." She continued, "I have *seen you before*. Several years ago." And with that, she gave me a knowing nod. Thinking that this was just a case of my typical forgetfulness, I asked if perhaps we had worked together before, but I had forgotten her. But no, we had not met before in the clinic. Betty simply laid emphasis on the fact that it was "*many years* ago."

A session or two later, I found that when Betty said "many years ago," she was talking about a vision she had more than 50 years ago, when she was only 18 (*before* I was born). I was amazed and intrigued when she told me that she saw my name, "Yama," she saw my face, and God told her I would be "a great friend."

The last part of Betty's premonition turned out to be exactly true: after a few sessions I gave up the prospect of doing psychotherapy with Betty, but we kept meeting, about weekly, maybe for 80 visits, until she finally succumbed to her last bout of cancer. In the end, we *were* great friends.

By the time Betty told me about her vision of me, I had learned a good deal about her past. She spent her early years in poverty and her main job was working for her father as a goat shepherd, up in the mountains of Idaho. When she was 16, a couple of women from her church fixed her up with a pastor—Betty always referred to him as "Mr. Anderson"—but her parents were against the relationship. Just as soon as Betty turned 18 she married him anyway. Her parents were right about this man: the preacher, now her husband, turned out to be a tyrant who was physically abusive. A few months after they were married, Betty and her husband attended church. Betty had just sat down in the front pew when she had one of the major visions of her life. Because of its importance to my story, I present Betty's vision exactly as it was told to me, transcribed from audiotape.

One—The Witch of Orofino

I was in prayer in the front of the church. And as I was doing this, this sensation came kind of floating into me. And I felt this kind of cool breeze on my face. And I realized I was not where I thought I was and this cool breeze gave me the impression that I was moving, fast. I did not sense any other being with me; it could have been an angel taking me there.... I just felt this on my face, and the next thing I knew I was standing in this beautiful garden under this great big huge tree. And the leaves on the tree were all shaped like hearts and they were thick, like pieces of leather. The tree was tremendous. It went a-ways, and around the tree were things that came down from it and were anchored to the ground like another tree, growing up. And there was all these little trees growing around this huge tree. And then I was aware I was standing under this tree looking out into a clearing where there was grass, beautiful grass, and there was a breeze, and there was a pathway, and there were some seats out there, and there were shrubs and other trees, in the, in the background. And as I was looking around I was wondering to myself, "Where am I? What has happened here?"

And then my eyes lit upon this pair of sandaled feet in front of me, a-ways in front of me, and then immediately my eyes drifted upward, and I saw this beautiful silver blue, it was waving in the breeze—ah, silver—and it came to different tones of blue, [in the] robe, and my eyes went on up and I saw this reddish-brown beard, and my eyes went on up and I saw these eyes looking at me. They were like coals of fire almost, but yet they were not on fire, they just looked right through me—kind of a grayish light blue, brown color. Anyway, I was looking right in the face of Jesus and He smiled at me. And I kind of broke the ice [Betty let out a laugh] and I was scared, I didn't know where I was. Anyway, I—I think He realized that I was scared, and then He smiled, and then He said to me, He said, He thanked me, He said, "Thank you for your sacrifice of yourself to me. And, and, and to—to God." And He says, "I accept your sacrifice," and then, ah, we started backing down this pathway together, and as we were walking He was talking, and He was saying, "I'm going to tell you what I'm going to do with you—with your life." And he explained these different things that were going to happen to me. And all the time we were walking together and then we sit together on the little bench that was there—kind of gray concrete-like stuff—but I noticed that the grass was different than it was on Earth, the grass was—was *alive*; it moved and it was not like grass on the earth. It was a lighter green color, and I looked up and I saw there really was no sun; there was just a white-light glow that was not sunshine. And there was this breeze that was just nice; it was different. I knew I was in a different place. It was not on Earth. I *never seen* a place like that in my life.

Anyway, He was telling me about all these different things that was going to happen to me. And I don't know if He wanted me to tell you these things, but He said I was going to live in a big huge city—I was not going to be out in the hillside anymore with the goats, and how that I was going to do church work and different things in the church, and He showed me pictures. Kind of like you would in a TV, pictures [in which] He was showing me these different things that would happen in my life, and I'd say, "Oh, I can't do that." And He said, "The I AM will do it.[3] You don't have to do it. It will happen to *you*." All these different things. So I didn't do anything but just listen. I did not try to talk much—I had given myself to Him. Now He was telling me all these things He was going to do with my life.

The Spirit Transcendent

And I was saying, "OK, OK, OK, and all right, and I can't do that, but *I can't do that*," and He'd tell me "the 'I AM' will do it." And He told me, "You'll have many, many problems to overcome," and "You will have to do things different." I would not be doing things like earthly people do, I would be doing things different, but I said, "I can't do that," and He says, "Yeah, we'll show you how to do it."

Yeah, He is telling [me] I would know how to do these things, and, ah, [he told me about] being the nurse, and at that time I was not [yet] going to nursing school—at that time—but He was showing me pictures of me being the nurse and doing this, that, and the other thing. And [He also told me] of being with Mr. Anderson, and not being able to do what I wanted to do—I always had to do what he [Anderson] wanted me to do ... and [He told me about] having my children. And showing me the different people and the different things in my life I would do. And how I would have 10 husbands, and I said, "Oh my, I can't do that! You are only supposed to have one husband, and be true to him." And He said, "This man is not your husband; he is a slave driver."

At this, Betty burst into laughter at the thought she would be speaking directly with God and He would come out and just flatly state that her actual husband was "a slave driver." Betty then went on to tell me how all these predictions had come true, one after the other, throughout her life, with the exception of a few at the end of the series, presumably because she had just not lived to fulfill them. She assured me that these too would happen in time. In fact, although Betty was not literally married 10 times, she did have 10 significant relationships with men (in the vision she told me, "I saw all their faces"), and she did in fact spend many years as a nurse. It was somewhere in this series of visions that I myself was represented: "I saw your name, I saw your face, and I knew we would become great friends."

Betty told me the conclusion to her vision. "Next thing I know I was standing in the Garden.... I was talking with Jesus and He told me I 'had to go back.'" "Okay," Betty continued with a laugh. "I really didn't want to go. Again, I did not feel or see angels. I felt that cool breeze on my face like I was traveling fast. Then I was in my body again."

"My husband was trying to wake me up. He was shaking me fiercely. He was saying, 'Wake up, wake up—stupid thing going to sleep at the altar.' That's what he did, and I tried to tell him what happened. He says, 'Oh, you're just dreaming; you just went to sleep.'" With this Betty laughed again, "like it couldn't be anything else," amused at the irony that her preacher husband would fail to grasp the true nature of what had happened to her.

Psychologically speaking, when Betty had her vision she was in a trance state. Naturally, the skeptic in me had difficulty accepting Betty's vision at face value, coming as it did from an altered state of consciousness.

One—The Witch of Orofino

Was it *really* Jesus, or was Jesus simply manufactured by Betty's mind? This is why the conclusion of Betty's story is so important—because spiritual events continued to present themselves to her, even in normal, waking consciousness. Here is how it unfolded.

> Then we left the church, there was no one else in the church, everyone else had gone home. We drove somewhere, it was around Spokane, and we had to go—no hotel or motel—it was somebody's house. And there was this great big, long living room, or dining room with a great big table and chairs on both sides, and there was great big windows on both sides. And on all the windows there were blinds, you know, the kind you pull back. And it was dark because it was nighttime. And Mr. Anderson says, "I can't park here. You go on in and I will park the car and walk back." And I went in and I stood by the end of the table. I put my Bible down on the end of the table. I started to take off my coat. And I was [having] a feeling of eeriness, like there was a spook here, somewhere—that was the sensation I felt. And I thought, "Oh boy, I wonder what that is." And all of a sudden, as I was standing there, all of the blinds went zip, zoom—scared me half to death. What's going on here? I knew they were supposed to be pulled down, so I went around, and I pulled them back down. I went over to where my Bible was, and as I soon as I stopped [by my Bible] they all went flying up again. All of them! It scared me. I said, "All right, God, why is this happening to me?" And I went around, and I said to myself, "If I pull them all back down again—I was talking to God at the same time—I said, now if they all fly up again, I will know it's you." And I went back, and I stood right there by my Bible again, and just about the same time I got there they all flew up again! I said, "OK, God, I know it's you," I said, "I know it's your power," and He said, "Yes, it's my power." He said, "Don't ever forget, I can do *anything.*"
>
> God was saying, "This is my power." And all I could do is *shake*. And I said, "Thank you, God, thank you, God, for showing me this. I will never forget it." And, of course, I never have forgotten it. Then we went to the bedroom and went to sleep, I guess. But my whole body and everything just felt so full of God's spirit, or the spirit inside of me was just overflowing with joy—that's the only way you can describe it. It was a warm sweet sensation of God being so close to me and He was so happy with me, that I was—that I had given myself to Him and He told me what He was going to do with me, and He showed me all, many, many things. And I said to Him, "I can't do these things, God." And He said, "The I AM would." And a lot of the things have come true.

The problem with visions is they are so completely internal. I think of Betty as coming from of a long line of mystics, all of whom were convinced they had tapped into another reality.[4] But who is to say? Yet Betty had other visions—visions of the future—that *did* have an anchor in reality, our reality, because they predicted things that *actually happened*. When Betty was poke, poke, poking with her walking stick, telling me she could *feel* the future, she was dead serious.

On May 18, 1980, Mount St. Helens erupted. It was a catastrophic

The Spirit Transcendent

event where the upper 1340 feet of the mountain was blown away and 1.4 billion cubic yards of ash was sent into the sky.[5] There was complete darkness in the city of Spokane 250 miles to the east. At about the same distance of 250 miles, to the southeast where Betty was living at the time, prevailing winds caused a particularly dense plume of ash to be centered right at her location, depositing a layer on the ground three to six inches in depth.

Betty knew beforehand that Mount St. Helens was going to erupt; she told me about this in one of our early sessions, and in a later session I asked her for more details about her vision.

"You remember when you had the premonition of when Mount St. Helens blew?" I asked. "When was it?"

"It was about five years before it happened."

"Was it a vision, or a dream? What was it?"

"It was just a vision. I asked a question. That's how I get my visions, by asking questions, mentally. Thoughtforms will come and I'll say, 'Well, I wonder, you know.' And, uh, well, I remember as a child we went past Portland, and over in that area somewhere is where Mount St. Helens is. And I said, 'Oh, that's such a beautiful mountain,' you see. And then we went on by. But I was *interested* by it. And it's out in No Man's Land, by the mountains, you see. Then the years went by, and every once in a while I'd think about that beautiful mountain. And somehow or another it clicked in my mind to ask about this mountain. And then when I was looking, I saw in a vision this mountain exploding. And how the sky went dark. And even the sun was blotted out. You couldn't see the sun."

"You actually saw all of this?" I was interested in how Betty's visions developed. "Was it like a snapshot, or what?"

"Ah, yeah, yeah, you see, visions don't always come all at once, you see. But you see something and then you will ask more questions about it, for greater detail. And that's what happens sometimes.... God was saying this mountain was about to explode, and it was going to get dark and everything. And then I asked God another question. How is this going to affect my goats? You see, I was *concerned* about it. And then God showed me that the goats were all covered with this silvery thing."

The "silvery thing" was the ash that blanketed everything. Livestock did die, mainly sheep and cattle. Here is what Betty actually experienced, five years after her vision.

"And then, you see, after the mountain blew, my goats were all tied up at the hillside and couldn't come in. And I had to run out and get the goats and bring them in. And I recall, you see, going out and bring[ing] in these goats, and the sun was getting darker and darker, all the time because of the dust in the air. And I remember holding a cloth over my face and trying to untie the goats and get them into the shelter. And here they were just silver color, with dust."

I had no reason to doubt Betty's story. There was no hidden motivation in her telling it to me, and the story itself was always exactly the same every time she told it, so it was clear Betty was relaying a memory. And not only that, but some parts of the vision ("goats covered by a silvery thing") only made sense *after* the actual event came to pass. The only problem is that there is no physical way to account for it! To me, such a glaring failure in our knowledge of the physical world was very troubling.

The only alternative is that it was coincidence. Okay, but without going into a statistical calculation, would you believe in Betty if this happened to her a second time? And if a second vision was true, and chance still seems to you to be the more plausible explanation, how about half a dozen times? This is why I found Betty so challenging. She had not just one, not two, but a lifetime of glimpses into the future.[6]

"I started having visions when I was about 20. At first it was if something would go by in a flash. Something would flash by and I realized it was a picture. I would say, 'Oh God, where did it go?' And I realized these flashes were something that actually happened later in my life, perhaps a month or two later."

Betty gave me more specific examples of her premonitions: "Between two weeks and one month before the assassination of JFK, I was at work in the mental hospital. I had a horrible feeling come over me that something would happen to him. I asked God what would happen, and I saw him in the motorcade."

"Before 9/11, I was in the library looking up something about towers. I wanted to know which were the highest towers in the world. This was two weeks before 9/11. I found there was one in China, and the ones in New York. Then I had an image of a game [this was like a video game] where planes were hitting the towers. I said to myself that something was going to try to hit one of those buildings. The reason was to knock the towers down, so they would not be higher than the one in China."

Betty also had a premonition about the *Challenger* disaster. In one of our meetings I had the opportunity to get the details. "Fifteen minutes before the launch of *Challenger*," Betty said, "I knew that something was terribly wrong. I had the sensation that they should not go. I tried to call

The Spirit Transcendent

NASA, but I could not get through. Later I wrote to them to suggest that we set up something so I can call if I know something will happen."

"Can you give me a sense of how you got that prediction, how it came to you—were you just watching TV and then all of a sudden you knew? Or what happened?"

"Yeah, we were all excited watching it shoot up into the sky, the kids and I were all sitting there in front of the TV watching it and I immediately felt this pressure."

"It was pressure?"

"Kind of a pressure that was saying, 'Uh oh, they shouldn't go.' This should not happen, you know, and I knew something terrible was going to happen and then I got on the phone and I tried calling them and I couldn't get through to them."

"So you felt strong enough you had to get on the phone right away?"

"Yup, yeah.... Before it went.... Before it went blasting.... And so I was calling and telling, trying to get through to them and they went ahead, you see, and did the different steps, you see, on the TV. I was watching them on the TV and even though I was having these terrible sensations and trying to get through to them, and they were lighting it up, and boom it went up into the sky, you know, and everybody was watching it. And we saw it sizzle and fall down. And that was the end of it. But I never could get through to them. The telephone operators—maybe there was just too much [call volume], or they were busy minding something. Anyway, I felt terrible bad about it, and the kids, you know, were watching it; we all felt bad about what happened."

Betty actually called NASA again, sometime later, trying to convince them that they "should set something up" so the next time she had a premonition, she could actually get through to them. She was frustrated when they brushed her off.

Later, I talked with Betty about the burden of having the gift of premonitions yet at the same time being disbelieved. She told me, "But I wish that people would believe me and trust what I had to say. See, it's because people in the past laughed at me and wouldn't do things or check on things. And they wouldn't believe me. So now I say why put forth the effort? Because they won't believe me. It's just a lot of stupidity, you know, that nobody's going to do anything anyway, even if I say something. So it's my own thoughts anymore—that why do it? And I came to that point where I was talking to God about it, I just says, 'Don't tell me things anymore.' Because why tell me, and why show me these things that are going

One—The Witch of Orofino

to happen, because what *good* does it do? See, I couldn't tell other people, and other people wouldn't listen even if I told them, and they wouldn't do anything about it anyway. And so God just kind of turned it off not to bother me with it."

I can see how people might have reacted to Betty. She so easily could be seen—with her threadbare, layered clothing, having no teeth and not caring to wear (or being able to afford) dentures, and that crooked staff of hers—as just a crazy old woman. Few would take seriously her insistence that she knew God seriously or that He had become her personal friend. I started out no better than Betty's neighbors because of the bias of my training and my assumptions about science.

Betty changed my mind about what I thought I knew. I believed she could actually see the future, at least at times. If that were possible, could her other visions be true also? Then the vision of Jesus could be real too, although perhaps in a reality different than that of our material world.

This was my reasoning at the time. Then something happened to me that was not at all on an intellectual level. I had a spiritual experience of my own! I always wondered if working with Betty had something to do with it and that she was somehow the key. I will say this, though: my experience came over me unbidden. It was overwhelming, and it seemed not of this world.

Here is how it happened: I was driving to work one morning in February, some four months after my first meeting with Betty. My thoughts first wandered to a book of science fiction, *Illium* by Dan Simmons.[7] It's a great and complex novel, and it works in the Greek gods as characters in the story, intermixed with references to Shakespeare. I found myself musing over a theme from the novel, that perhaps the gods themselves could have been the creation of human genus, of men like Shakespeare and Homer. Basically, the idea was that great art, a product of the human mind and human history, could make a god, and that these gods, like the characters in Simmons' *Illium*, could actually become real.

As I continued on my drive, my next thought was that Christ could appear anywhere. He could be incarnated in the most humble person, a person like Betty, and it was important to see beyond the humble origins and not be put off by them. I suppose 2000 years ago the same could have been said of Jesus, who was also of humble origins. He too was probably disregarded by the members of the upper class in his time, the philosophers, the powerful, and the literate.

And then, driving along, the thought occurred to me that God could

The Spirit Transcendent

be in me but also that I could be in God too. This thought then became more concrete. It went from a thought to a direct sensation, that God *was* in me and that at the same time I *was* in God too.

Some months later I came across a saying of the 13th-century German mystic, Meister Eckhart: "The eye through which I see God is the same eye through which God sees me; my eye and God's eye are one eye, one seeing, one knowing, one love."[8] In another of his sermons Eckhart said: "God's ground is my ground and my ground is God's ground."[9] This captures better than I can possibly express what I felt was happening to me.

When I arrived in town I spent some time in an eatery where I often stop to have coffee. I wrote a bit about what I was experiencing (my description is from my notes). I had the feeling that I was being touched by a divine spark, and another part of my perception was that whatever this was, it was really transcendent, that it really was something *other*.[10]

I am not devoutly religious, but on instinct I decided to drive to my church, as it seemed to be the best place to be. All this while, I felt overcome by what was happening, so I had to pay particular attention to just the act of driving, feeling as if I might go off the road. Then, as I sat in the empty church, the feeling that had come over me developed more fully. An older gentleman crossed the space in front of the altar, opened the tabernacle, and took a moment to pray. I had a sense of everything being open, of *being* in its barest sense.[11] There was a direct, immediate perception, mixed with awe, that whatever this thing was, it was good by nature. Goodness was its *essence*. In awe, I felt myself asking, "What *is* this?" There was an answer that was half produced from within my own mind: "I am who I AM."

At the time I felt I was given direct knowledge. I looked at the architectural lines inside the church, how the space was pointed upwards, and I thought of it, intuitively, as a reaching toward God. I felt that there was meaning in this, and that it was that the church was shaped by the holy, but at the same time that it was blind. It seemed to me that all the rites, all the efforts at worship, and all the words in the Bible missed the essence of God. What I was touched by was on an entirely different level. Sitting there in church, I thought of the phrase "manna from Heaven," and how on the mundane level a reader of this passage in the Bible could interpret the miracle of manna on a physical level, as being kept from starvation by food falling from the sky. But face to face with the experience of it all, I saw the meaning of manna as being about grace itself.

One—The Witch of Orofino

Most people would first entertain that what I experienced was the product of imagination or perhaps of wishful thinking. However, all I can say is that I am certain this cannot be true. I did ask Betty about it—did she think my experience was enabled by her, or could it at least be influenced by her? She said, simply and bluntly, "It had nothing to do with me. That was from God." When I persisted in my questions, Betty did allow that she might be involved indirectly, to the extent of showing me "that such a thing was possible."

At the very least, I am not alone. St. Teresa is a perfect example. She wrote about an experience that seemed exactly like mine and called it an "intellectual vision." Trying to describe it to her confessor, she wrote: "I see Him neither with the eyes of the body nor those of the soul." She understood she was not having a human visual experience, and she did not see God in any particular form. Yet, she went on to write, "how is it that I can understand and maintain that He stands beside me, and be *more certain of it than if I saw Him*?"[12] For St. Teresa, the sense of reality was direct and immediate, just in the way I experienced it.

After working with Betty for a short time, strange to say, I encountered many other clients with their own spiritual stories to tell. It was even pretty amusing: I would go to work expecting to do pain psychotherapy, and by the time I left for the evening I found I had been investigating visions, spirit guides, and talks with angels, related by several of my patients, all in the same day. And there was nothing to cue these patients—the clinic was your basic professional, sterile medical setting: no religious pictures hanging on the wall, nothing of the sort. Although by now I was working on a book, *not a single client* knew of my interests beforehand. Spiritual stories simply came up in the course of my ordinary work.

Again, it is easy to pass it off as coincidence. But I have wondered if Betty might have been at work on a spiritual level and that there was some reason all of these spiritual stories seemed to find me. Betty had a deep wish, to get people to know that the spirit was real and ought to be cultivated. It was the key to immortality, she believed. But how to get the message across? Betty had tried and tried but was always dismissed as crazy or as a crank. Telling people about the spirit was like "digging in concrete with a plastic spoon," she told me. But now that we had met, she thought that perhaps there was hope. Maybe I could be the one to deliver the message. "My hind-ender led me to you," Betty told me, speaking of her rectal pain from metastatic cancer. "And that's the way God works!"

Two

Hallucinations of the Angelic Variety

Betty, after all, is just one person. Her stories, remarkable as they were, were from a single source. I might have been able to file my encounter with Betty away and rest undisturbed if it were not for the fact that, after having found Betty (or perhaps after she found me), I was visited by so many others, all with spiritual stories to tell. They came to me unbidden, without any direct searching on my part. Perhaps, I thought, as I went about my clinical work, there were all of these experiences waiting to be unlocked, and often I was sitting right next to them, but until now I was not sensitive enough to tune into what a client was trying to say. Only after my own spiritual experience did they emerge, now that I had eyes to see and ears to hear. Maybe the stories were there all along and there was something in my manner, picked up consciously or even unconsciously by the client, that said, "You had better not tell *him* that; he'll think I'm crazy." But now they were popping up, seemingly all over the place.

Damon, a 16-year-old boy I interviewed along with his father, Erik, was one of many examples. I was cued, during an ordinary interview, when Damon announced, "See those scars? I got those when I heard the voice of God and ignored it."

Damon looked like a typical 16-year-old, wearing a baseball cap backwards, with longish dirty blond hair that partly covered his blue eyes. Around his upper lip there was a whisper of what would later be a mustache. Even though he was here with me in a clinical interview, there was nothing particularly wrong with Damon. He was not mentally disturbed in any way. True, if you went back eight years or so there were some behavioral issues, but these were mostly the result of a chaotic home environment, and the home situation was now much improved.

The voice Damon heard was during an episode about five years ago,

Two—Hallucinations of the Angelic Variety

when he was 11 and was mauled by a pit bull. Once this much was clear, I asked for permission to switch on a recorder.

"Let's take it from the beginning, so that I can get this straight. And thanks for letting me make a tape of it," I said.

"Okay, so one morning I was walking," Damon began, "and I had on brand spanking new Adidas, like white and purple, and I had a feeling something bad was going to happen that day.... It was like 8:07 in the morning.... I had to get home before—so I could get ready and go to school."

"Go home *before* you went to school?" I asked.

"Yeah, I was staying at a friend's the night before.... And I get up and I'm walking towards Albertsons and this big voice in my head—like, it was weird. It totally—something stopped me. And it's like, this big loud voice said, 'You need to turn left right now,' and I just put it in the back of my head and I started walking again."

"You told me you thought it was the voice of God?"

"Yeah," Damon replied. "It was, like, holy something. An angel telling me—God sending an angel or something. But it was definitely a girl. I could tell it was a girl—she had such a high-pitched voice. She was screaming!"

"She was screaming? Was she outside your head? Or inside your head?"

"Outside my head. I, like, stopped and she yelled at me and I look around and nobody is there. And I just keep walking. And, like, as I'm walking, the voice gets smaller and smaller … it's like TURN LEFT … TURN LEFT … turn left … turn left … and then I finally got to the house where the pit bull was and the voice finally quit. It, like, gave up telling me to turn left and then it [being mauled] all went down."

Hallucinations of voices can appear to be outside of the person, but I had never heard of a hallucination that *behaved* as if it were an actual sound source, a sound that became "smaller" as you walked away. Not at all what you would expect from a hallucination. I fumbled for more details. "Did you say it was a girl's voice?"

"Yes, a girl's voice—it wasn't a lady's voice—it was a girl's voice. She was, like, yelling at me; she was like 'TURN LEFT NOW!!!' and I just kept walking and then I saw the dog and I was like, 'Now I know why it told me to turn left.' And that dog just got the weirdest look on its face. And it walked towards the steps and almost into its house then turned around and bolted straight at me, and I went to go run, but there was a big red truck in my way."

"This is when it bit you, right?"

The Spirit Transcendent

"Yeah, but it did not get lock jaw [its jaws were not locked on to me]—something pulled it off of me. Like, literally one second it was like vicious foam coming out of its mouth, biting on me, and ripping me apart, then all of a sudden it was all quiet. And the dog looked around twice, and then walked away like nothing happened."

"That's weird—doesn't that seem really weird to you?" I remarked. "It's like it has got this entirely other personality all of a sudden."

"Yeah, it was weird. He was, like, vicious and biting me, then two seconds later, it, like, heard—it sounded like it was looking around like it heard a voice or something. And it did that thing where dogs they shake off the water. That's what it did, it, like, looked around twice and then went like this—" Damon shook his body. "And then walked off."

This seemed like unusual behavior on the part of the dog. It was as if some unseen intelligence was trying to help Damon: he failed to heed the first warning, so now direct intervention was necessary. Rather than interrupt Damon with thoughts of my own, I simply asked, "Did somebody call the dog off?" This would have been the simplest explanation.

"No. All I was hearing was a little boy yelling, 'OH MY GOD! OH MY GOD!!!' Nobody yelled for the dog to stop. The grown-ups were both inside with the door closed, so they couldn't hear us outside…. And finally the little boy ran inside, but that was already after the dog was off me."

Damon's father, who had been silent to this point, exclaimed, "His teeth actually went into his chest cavity." After a brief three-way interchange among us concerning teeth vs. claws, Damon returned to his story.

"And the kid goes inside, and gets his parents outside. And there's this really skinny dude. And I ask for a towel. And he was like, 'Hold on, I need to look at your ribs. They are bleeding really bad.' And I was like, 'No, you need to look at my arm.' And I rip the sleeve clear off—even though it was my favorite shirt, and I didn't really want to do it, 'cause I loved Pokémon at the time. I had my Pokémon shirt on and it was long sleeve. I just ripped the sleeve off because it was burning so bad, and I needed to figure out what was there and I couldn't…. So I just ripped it down. And the guy looked at my arm, and hits the ground. [He faints dead away.] And this big, really heavy-set women comes from the back room with a bat that's all bloody."

"She actually beat that dog," said Damon's father.

"Yeah, she beat that dog bad," Damon continued. "She was like, 'Can I help you? What do you need?' I was like, 'I need a towel and phone.' And

Two—Hallucinations of the Angelic Variety

then I just sat down and waited for the towel. And she already had the phone in my hand."

Then Damon showed me a long scar from forearm to above the elbow. "You had stitches, didn't you? How many did you have?" I asked.

"Fifty-two on my arm, and three in my ribs…. It was like a slice of pizza from here to here. This part of my skin was all the way up here." Damon showed me graphically.

"So your skin looked like it was flayed away from the bone?"

"Yeah! Flayed away from the bone…"

Contained in this single story is much that traditional psychology cannot explain. Just how would a traditional explanation go? The usual approach would be to assume the girl's voice was a hallucination. I don't think Damon was mentally ill, so that negates one major reason a person might hallucinate.[1] True enough. But there is a recent view in psychiatry that recognizes sometimes a hallucination is "benign," meaning hallucinations can be innocent, without indicating mental illness.[2] You could make an analogy with a cough: sometimes coughs are symptoms of a disease, but sometimes they are simply coughs and have no particular significance. The same might be said of Damon's perception of the girl's voice.

Well and good—but psychiatry is silent on *why* Damon would have heard the girl's voice. There is no reason for a hallucination, defined as a kind of brain artifact, to have any kind of purpose, but this particular hallucination was obviously bent on trying to save Damon. And the challenge goes deeper: if the girl's voice—which showed clear intention—could be said to belong to a *she*, that is, something or someone with a will and some kind of *identity*, how would "she" know what was about to happen? Therefore, there are two challenges to the traditional scientific interpretation: the first is having a source of intelligence without an apparent body; the second is being able to access knowledge of a future event. A traditional view is going to have to explain away both of these possibilities.[3]

The skeptic could try to take refuge in the fact that this is a story told by a 16-year-old boy about an event that happened when he was 11. Could the story be unreliable? Yes, yes, it could, and that will always be the case for a single story. So here is another example: it was told to me not by an adolescent who I met only once in a psychological interview but by a university professor whom I have known for many years. I had shown—let me call her "Dr. L"—some of my writing about spiritual events like these. I remember having the usual trepidation from not knowing how a colleague would relate to material which, I will admit, is more than a little weird. But

The Spirit Transcendent

I was placed at ease when my friend and colleague proceeded to relate a personal event that happened to her a few years ago and for which she had no explanation.

Dr. L had just finished a quick meal at a fast-food restaurant. She got into her car and was about to back up. After shifting into reverse, but before lifting her foot off the brake, she heard, very clearly, her name being called—to her it seemed to be the voice of her grandmother. This caused her to freeze for an instant, and at that very moment a child ran across the parking lot directly behind her car. Now, my friend is not in the habit of having hallucinations, but if it were not for her name being called, she would have run over the child. Maybe it *was* a hallucination. But tell me, how do you account for its purpose in saving the child?[4]

Betty too had stories that showed her visions had a purpose, and for this reason it was impossible to explain them away as simple hallucinations. In our meetings, Betty and I would often get lost in friendly debate. Ever the skeptic, one evening I asked her, "How can you be so sure—how can you be so sure that God exists?" Betty made her point by telling me a story. It had taken place during a time in her life when she had just moved back to Idaho from Denver and was a single mother with two young children and an older son. Betty would insist, how can God *not be real* given the following events?

"Oh, I was so tired," Betty said. "I had worked myself to death. I was so tired. Yet I had made an appointment to be at my son's house for dinner, but I was driving. And you get so tired, but you're still driving. Your eyes roll up, and you know how all of a sudden you're still on the road, but you're asleep. And I knew I had to get some rest, some way or other, so I pulled into a park. And I pulled in and underneath this pine tree, 200 feet up, and I thought, 'Well, this is a good place.' The kids went in the park and played. And I thought I would take a nap. So I went in the back, laid down and went to sleep. And was just dozing off.... It couldn't have even been 10 minutes, that I laid down, and God's voice said, 'Get up!'"

"Well, I *just* laid down."

"Get up! You've got to go on. You can't stay here," God said.

"And I says, 'Well, I'm so tired, please, please, let me sleep.' The sensation went on. I wished I hadn't, but I dozed off and again this comes to me."

"Get up, go on!"

"And I says, 'OK, OK,' and I get up and crawl out of the back. And I called the kids.... I had to finally go over to where they were playing and drag them in the van and say, 'Come on, we have to go.' I said, 'I don't know

Two—Hallucinations of the Angelic Variety

why, God says we have to go.' So we got in the van and we took off, down on the road..."

Betty leaned forward and continued. "I drove all the rest of the way to my son's house, from Weiser to Nampa, down the big highway.... I went into the house and the news was on. And it was about 6 o'clock when we got there.... And I said, 'A tornado! In Weiser?' 'Cause it was all over the news. And it was local news. And my son was sitting there, and he said, 'Yeah, there was a tornado over there and it tore up the whole park. All the trees in the park are pulled up and laid on the ground.' Sure enough, that's what they were saying on the news. And I said, 'We were just there a little while ago—it was God's forewarning. There's going to be a tornado.' And right under that big tree, 200 feet tall, was where my van was parked. And the trees where the kids were playing. It was just like a whole bunch of toothpicks lying down when I went back through there.

"So explain that without God!" Betty finished. And I had to admit, there was no good counterargument.

As a psychologist, I naturally tend to see people who have, or in the past have had, some form of mental disorder. They too have told me about spiritual experiences, and why not? It is too facile to use the simple fact of a mental disorder to explain away what we cannot fully understand.[5] Karen is an excellent example. I met her when she was in her 30s and performed an assessment; her story emerged within a single meeting.

Karen had a very rough upbringing, suffered neglect as a child, and was a victim of abuse. When she was 19, she managed to escape a terrible home environment by getting married. Thankfully she found a husband who cared about her, and before long she had developed a close relationship with her mother-in-law, Judy, who became her best friend. Karen was doing well emotionally at that point in her life, but then Judy became ill and passed away. This was devastating to Karen, and at some level it must have been that Karen was confronted with a double loss. First there was the real mother who was unavailable to her as a child, and now as an adult she suffered the loss of the mother she had found in Judy. Right at this time Karen was hospitalized for depression. Even after she was discharged from the hospital she was still in a depressed state; she felt hopeless and had basically given up on life.

When Judy, her mother-in-law, was alive, Karen and her husband lived together in the same home with Judy and Judy's husband. Both of the men were loggers. This is seasonal work in the Northwest, and during logging season it involves working very long hours, where you need to make

The Spirit Transcendent

a very early start so as to make the several-hour drive to the worksite. The routine was for both women to wake early in the morning—3:30, in fact—so they could cook breakfast for the men. Each morning began with a kind of ritual where Judy would wake Karen up by pulling her big toe.

A familiar part of a standard psychological assessment is to ask the client if he or she has ever had a hallucination. I remember that Karen paused when I asked this question, and this was my cue that she had something to say. It turned out that she did have an important experience that was obviously out of the norm, but she was afraid to talk about it for fear of having it reduced to a mere sign of mental illness.

Karen finally explained: after her mother-in-law's death she had, in her words, "a nervous breakdown." Karen could not care for herself, let alone anyone around her, and she admitted herself to the hospital. After a few days, Karen was released, and then one night soon afterwards she was awakened from her sleep—by her mother-in-law pulling her big toe! Karen was now completely awake, and she looked over to see Judy fully present, exactly as she would be in real life. Not only that, but Judy had a message for Karen. She told her, mincing no words, "to knock it off and take care of your kids." In other words, the message was for Karen to quit dwelling on the loss, lying in bed and feeling sorry for herself—she had work to do, and she had best get on with the business of living.

If Karen revealed her vision to anyone who was working with her from the hospital it would easily have been taken as just a symptom. Makes sense, because people who are severely depressed have been known to hallucinate—although usually their hallucinations are "mood congruent," for example, images involving death, decay or destruction. It is an anomaly to have a hallucination that is positive along with severe depression, so it is very unusual that Karen's hallucination involved the woman who was like a mother to her.

However, what is really striking about the hallucination of the mother-in-law is not only did it have the appearance of Judy, as if she were still alive, but it *acted* the way Judy would have acted. Karen was literally woken up by her toe being pulled (what a greeting!), and at the same time the toe pulling gets a deeper message across: "Come to your senses! Get moving! You have responsibilities!" In the past, when Judy was alive, the message was to cook breakfast. Now, it was as if the mother-in-law was saying, "Get out of bed! Quit lying around and being depressed!" This is just like a mother might have acted in real life.

These apparent actions on the part of Judy were by far the most po-

Two—Hallucinations of the Angelic Variety

tent "therapy" that Karen experienced, despite her stay in a psychiatric hospital. There is no reason to expect, on the thesis that Judy was a hallucination and a product of brain pathology, that she (or it) would have had a therapeutic function. And what about the fact that the vision of the mother-in-law is showing actions as if motivated by its own will? (Karen would rather stay in bed, but Judy had other plans for her!) Psychiatry tells us that sometimes hallucinations can act something like (alternate) personalities.[6] But what if the source of the personality *actually was* Judy? Faced with story after story from my clients, I was beginning to take this possibility seriously.

Karen may or may not have had a mental illness that could explain her vision—my point is the "illness" can explain the vision only up to a point. It is as if you can use a psychiatric framework, or a spiritual one, depending on your preference, and then choose the one that gives the best overall sense of the truth of what is happening.[7]

So far, we have been up against the fact that visions and hallucinations can be very similar, and it is hard to distinguish between the two. Psychiatrists are familiar with a class of hallucinations that command the patient to act in some way, often a way that is harmful (they may be told to walk out in traffic; cut their wrists; and so forth). These types of hallucinations are taken as clear signs of mental illness and are notable because of the possible connection with dangerousness.[8] Betty told me a story that was similar in that it concerned a vision or hallucination that commanded her, but in this case, the "command" she obeyed was *the will of God*. Here, then, is an experience that a psychiatrist might call a "command hallucination," but it was not destructive, as you would expect in mental illness. In Betty's case it was *helpful*. This story comes from a time in Betty's life (about the same time she was saved from the tornado) when she had escaped her ex-husband and had traveled back to Orofino with her three young children.

Betty was back on her old property, some distance out of town, living in a house at the base of a hill. Around this time, without Betty's knowledge, Mr. Anderson was busy trying to convince Health and Welfare that Betty was an unfit mother so that he could gain custody of the children. Shortly after these efforts by her ex-husband, Betty was summoned by God.

"It was midnight or one o'clock in the morning and God was saying, 'Get up.'"

Betty argued with God. "I don't want to get up, I want to sleep."

The Spirit Transcendent

"No, *get up*," God persisted, "you need to work—you need to do something."

"Well, what am I supposed to do?"

"Take the tent and go up on the hill."

"So here I was," Betty explained, "in the dark, no flashlight—'Just take the tent and go up the hill.'" God was unwilling to give further explanation. "It took me an hour, at least," Betty said with a tinge of the exasperation in her voice. "I came back down off the hill and went to bed—I'd obeyed God and did what he wanted me to do."

"And then the *next* night He wakes me up again at 1 o'clock and says, 'Take the carpet up with the tent.' It was the next night when He told me to take groceries up. And then I got this bell ringing in my head. I thought, 'Somethin's going on—somethin's going to happen. Now why should I do all these things?'"

A night or two later Betty was prompted to take *her children* up the hill, but at this point she had definite grounds for an argument with God: "The thing was the kids were all down with the *measles.* They were sick. They had a temperature of 102, 103. Why should I take those kids up on the mountain when they're sick? There's snow on the ground."

"'Do it. Do it,' God says."

"So I says, 'OK, God, I obey You.' And so I got the little kids up and got them all dressed and we went up on the hill. I said, 'We're going to go camping with the little tent.' And I had the sleeping bags so I put them in the sleeping bags so they would stay nice and warm. You see, it was in March. It wasn't terrible cold, but it wasn't warm either. And I took care of the kids up there. Every day I would be asking God, 'Why—what are we doing up here?' And He would say, 'Stay—just go feed your kids. Give them peanut butter and jam sandwiches.' And I took a little stove up there so I could warm up soup and stuff for them."

This went on for two full weeks. But finally, it all made sense. Betty found out that in the meantime Mr. Anderson had come from Denver, and after convincing Health and Welfare it was for the best, was out at her house with the intention of taking the children away. It was exactly one day after Anderson had given up trying to find her, after he boarded a flight back to Denver, that God finally said to Betty, "OK, OK, you can go home."

"So it was perfect," Betty concluded. "It was perfect, you know."

As I listened to Betty's story, it seemed to me that the idea of a "command hallucination" really explained very little. Betty would have told me

Two—Hallucinations of the Angelic Variety

it was obvious that God knew what He was doing. Perhaps the psychiatric idea of a benign hallucination needs to be expanded even further: from hallucinations that are *benign*, to command hallucinations that may be *beneficial*.

The same ambiguity between psychiatric and spiritual explanations was apparent for Raymond, another of my pain clinic patients. Raymond is a large, burly, bear of a man who continues to suffer from chronic pain because of the extensive injuries he sustained when the truck he was driving went off a cliff. What makes Raymond's story interesting is that it is yet another example of a purposive hallucination—a hallucination that literally saved his life.

"Tell me again about the crash you were in and when you saw your grandfather," I asked, after fumbling with my recorder. "So what was it you were driving, a chip truck [a truck designed to haul wood chips]?"

"Yeah, 2003 Kensworth, with a 53-foot trailer on four axles."

"Well, tell me about it. Where were you?"

"I actually had the wreck when I was three miles west of Newport, Washington, up near the Canadian border. They have these Motorola repeater radios and there is one spot up on the mountain where they can talk to you and get your dump weight. I was on a big wraparound curve and I reach down for my phone which was somewhere on the floor, and by the time I look up, my tires were in the ditch on the passenger side. Well, I got my truck up out of the ditch but by then the top back corner of my trailer caught the cliff going up, and when it did, it tweaked my trailer because I was empty; it took the back tires up that were driving me forward, and I jackknifed and went off the cliff."

"The truck and me fell a good 200 yards, 'til I hit the tree line. When I hit that first tree, the tree picked up the hood, and it drove the hood through the windshield, ripped my face off. By the time it got stopped, the truck was facing up the hill." Raymond showed me the orientation of the wreck with his hands. Soon an ambulance was on the scene. "The ambulance driver came down the hill, and he said, 'Wait here, and when the fire department gets here, we'll put you in a backboard and a neck brace, and we're goin' rope you up the cliff.' As soon as he [the EMT] said the word 'cliff,' the floodlight, the white light, came over his head, and in the bright white light was my Grandpa Johansson, who had just passed away a little over a month before the wreck ... and he appeared with halo and wings. He looked to be in his late 40s (my earliest recollection of him)—even had his waxed handlebar mustache. And then my Grandpa said to me, 'Raymond,

The Spirit Transcendent

you have your two boys to raise and if you wait for the fire department you're gonna bleed to death. You need to climb the cliff to the ambulance or you're not going to make it.' So at that point I climbed the cliff to the ambulance, and even walked up into the ambulance, and sat down on the gurney holding my face ... everything from the tip of my nose to the bottom of my teeth were all just hanging by this skin here. It was all completely ripped off my face ... the whole sinus cavity wide-open."

Raymond's ability to climb that cliff was nothing short of a miracle. He lost a large quantity of blood, and since he was holding his sheared-open face with one hand, he had use of only one hand to help him climb. The seriousness of the accident was brought home a few days later, when, laid up in the hospital recovering from his injuries, Raymond was visited by the patrol officer who had been directing traffic above him, at the point in the road where the truck went off the cliff. The officer apologized to Raymond for not coming down to the wreck to try to help. He had just assumed, having seen the extent of the crash, that Raymond could never have survived.

Physical recovery had been hellish for Raymond. He had dozens of surgeries. "They've been burning nerves for the past six years," Raymond explained, "and had my jaws wired shut three different times, three months at a shot—I was only able to eat through a little rubber feeding tube.... I lost 85 pounds the first time my jaws were wired shut, and the other two times 45 pounds and 40 pounds." Pointing with his hands, Raymond told me, "They removed all of the teeth fragments and put in a silicone eye socket." When Raymond and I first started working together, his face was lopsided and there was still a very noticeable amount of scarring. The surgeries continued, and after the surgeon was able to move the eye socket back to its original position, Raymond's features returned almost to normal. Looking at him today you would not guess all that he had gone through.

After Raymond had finished telling me about the wreck and his physical recovery, I directed our conversation back to the surprising part of the story: the vision of Grandpa Johansson, with wings and a halo no less, and the fact that it was this vision that saved Raymond's life.

"What do you make of what happened to you?" I said.

"I really felt it was divine intervention."

"Really?"

"Well," Raymond replied, "if it wasn't for guardian angels I wouldn't be sitting here talking to you, I think."

Two—Hallucinations of the Angelic Variety

This is an honest and straightforward interpretation. But, of course, my background and training required that I try to make sense out of it without resort to spirituality. Couldn't there be an ordinary explanation? My natural inclination was to explain the vision based on known psychological principles and what I knew about Raymond. Assuming that Grandpa Johansson was a hallucination, was there was something in Raymond that would have made him hallucinate? But Raymond did not suffer from any serious psychiatric disorder—schizophrenia, for example—for which hallucinations are symptomatic. Raymond was not on drugs at the time, and although he had some experience with hallucinogens, that was decades ago. I could fall back on the fact that the accident, and having one's face sheared off, was traumatic both physically and psychologically. But the literature on trauma is certainly not filled with reports of hallucinated angels. Therefore, this would appear to be another example of a "benign" hallucination, that is, one that does not signify mental illness or disorder.

I was then left with the original problem: how to account for the fact that the hallucination had a function or, to put it baldly, that Raymond could have had a hallucination that took intelligent action. As a psychologist, I was least disposed to a truly spiritual explanation to this puzzle. It did not register nor did I remember the fact that Grandpa Johansson, in real life, had passed away about a month earlier. It seemed irrelevant and only became important later as the story developed.[9]

I continued to think about the case in psychological terms. Why, I wondered, assuming it was Raymond who had generated the hallucination, did it take the form of Grandpa Johansson? An answer presented itself when Raymond filled me in with some personal history.

It turns out that Raymond had a special connection with Mr. Johansson—Raymond told me that Johansson and his wife were his godparents. He was called "Grandpa" not because he was a blood relation but as a term of affection. During our session, Raymond went into an example of how Mr. Johansson had come to his aid when Raymond was much younger and had nowhere to turn. According to Raymond, when he was a sophomore in high school he was in the habit of sneaking out of the house at night and partying. Raymond had a system: he oiled the hinges of the front door, and so long as he snuck in before 6:45 a.m.—this was when his father returned from working the night shift at Boeing—he was safe. The plan worked well until he came home stoned one evening and forgot to remove the instrument of his partying—his bong—from the car. He was discovered and his

The Spirit Transcendent

father announced "he wasn't going to let a pothead live under his roof, and I had until noon to get all of my things out of his house." With nowhere to go, his godparents took him in and Raymond lived that entire year with them, until he could graduate from high school.

Grandpa Johansson, then, was a father figure who, unlike Raymond's real father, was someone he could rely on. In real life he had rescued Raymond—just as in the vision when Raymond was rescued by Grandpa Johansson in the form of a guardian angel.

Talking with Raymond during the session, I kept my interpretation to myself. Why challenge his belief in a spirit? I probably also felt a bit smug thinking I had a solution to why it should be Grandpa Johansson that would turn up in Raymond's hallucination. This small "ah ha" moment allowed me to feel comfortable with all those unanswered questions. How could a mere "hallucination" save Raymond from bleeding to death? Why would a sane person hallucinate? These were questions that made the story so remarkable.

But when we met months later, Raymond let me in on another, critical part of the story: Grandpa Johansson was very close to his own wife, Lily. By Raymond's account, it was a model marriage, the way he thought a marriage ought to be. Three years after Grandpa Johansson passed away, Lily also passed, and Raymond attended the funeral. The couple had three boys, and the middle son, Paul, had been Lily's caretaker up until her death. After the funeral, Raymond spoke with Paul. The conversation turned to spiritual matters, and then Paul revealed something he had never told anyone else because, he said, "I thought I was going crazy."

The evening before Lily died, Grandpa Johansson came *to Paul* and spoke to him. His exact words were "Thank you for taking such good care of my bride." This second sighting was *years after* Raymond's own experience with Grandpa Johansson.

What would account for the two separate appearances? Obviously, the most likely explanation cannot be in material terms—the independent (and real) existence of Grandpa Johansson! The alternative, a hallucinated Grandpa Johansson, generated by Raymond, and a second hallucination by the son three years later—without any reason to connect the two—seems extraordinarily unlikely.

Several of my clients have had "ghost stories" to tell. Here is one of my favorites, and I love it because, as with Raymond's story, when you think about it, it establishes the reality of a non-material entity by a kind of mental triangulation.

Two—Hallucinations of the Angelic Variety

I was interviewing a woman, Jean, who was in her early 50s. I found Jean to be rather personable, and we began with some pleasant banter about the purpose of our meeting, and the need to have an assessment for the sake of her insurance, even though she could not see the point. Eventually, I got down to business and asked if she had any symptoms of a psychological nature. In response, Jean told me that she sleepwalked. Not only that, "*things move around*," she chuckled.

Jean informed me that she often made some rather amusing discoveries the day after. Once she found that someone had poured cat food in her son's shoe; another time she found a single shoe in the refrigerator. Joking about what must have been her nocturnal wanderings, I asked, "Do you believe in ghosts?"

"Do *you*?" was her response.

There was an undertone to Jean's question that suggested that the conversation might turn a bit more serious. I paused for a second, and then, more carefully, answered, "Yes."

"Why?"

"Well," I replied, "I've never seen one myself, but I've talked to people whose reports I trust, and it seems that a spirit is the only way to describe what they have seen."

Now that Jean realized it was safe to trust me, and knowing she would not be ridiculed, she proceeded to tell me a story from when she was a girl of 16. Jean lived (and still lives) in a small town, population of about 500, that is in fact not far from the little town that is my own home in rural Idaho. She was at home with her mother, and about 1 in the afternoon both women heard a loud crash coming from their porch. They checked to see what might be the matter and found that Jean's father had fallen and gashed his head on a freezer. They found him dead, the victim of a massive heart attack that killed him so quickly the gash on the head produced little blood.

About an hour later, still in shock, Jean and her mother went over to the local diner about where Jean's aunt, Kelly, worked as a waitress, figuring they should let her father's sister know the news right away. When they arrived at the diner, Jean's mother broke the bad news. "Your brother is dead."

"What do you mean?" Kelly replied. "He was just here."

In fact, patrons of the diner had just witnessed some odd behavior on the part of Kelly. She had served coffee as if there was a customer in an empty booth, and there she was, chattering away, but obviously no one was there.

The Spirit Transcendent

"They thought she was nuts," Jean declared. All the while, Kelly had been talking to and serving coffee to her brother as she had done so many times before, just as if he were alive and in front of her.

Perhaps it goes without saying, but Kelly's experience is about impossible to explain without invoking the spirit of her brother. The timing was exactly around the time of death, and several people observed—and commented on—the odd behavior which could only be that she thought she was serving her brother. It is this kind of story that provides the missing piece that allows a reasonable explanation of Raymond's story—as long as the existence of a spiritual entity is counted among "reasonable" alternatives.

In their visions, Raymond and Karen were rescued by a figure who was like a parent, and for all the world it seemed to me that it was as if the love and care of a parent could transcend the grave. I have been told still other stories that lead me to believe that somehow love is at the core of a spiritual experience.

There was a bright and articulate woman by the name of Ari, with no mental disorder I could determine, who was in her late 20s when we met. I was much taken by an event in her life that happened when she was eight years old. It was so profound and so significant that it has always been clear in her memory.

"It was morning after waking up from a night of sleep," Ari said. "It was really early. It was in a room I shared with my sisters, who were not awake yet. And so I remember the sun was just rising and I slowly became awake out of my sleep. [I was awakened by] the sensation of someone caressing my cheek. And the sensation lasted maybe about 10 seconds. And the feeling I got, even before I opened my eyes, was absolutely the most incredible feeling of love. And concern. And tenderness. And before I even woke up, before I consciously woke up, I remember feeling so happy and so contented and so safe.... As I woke up I thought, 'Oh my gosh, who is touching my cheek?' And it was not just a feeling, but it was a physical sensation."

Speaking with Ari, I had the feeling, hard to define, that this was no ordinary memory. It seemed so clear, even after so many years. "You felt a caress on your cheek," I said. "Tell me more. And what do you think it was?"

"It was a feeling of love and the feeling of concern, and I woke up feeling so happy and so safe, and it was an unfamiliar feeling to me at that point in my life. And when I opened my eyes I was just—stunned. And I

Two—Hallucinations of the Angelic Variety

looked around, 'Wow, what was that?' But even while I was thinking that, there was no question in my mind it was an angel. Absolutely felt that way. And the room ... had the most beautiful sun in it. And I woke up feeling really contented and secure, like I knew someone was watching me. I felt safe."

"Unfamiliar to feel happy and safe?" I reflected. "So you were in a rough spot when you were that young?"

"It's just—I wouldn't have known at the time but, you know, starting at age eight until about age 14, I just had horrible experiences in store for me. And I really struggled with losing my faith when I was about 13. And being able to get it back. If I hadn't had that experience, I don't know I would have been able to fully get my faith back."

Thinking about Ari's angel, or whatever it was, that seemed to appear because it was needed made me think about one of my other clients. Around the time I spoke with Ari, I was working with another woman, a kind, gentle individual in her early 30s. She too had a spiritual story to tell from when she was a young girl of eight. Let me tell you, then, about Melissa. Unlike Ari, Melissa did have mental illness. She had been hospitalized in the past for bipolar disorder, and although she was now much improved, she was not yet at the point of being able to hold a job and be completely independent. Despite her history of severe symptoms, if you met Melissa, she would strike you as clear thinking and she would not seem "emotionally disordered" in any obvious way.

Because Melissa did have a serious mental disorder, it is even more difficult to distinguish between spiritual phenomena and hallucinations than it would be in an individual who (apart from the vision) shows no symptoms of mental disorder.[10] After all, the seriously mentally ill can have hallucinations with religious content—angels, devils, and so forth—that are nothing more than symptoms. (In those cases, usually the experience is destructive and not helpful in any way.)[11] But by now I had heard enough visions and unexplained events among those *without* mental illness that I was no longer so eager to reject out of hand an experience that seemed spiritual, even in the mentally ill.

The real story begins with an event when Melissa was eight—the same age, coincidentally, that Ari was when she had her early spiritual experience. Melissa recalled that she had gotten upset with her brother and, wanting to be alone, went off to play by herself near the edge of a cliff. Melissa remembered walking along the edge, looking over the cliff from time to time, but not really feeling she was so close that she need worry about

The Spirit Transcendent

falling. However, it had just rained and the grass was still wet. Too quickly to react, she slipped off the edge. She kept tumbling and fell 35 feet, hitting rocks on the way to the bottom. Melissa blacked out. She did not know for how long. She was bleeding from the forehead, "blood just running down my face," and she believed she was in shock at the time because she was not feeling pain from her injuries. At least not yet.

When Melissa regained consciousness, she was disoriented. Since she could not climb back up the hill, she found the highway and began to walk toward it, which "felt like it took forever." Then the story became interesting.

"I started walking along the highway ... and a lady stopped in her car and opened the passenger door and asked if I needed help, and I said, 'Yeah, I need to get home.' And so she let me crawl in and I told her where I lived and stuff."

I was struck by how concrete these events seemed, just as we might expect from an actual memory. To my ear, they seemed real and not invented. "Well, tell me about this woman," I managed to say.

"She was probably in her mid–30s," Melissa replied. "She had long, blonde wavy hair and just looked like a regular person. And I don't know, I remember her being very pretty, though." Next came my first hint that this was no ordinary experience. "She talked to me, mainly just about the things that had happened to me, things that I remember happening, but I never told her what had happened before."

"What things do you mean?"

"Well, like about me living with my grandma, and being taken away from my mom, and just about hardships I have been through and things that were hard for me. And I don't know, just things I had never told anybody."

"Was this woman anyone you knew?"

"No," Melissa replied. "I didn't know her from before, I didn't [know her] from Adam." And then Melissa filled in yet more details of how this woman talked with her of other trials in her life. "Yeah, about my dad and stepmom marrying, and that was a really hard thing for me. I—I remember not wanting my dad to get married to her and stuff, and when my dad married my stepmom and got me taken away from my grandma [Melissa's only decent relationship], both me and my brother did.... Me and my brother were always close to our grandma, so being taken away from her was really hard."

Melissa's rescuer drove her to a bus stop near her home so she could

Two—Hallucinations of the Angelic Variety

walk the rest of the way. This also didn't make sense. Given the extent of the injuries to this eight-year-old girl, you would rather expect a bystander to drive Melissa to a hospital rather than to a bus stop. Melissa wanted to talk with the woman further, so they walked up the hill, toward her parents' home. Melissa said, "She told me, 'Just to put all my trust and faith in God, and that I would go through some hard times in my life, but God would see me through them.' And she talked about how everybody pleasing to God has hardships, just like it is part of human life to have hardship and stuff, you know and [she] said something about how 'life isn't as long as you think it will be.'"

"We were walking up the hill and she stopped in the garden and told me to go on home and get help," Melissa said. "Yeah, she left me in the garden and I took a few steps and turned around to say 'thank you' and she was gone, she was totally gone! And you know, mind you, this is on a hilltop where you can see all around, and I could see the whole trail doing down the hill, and everything, and she was gone, I mean, totally gone. And I remember looking around for her, and then after she left it didn't really dawn on me right then what really had happened until I went on up to the house and told my dad and stepmom about this lady. And they were like, 'We were watching you come up the hill and we didn't see no lady,' you know."

"My dad was freaking out and when he gets mad he cusses a lot, and he was just freaking out because I had blood just running down my face and so he was just trying to get me to the hospital.... I was a mess ... but we talked about [this lady] the whole way to the hospital."

"Do you think she was real?" I asked. "Could it have been in your mind?"

After thinking carefully and hesitating for a moment, Melissa said, "It was real, it had to have been." Melissa believed that her experience was one of an actual angel, sent by God, to rescue her, to give her comfort, and to provide courage to withstand trials to come.

Because Melissa had mental illness, I had to consider that her story was part of a delusion. Could what she was telling me, and even the story of the 35-foot fall, be invented? But some years later, I had the chance to speak with Melissa's sister. It turned out that Melissa really did fall off of a cliff when she was eight; she really did find her way home after the accident; and she spoke to everyone about the woman who helped her. The woman that Melissa said delivered her was nowhere to be seen. The family's interpretation of these events was the same as Melissa's—she must have been rescued by an angel, one that they never saw.

The Spirit Transcendent

Melissa was taken to the hospital, where she was treated. "They stitched me up, and then I went home." Melissa told me she could not remember the details after the accident "because I kept blacking out.... I mean, I obviously had a concussion or something." To this point, I was still of two minds about what to make of her angel. Besides the spiritual interpretation, the psychologist in me wanted to argue that it was just a hallucination. But there was an end to the story that tilted the explanation toward the spiritual.

About two weeks after the accident, Melissa went to church. "I got filled with the Holy Spirit." This was an unexpected turn to the story. But it seems that the meeting with the angel had prepared Melissa spiritually: "After seeing that lady—and I had two weeks to think about that lady, you know—and the more I thought of it I knew she had to be an angel." When in church, she was inspired to pray. I asked Melissa about the nature of her prayer. "The jist of it," she replied, was "I asked for forgiveness for my sins and [I asked] Him to come into my heart to live. Then I wanted to serve Him for the rest of my life." This was the moment when Melissa became filled with the Holy Spirit. "I remember right after I said that prayer I felt this warmth that started in my heart and I just felt this comfort in my heart and it felt like warmth, and it spread through my whole body, and then the pastor prayed on us all, and I spoke in tongue for the first time."

The cases I have presented thus far are only a sample of the stories, all with possible spiritual meaning, that have arisen over the course of my clinical practice. Some of the cases are fragmentary and came out of my meeting with a client for a single session, typically for the purpose of performing an assessment. The following brief story is interesting because it involved a feeling of warmth that might be like what Melissa felt when she dedicated herself to Jesus.

Leah was in her 40s when I saw her, and in that one session she told me of how her lifetime was filled with terrible event after terrible event. As a child she was sexually abused. As an adult she was left to care for her young children when her husband was killed in a logging accident. Then one of her daughters was trapped in a house fire and died of her burns. She was with a boyfriend who was violent, and he had just beaten her up one more time. Finally, she couldn't take it anymore. She had decided to end it, she wrote a suicide note to her children, and she had the gun in her hand. "What use am I?" she thought at that moment. "Am I only a piece of meat to be abused?" But then, with the gun still in her hand, a warm feeling overcame her. The gun fell to the floor. "I could not physically lift it," she

Two—Hallucinations of the Angelic Variety

said. Instead of anguish, Leah felt "a real calmness," and she thought she heard someone say, "No, you don't want to do this."

I have saved one brief case for last because the quality of the patient's experience seemed much like my own. To use St. Teresa's terminology, it was another example of an "intellectual vision," where there is no specific form to the vision, but rather a sense of being overwhelmed by something holy.

Sean was in his mid–30s and another patient I met once for the purpose of performing a Social Security evaluation. Sean had been an alcoholic a good part of his life. He battled depression and anxiety, and he had already been found disabled because of his PTSD. Over the last couple of years, Sean told me, he had managed to clean up his life. He had quit drinking and had stopped doing meth. "My body was pretty well cleansed, and my mind had cleared," he said.

Sean told me about a service dog he had, as his lifeline during times when he was profoundly depressed. "There's this big parking lot behind Walmart, I'm out exercising my dog. I've got two sticks, and I'm throwing them. He brings one back, I throw the other, and so on.... Well, I reach my hand in my pocket and I find my marijuana pipe. I hadn't been smoking for a good while—I'd forgot it was there. So I decide it's time to get rid of it too. There's this little hole in the ground, and I stick my pipe in there and cover it up. I stomp on it, once, twice. With the third stomp I felt this electric shock went right through my body. I get this feeling of His presence, and I look up at the sky, and it was, like, *on fire*. I didn't see anything [he didn't see God]. But *it was this light*. It was like Jesus gave me a hug; I could feel His presence." An intuition came to Sean, like a thought in his head. It said, "I've got you now—everything is going to be OK."

"I've tried some of the best drugs," Sean said, "but there is no euphoria that comes close to that. Nothing before or after never come close.... It's so hard to get anyone to believe me. Even my pastor—they all assumed I was on drugs."

Sean, and along with him all of my spiritual clients, would say that their experience went beyond the human. Whether a guardian angel is seen, or God speaks, or His presence is felt, it seems to go beyond mere hallucination. When Sean said his elation was better than any drug, he meant it was *different than* the effects of any substance. This gets to a central thesis about spirituality: if the spirit is real, then its reality is on a different level than common perception or common emotion.

William James, writing at the turn of the century, understood that spiritual experience could not be grasped in human terms, and he hinted that the difficulty was much more than the general problem of trying to describe the sublime, but that being in contact with the ineffable was central to the experience itself.[12] He clearly had a kind of dualism in mind when he spoke of religious experience as the opening of an alternative reality.[13]

As a scientist, James was interested in all kinds of phenomena that might shed light on the spiritual. He attended séances, dabbled with inhaling nitrous oxide gas, compiled accounts of religious experience, and did much more. But James did not know about near-death experiences (or NDEs, as psychologists today call them), maybe because in his time there was no good way to resuscitate individuals at the brink of death. It was only with Raymond Moody's book *Life After Life*, published in the '70s, that NDEs became well known. So well known that almost everyone today is familiar with visions of going "towards the light," passing through a tunnel, meeting a divine being, having a life-review, and making a decision to return.[14]

Were he still alive, William James would have dropped everything to study near-death experiences. They show, best of all, the possibility of a reality that is different than, and that goes beyond, that of the material world. They are also *common*—depending on the study, between 9 and 18 percent who suffer cardiac arrest and are resuscitated will have them.[15] I myself have had about a dozen of my patients tell me their NDEs. There is nothing like them for giving a feeling for the separation between the material and the spiritual. I now turn to an examination of these experiences as told to me.

Three

Death and Transcendence

My first exposure to a near-death experience came not from one of my clients but from Richard, an older gentleman who worked as the janitor at the pain clinic where I consulted. This was back in 2004, before I began to focus on spiritual events. I recall lingering by my truck at the end of the day, talking with Richard in the fading light. One part of his story stayed with me: after nearly dying, Richard told me, paradoxically, that he no longer feared death.[1]

Maybe six years later, after receiving what seemed like a flood of spiritual stories, I sought Richard out. I already had a collection of near-death experiences and I was convinced there was something powerful in all of them. I wanted to record Richard's. Maybe, I thought, I would write about them one day. I managed to carve out some time toward the end of the day so we could sit together and I could get his story.

After switching on a cassette tape recorder, we got to the story itself. "I guess I'll take it from the very beginning," Richard said. "My brother and I owned a manufacturing business and we were chaining down a load on a trailer. And the idiot that I was, I didn't use a cheater bar on my chain binder. So I had my face right by the binder and it didn't latch and consequently snapped and crushed my face. So I was bleeding really bad. It was early in the morning and the doctor wasn't in yet. This medic, who was just back from Vietnam, recently back from Vietnam, was unlocking his office. So he stitched me up, and that's why I only have a few little scars. Sent me home."

"Well, the bleeding didn't stop. It wasn't bleeding out the nose—he had packed that—but it was bleeding down my throat." In actual fact, a fragment of bone had pierced an artery in the back of his throat, but Richard did not find this out until much later. "So about the point when I turned gray—we were living in Buell at the time—which is, what, 11, 13 miles west of Twin Falls? They rushed me over to the hospital; they take me in the emergency room, give me X-rays, and the doctor says, 'Well, you broke your nose, if you didn't know that. Go home, take a couple of pills, and lay down.'"

"Well, back to Buell we go. Laying down, a few minutes, I no more than hit the couch, I'm vomiting up blood and it's not a small amount—it's a large amount and I can't stop. So back to the hospital we go. They decide they've got to admit me, so they put me in. Over the course of the next three days they put in seven pints of blood. It was on the third day, of course, I was pretty much out of it most of the time because of the pain, but the third day my wife was there and all I recall I was throwing up more blood. And the nurse she come in and she said I was going into cardiac arrest again. So they threw me on a gurney—"

At this point in the telling of the story Richard's voice caught. It was obvious to me that it was hard for him to go on. The conversation wandered to a humorous, unrelated event. I simply waited, like any clinician would wait, giving Richard some space before he was ready to get to the main point. Another pause, and then "it was just ... back to the elevator. We were starting down the elevator. That's when everything stopped." Richard had tears in his eyes. Feeling a bit uncomfortable myself, I asked if it was okay for him to continue. He said yes, that it might be hard, but it was important that I know what happened. Richard picked up the thread of the story.

"I'm lying there, of course. Everything turns black. Last thing I remember is…. Anna says, Anna says, 'You can't die, you son of a bitch—I can't raise those kids alone.' So this—it's like everything just stops. This blackness comes in, the pain dissolves. The pain is intense ... the pain goes away, then it dissolves. Then there is nothing. It's like there is a total black void of nothing. And I didn't understand what was happening. Trying to figure, to figure it out. There's no—I don't believe there's any frame of time reference, 'cause I don't recall being able to say it was five minutes, an hour—I have no idea. There was no sense of time…. And then way off in the distance I see a little prick of light. And I focused on that. And that light began to grow."

"You mean an actual light?" I asked, pointing upwards. "Like this one overheard?"

"It was visual…. It's like you would take a pin in a totally black box or a totally black room. You would punch that pin in the wall and in that little hole is suddenly that light. That light—grew—steadily and seemed fairly rapid to me. And the closer that light got—I never heard of a near death experience—no, this, this was 40 years ago."

Three—Death and Transcendence

"Yeah, that's just it," I said. "Forty years ago, no one had ever heard of near-death experience, but here you have that sense of light everyone has talked about. But let me ask you about something else: why do you think you could remember it so clearly? It was 40 years ago, you know."

"This is something you'll never forget," Richard replied. "It's embedded into you. I mean it's in your heart as well as your mind. It's a total experience in your body."

"As that light grew—it's like, at that time I thought the light came to me. I've heard people describe it today as they're going to the light. And at that time I honestly believe that the light came to me.... There was no sensation of motion. I didn't feel like I was traveling through a tunnel. I was in total blackness and here came the light. And as it grew, it was like *rays*, and these rays went *through me*. It was like I wasn't—if I was material, they were flowing right through my material. And that light—it's not like this light bulb here." Richard pointed overhead. "This light is alive. This light—I think it's from the Creator. I don't think it's God himself. But I think it's his messenger, or a courier, or however you would interpret it, that's how I would interpret it."

Richard elaborated on his experience of light. "This light, to me it was like a golden light. It was warm, it enveloped me, it's like, like it flowed through me, yet it wrapped around me."

"You knew it wasn't like a physical light?" I asked.

"No. It definitely wasn't like someone shining a light in my eyes," Richard responded. "Definitely not. As that light grew, and I began to feel that flowing in me, I felt this feeling of comfort and well-being and then there was this overwhelming feeling of love. It's like they were *cradling* me."

Richard was overcome as he said this, the words catching in his throat. "It must have been beautiful," was all I managed to say.

"It is. It's an unbelievable experience—yet it happens. Ah, I think you could use every good word in the dictionary. Combine all them together. And it still wouldn't come to that feeling."

Richard was crying. At the time, I supposed this was because he was recalling a traumatic event, that is, his brush with death. However, I was completely wrong. Richard's tears were actually because of the *beauty* of the experience.

"It's deeply—ah, it's comfort—I don't know. Beauty and joy. Happiness. Knowing that He's there—or at least something's there. That this life is not the end. That death itself is a doorway. I honestly believe that and always will. You go from that transition of total pain, to nothing, to light, to comfort, to total love.... At least in my mind I saw that I am dying and *gosh this is great*—this is great, this is *the way it should be.*"[2]

But soon Richard reached a point where he had to return. In the middle of his journey he had the thought, "Wait a minute; my family needs me." Richard continued, "And I don't know whether I was talking physically or if you're thinking this—if this is actually your soul speaking—that you're at that point where you actually *are* your soul—that's what I think, that is why I feel it so deeply in my heart." After he collected himself for a moment, Richard continued.

"I thought that, and I repeated it several times, and then—no one spoke to me, it was just the comfort of that light, that over—overwhelming feeling of love. And then, when I'm thinking this, I kept thinking, 'Wait a minute, I can't go, they need me, but this feels so good. I don't want to go, but they're pulling at me. I got to go back. Can I go back?' And when I asked the words 'Can I go back?' it's like the light froze. This flow of light just stopped. It didn't go away. It stopped. And I kept thinking, 'I gotta go back.' And then it reversed. And it slowly started to go back. And at the point it went back, and the second it disappeared I was hit with pain. I was back in that intense pain and that blackness. And the next thing I know, the doctor's givin' me, whatever it is they're doing, pushing on my chest. We're in the emergency room. He's saying, 'You can't die.' He's saying, 'I've never lost a patient to a nose bleed before.' So I came to."

Richard didn't talk to anyone about what had happened to him at first, especially because he had never even heard of a near-death experience. "And after nine days in the hospital I told my wife about it, and then I told the doctor. And I didn't tell anybody else. I didn't want people to think I *was a nut*. The doctor says, 'I don't know what happened to you, but there was about five minutes there when you were totally out of my hands. There was nothing I could do for you.' And he said, 'When you came back it was my last-ditch effort.' All I remember he was beating on my chest."

Richard and I first talked about his near-death experience many years before I met Betty. After Betty, I was confronted by many of them. Every one of my clients who related a near-death experience were convinced they were face to face with something divine. All of their experiences seemed woven of the same cloth.

For example, there was Monica, a middle-aged woman and divorced mother of four who was another of my clinic pain patients. I had worked with her on and off for years. I asked if she would be willing for me to de-

Three—Death and Transcendence

vote part of one of our sessions to recording her near-death experience. She told me the following story.

> Well, this happened on March 19, 1981. It's the day I had my first child. And I woke up at two in the morning. And I was in labor. I didn't know because I was seven weeks early. And we were to take the first childbirth class that night. And anyway, I woke up and I had severe back pain. I went to the bathroom and I was bleeding heavily—which I didn't know at the time was abnormal. But we called the doctor and he said, "Come right in." I was in such bad pain. We lived seven miles out of town ... so we got there to the hospital.... They were remodeling, so I had nowhere to go except in the hallway on a cot. And I was losing a lot of blood—I was in a state of shock—I was in such bad pain from the word go. They had a port-a-potty and I kept having to use it, and blood was just everywhere. They came in and told me they were going to fly me to Spokane. But the baby was coming too fast...
>
> So all of a sudden all I remember they're rushing me to the operating room. There were doctors and nurses everywhere. And, uh, baby was just coming too fast to do anything and they couldn't give me anything for the pain, and, uh, it was just all kind of a blur. They're telling me to push—baby came real fast. And all of a sudden, I was in this tunnel thing. I remember it was a grayish color—it was like rocks but more uniform and ribbed. And it was kind of dark. And all of a sudden, the next thing I know, I was, like, on this cloud. I was in this bright, bright light. It was like a sunlight, but it was lighter or something—it was just brilliant. And all of a sudden, this overwhelming joy, happiness. And I could see, I could see the baby at this point. And I, I didn't know, you know, it was just this feeling that I had never experienced since, but best way I can explain it is the best sexual experience you ever had *times thousands*. That happiness, the joy—it—it was so warm. I didn't want it to end.
>
> Then all of a sudden, I'm back in the operating room. The doctors had the baby over, were examining her and they had shocked me to get my heart going again, so then I had a heart monitor on me.

I was curious about Monica's vantage point. She was looking at her baby but was not yet conscious in the ordinary sense. So how could she see? "Were you outside of your body when you saw her being born?" I asked.

"Yes, I was kind of looking down," she replied, "and it was kind of dark. I didn't want to come back. I really didn't. It was so cool, this place I was in—I don't know, it just happened so fast. And I've never been that happy in my whole life. And to me, you know, after this happened, I wouldn't tell anybody because—it was weird, you know, and I thought maybe I was in a dream—or I don't know."

"You said a dream. But did it seem real to you?" I asked.

"Yeah," she replied, "it was very real—very real."

The Spirit Transcendent

"Was it as real as that chair sitting there?" I asked, pointing to a chair beside her.

"Yes, yes definitely," she replied. "I can tell you this—this was Heaven. I know I was in Heaven, I know it. And I don't want to die, I'm afraid of dying, but if I'm going to Heaven this would be so wonderful. And they say you live eternally in Heaven, and I believe it. I'm scared about the eternity part because we know everything has a start to a finish—eternity doesn't have a finish, you know? But this, this place [was eternal]—then a few years later I watched this TV program where these people have these experiences and they see a kind of a tunnel, and *they're right*. That's just exactly what happened to me."

It turns out that Monica, like Richard, knew nothing of out-of-body experiences until she had one, and therefore she had no expectation to bias her. Also like Richard, she kept her experience a secret, out of fear that people would think she was crazy.

"I know I was with God. I *was*," Monica told me. "I didn't see Him, but I was in this place where He was. This is almost 30 years ago and thinking about it, you know, just puts me in awe. I never forgot it."

When I present stories like these to my colleagues, I never get very far. Always, my fellow academics, in a place like the Department of Psychology, will begin with the assumption that whatever did happen, it could not be *spiritual*. So they reason backwards. Couldn't the perception of the tunnel be the result of lack of oxygen in the occipital lobe? And that feeling of joy? "It must be an endorphin response." These explanations do not fit the actual experiences of my clients, if you take the time to listen. For example, Richard talked about love, and I don't think he would have mistaken that emotion for relief from pain. And then there is the problem of lucidity. Think about it. How do you get *lucidity* in a brain that is close to death? Most of us know first-hand what cognition is like if the brain is compromised. We might have experienced it, say, after a concussion, or in a high fever, or perhaps in a state of intoxication. These circumstances do not produce lucidity! Nor would events occurring in a compromised brain create such an indelible impression that they would be remembered so exactly decades later.[3]

Next is an example that defies all attempts to reduce a near-death experience to some sort of biological dysfunction. Debra was a middle-aged mother of two young girls. In one of our sessions she told me about her mother's final battle with chronic obstructive pulmonary disease (COPD). Debra was having a particularly difficult time with her mother's terminal illness because her father had died of the same cause not long before. Debra was at her mother's side as she lay in the hospital bed.

"My—my mom was dying. And she was having a hard time going."

"You felt this?"

"Yeah, something was holding her back. So I called my mom's friend. She said to me, 'Sing to her.' And she'd been in the hospital for four days and my adopted dad had just passed away before from the same thing. He'd had lung cancer but they're dying in the same way. I was having a real hard time watching her hang on like she was, 'cause I had just gone through it with Dad, and I just wanted her to go. And so, when her friend said, 'Sing to her,' I was like, 'What does that mean?' Well, my sister Sarah, my little sister Sarah, was on one side of the bed and I was on the other side of the bed and we were each holding her hand. Sarah started singing church hymns, and of course I didn't know them, so I was just listening to Sarah. And then Sarah starting singing 'Amazing Grace.' Well, that was one that I just happened to know. And we were singing this amazing harmony. We've never sung with each other before. We barely knew each other. And, um, it was beautiful, it was beautiful harmony. And neither one of us were great singers. But it was—I remember it being just beautiful."

"And then all of a sudden I was in, like, a Heaven-ish place—I don't like putting labels on things. But it was like a glowing yellow kind of a cloudy foggy glowing yellow and there was a Jesus-type figure and there was like an *acknowledgement* between my mom and Him. She grabbed His hand, and, well, she grabbed His hand, and they had the acknowledgement, and then she let go of *my hand* and I came back down. Like I had handed her off. But the feeling there was the purest form of love there is. And I was back in the hospital room and she was gone."

It was exactly at this moment, while Debra was in the "Heaven-ish place," that her mother breathed her last.

"Now, what is it exactly that you saw up there?" I asked, wanting more details.

"I did not *see* it," she replied. "It was just sort of a glowy hazy yellow.... It is this feeling. Oh, yeah—yeah. It was all the love ... and just all the most heartfelt, deepest, richest, wholest, truest, purist love—the most intense love. Just exactly the way it's supposed to be. Love. And that's ALL there was."

Unlike a dream or a fit of the imagination, Debra's experience was as concrete as actual perception. By now I had come to recognize this as a hallmark of a vision. In fact, some will tell me visions feel "realer than real." In Debra's case she naturally assumed that her sister must have had the same experience.

"And I went to Sarah and I went, 'Oh my gosh' and it took me a minute to realize that Sarah wasn't there [did not go to Heaven]. I just assumed she was there." The reason she, and not Sarah, went with her mother to Jesus dawned on Debra later.

"It was that day," Debra explained, "maybe a couple of days later, that I realized what happened. What I assumed happened was, my mom wouldn't go without—without making sure that I had my right to go to Heaven too. That she wouldn't let go without knowing, that even though I did not go to church, that I was OK to go to Heaven, even though I did not know God. I think she was afraid that I was going to go to Hell, because I didn't go to church. That was the deal."

"So your mom dies, but you're the one with the death experience."

"*I went with her.* I handed her off to Jesus."

So here Debra is having a near-death experience, but she is not the one dying! It all makes sense, but only if material explanations are left behind.[4] There is no reason to search for some biological reason for the feeling of love, or the perception of light, because love and light in NDEs are not at the level of human emotion and perception. They are part of a spiritual experience, discontinuous with ordinary reality, that is translated into human terms.

One of my favorite near-death stories was told to me by Shannon, a 69-year-old woman I met for the purpose of an assessment so she could be cleared to have a medical procedure. During my evaluation, Shannon let slip she had a profound experience when she nearly died. In a follow-up session I had the opportunity to ask her more about what she felt had happened and to make a recording. After some brief preliminaries at the beginning of our session, Shannon told me:

> I got septic shock in the hospital and I went into a coma. And they really did not think I was going to make it. My family was called and, um, they thought I was going to die.... This was in May of 2011.... And, um, then while I was there and they were all fussing around me *I had the most wonderful time.* I had the most awesome vision. It all started by all white. Just all white. I could see snow everywhere. It was kind of like snow blindness. And off to the right side was a train depot and it was covered in snow and there was a lady standing there in a big heavy coat because it was so cold. And off in the distance the vision through the snow, even though it was so heavy, you could see this train coming. And it was a very prominent, very spectacular Indian face that was the nose [of the train]. You could just see every detail of this face. And he had—it was an Indian chief. And

Three—Death and Transcendence

he had the most awesome headdress on that covered the first car of the train. It was all his headdress. In colors that were *beyond belief*. Beyond belief—I have never, ever in my life—and I have been all across the United States, north and south of here—but I have never ever, *ever* seen colors of this magnitude. The yellows, the reds, the browns, the blues, the greens, were just take your breath away, take-your-breath-away colors.

And this woman—she thought it was gonna stop and pick her up. But it didn't stop. It just kept going. She wanted to go with it really bad. She wanted to get on that train.

"Who was this woman?" I asked.

"I think it was me," Shannon replied, her voice cracking with emotion. "I wanted to go. I wanted to get on that train so bad and go where it was going. All you could see if you looked in the direction where the train was going it was still all white, but I wanted to go really bad. Really bad."

And a little later Shannon laughed and told me, "If I ever see that train again I'm gonna run in front of it. And I'm getting on it. I am getting on that train. I'm going to make it stop." Shannon's memory of the vision, even months after the fact, seemed so clear it was like something that had been registered inside of her. She couldn't stop talking about it. She gave me more details about the train.

> I could see [the first car] from the side. It was the side of an Indian. Beautiful male Indian person, American Indian. And, uh, the headdress. Oh my gosh! It was magnificent—just magnificent.... The second car was a female. The whole train were Indians. The second car was a female. She was just in a beige—she wasn't so predominant. But the color of brown I can't even describe it. I guess you might say it was the color of the bushes out there. It was creamy tan. But it was brilliant! Just brilliant. She was kind of nondescript as far as anything else about her. But the second car [the second car after the engine] was another Indian male that was one down from the chief and he also had a headdress on. So the chief's headdress kind of covered up the female somewhat, because it was so magnificent. Then the second one was not as big as his, but the colors were still just as brilliant. And then after that, to me, it was just cars.

The next part of Shannon's vision was less distinct. She had the feeling "that people were trying to explain things to me about something that had happened or was going to happen ... and the more they talked and the more they tried to make me understand the more confusing it became." And then, at the end of the vision, according to Shannon, "the last thing I can remember before coming out of the coma was asking God to please take me and He said, 'No, not yet.'"

"You spoke with God?"

"I just heard a voice," Shannon replied, "and since I was appealing to

The Spirit Transcendent

God to take me, I would assume it would be Him. And it just said, 'No, not yet.' And then after that is when I came out of the coma."

Shannon was unconscious for two and a half days. When she recovered, she told some of her family about her experience and about her real regret at not having been able to "board the train." From her family's point of view, Shannon was longing for death—they thought she was suicidal! They even tried to have her admitted to the psychiatric wing of the hospital. What a complete misreading of Shannon's experience! Unlike a suicidal person, Shannon was not unhappy with life or with herself—she was grieving the loss of a spiritual union. In my session with her, Shannon was still trying to cope with the loss. I was able to provide some comfort by telling her that the great mystics of the past understood this exact feeling and that St. Teresa of Avila had written of the same variety of grief hundreds of years ago.[5]

Shannon's family never was able to understand her. She argued with them, telling her family the psychiatrists were a waste of time. As she spoke, Shannon lifted her hand and said, "I have a 'little revolver, that just *fits my hand perfectly*, and it would make better sense for them to take *that* away, if they were really worried.'" At the same time, it was a reminder that I practice in North Idaho, where grandmothers and handguns sometimes still go together.

All along, I had been operating under the assumption that a spiritual experience is at a different level than the human. I asked Shannon about this, directly.

"Why would you tell someone it was more than a perception?"

"Because of the way you feel inside." Shannon seemed emphatic. "It's a spiritual feeling inside you." Again, there was talk of love. "I guess what comes to mind is my heart felt so good. You know how when you do something, you just feel good all over? You're really happy you did that and it makes you feel really, really good. That's the closest I think I can come to explaining it, but it's far beyond that.... You can actually live better having felt that."[6]

Shannon was changed by her experience, and I had the impression it was not on a superficial level but deep in the core of her personality. This, I believe, tells us that something was working at a spiritual level, at a level beyond simple human concerns.

Another of my patients, Sandra, showed more directly a spiritual experience can begin a process that unfolds and transcends the human.

Everyone would say Sandra had a lot going for her. She was so bright that by age 15 she was already in college and she obtained a doctorate in Special Education at a younger age than any other student in the history of her department. If this were not enough, Sandra was extremely attractive—tall, blonde-haired, blue-eyed, with fine, slightly exotic features that reflect a heritage that is one quarter Cherokee. And on top of it all, she is an accomplished musician, playing classical harp at a professional level.

Eight years ago, on Christmas Day, Sandra was skiing with friends when she slid past a marked trail, went out of control, and hit a tree going 45 miles per hour. She was wearing a helmet, which certainly saved her life, but her face felt the full impact. Every single one of her facial bones were fractured, as was her skull in four places. Given the severity of Sandra's injury, the prognosis is usually death. But not only did Sandra survive, her accident was the beginning of a spiritual journey and a personal transformation.

After the impact, there was a very brief period of unconsciousness. Sandra found herself lying in snow that was red with her blood. She was at the top of the mountain and the weather was bad enough that an airlift was impossible. Instead, she was loaded onto a gondola for a ride to the base of the mountain. This particular gondola ride is advertised as the longest in the world—great for the tourist, but terrible for Sandra. By the time she got to the base, she was in incredible pain, and the whole gondola cart, and the members of the ski patrol who were with her, were covered in blood.

Sandra was first taken to a local hospital. By now she was begging for pain medication, but this was withheld because of the fear of neurological damage.

"I was laying in bed," Sandra told me, "and just hoping I would die so I could get out of this situation, when all of a sudden I was on the other side of the room."

At this exact point in time, her pain disappeared. "I was in this other corner and I was looking around and I could see the doctors working on me ... there were a lot of people in this little room and my body just looked lifeless and bloody and gross."

Sandra had the sense that her spirit, or soul, had left her body. "My spirit was by the door." And it was not just that she did not perceive pain—it was much more than this. "I was surrounded by peace and love." Sandra continued her story.

> Then everything melted away and there was this very bright light. I was elsewhere but I was in the room and looking. Then everything melted away and there was this very bright light, brighter than I had seen before, like a sun-lighted area—just

The Spirit Transcendent

white all around me—and I remember looking into this light that is all around me. I had different clothes on, I had this golden outfit that I sometimes play music [the harp] in, like a golden blouse and shirt that I go to play music in. And I remember I was wearing this golden outfit ... and I was looking into this light and this time I am saying I don't want to die—I don't want to go. I am not done here yet. I was telling this to God, and I couldn't see God, and I couldn't hear His voice, but we were communicating without words.

Sandra then began to bargain with God. "I don't want to die. I don't want to go," she cried out. "I remember holding these sheets of paper in my hand and looking into the light saying, 'See, I *can't* die yet because I have to complete my Ph.D.—it's almost done.' I have my harp, my friends, my family, and my son ... a sheet for each thing." Sandra tried to argue that she needed to remain on Earth for each of these reasons, but with each sheet of paper "God just said, 'That doesn't matter.' And soon all these sheets of paper were just gone, and the only sheet of paper that stayed was my child and the other was a close relationship I had developed—and I loved my harp, but even that didn't matter. Only two sheets of paper were left." There was a purpose to the vision: "I was reminded of my potential and what I should be doing with my life."

It was not yet time for Sandra to go back into her body. In the next part of the vision Sandra had a life-review. "God showed me what I had done, and how I had helped people, and how I had hurt people.... There was a time when I was a child and I called a little girl fat. I saw her cry and I could feel her feelings from her point of view. I saw a man I had met in the nursing home, and I could see how happy he felt to be visited." There were countless snapshots of Sandra's past life. "It was like being in a warehouse, and it's all dark, and then someone suddenly turns the light switch on, or it was like watching a fireworks display." It was as if the replay of experiences was like so many illuminating explosions overlaid one upon the other, firing in brilliant sequence.

Sandra told me that prior to the accident she was vain and self-centered. "I was interested in being an arrogant academic," is how she put it. Adding to that vanity was the fact that Sandra always had lots of attention: she was very pretty; she was the youngest student to graduate from her department with her doctorate; she was a professional musician. But in the few moments that she conversed with God and had her life-review, Sandra was changed. "I felt like I was shown those things so I could go back and live a full life that mattered."

"Despite how terrible it was, I'm thankful for that because I realized after that I could live a real life and I could be a better person. I can show love, I can show compassion, and I could do my part to make the world a better place because that's what matters—it's not all the stuff you have or all the degrees you have."

When Sandra went back into her body she returned to terrible physical pain. "I felt like I was a patchwork quilt," she said, speaking of her face, "and the patches were tearing apart. That terrible pain that wouldn't stop." So Sandra prayed. She prayed to be relieved of the pain; she thanked God that she was not paralyzed (a real possibility); she thanked God that she still had her senses and was not brain damaged. She felt that her prayer kept open a channel to God.

But then Sandra told me about another kind of suffering she was fated to endure: lying there helpless, her face crushed so she had no way to speak, and completely under the control of a supposed caregiver, she was sexually abused. Finally, Sandra's father arrived and saved her from the abuse. But there was still another trial: Sandra's father was a Vietnam veteran who suffered from PTSD. When he saw his daughter so disfigured, with trauma that was like what you would see on a battlefield, it triggered his PTSD symptoms and took him back to his own wartime experience. Worse, Sandra's father held extremely dogmatic religious views and thought that Sandra's accident must have been the result of her being "sinful" in some unknown way. He deprived her of her pain medicine, and he "forgot" to take care of her basic needs—giving Sandra food and water. He even destroyed the landline so she could not call for help. Sandra was trapped again.

Sandra prayed. She asked God, "Why not let me die? What do you want me to do—I called my family and they did not help."

God answered, "But you haven't called your *real* family." By this Sandra understood God to mean her *church* family: right after the accident Sandra was having her son stay with a Mormon couple. Sandra found her cell phone and was able to make a call to them. She was rescued, and from that point forward she finally had someone to watch over and protect her.

"I never would have been able to endure the pain," and by this Sandra meant not just physical pain, which itself was unbearable, but the emotional pain of being abused "without God's help." Sandra felt that a direct connection with God had opened up from the first, and the channel remained open. "It was as if my spirit was fortified, poured out and then replaced with something stronger.[7] That was how I could survive."

Sandra's story did not end there. After she returned from the brink of death—she would say after God allowed her to return—Sandra came back with gifts. "When I came back from that experience," Sandra told me, "it's like my intellectual capacity went up." This first became clear to Sandra about 10 days after surgery. While still in great pain, she sat down to play her harp. "I played perfectly ... and I didn't mess up, and not only that, but when I actually started playing I was playing almost repertoire quality—all of the songs where I used to have sheet music to do anything with were now *there*."

Sandra found she could play perfectly from memory, effortlessly, fluidly. And her enhanced memory was not just for music. She also began to remember events from her past, exact records of memories previously unavailable to her. Many of these memories were confirmed by her mother, so they were in fact real events that she was now recalling.

And there were other cognitive skills: "When I was in the hospital, when I first started speaking, they said, 'She speaks like a five-year-old professor,' because I was high as a kite [from the pain meds] but incredibly articulate in the way I was speaking—I didn't have to search for words—they just came.... I still have intellectual skills but what I had then was incredible ... the way I was speaking was so fluid and so easy, and the vocabulary I was using was so complex, and it was so smooth to put this all together. It was incredibly witty, using satire, playing on words." Sandra's friends, who knew her (rather considerable) abilities prior to the accident, were witness to, and impressed by, her new mental agility.

Sandra's gifts appeared not long after a trauma that was so severe that the usual prognosis is death. Yes, Sandra had a helmet on, but her skull was severely fractured. How is it that someone not only survives this kind of injury, but then is intellectually *better* than before? There are some cases in the neurological literature which, on the surface, are somewhat like Sandra's. These are cases where a traumatic brain injury seems to have released special talents, among them artistic gifts.[8] However, these are so rare—perhaps only a handful of such cases worldwide—that although they appear in the literature, probably most clinicians have yet to see one firsthand. So while Sandra's increase in ability is not impossible, I think of it as being on the order of being struck by a meteor. Well, such a thing has happened, to someone, somewhere, but the chances are so vanishingly small that you will never meet someone who can tell you personally about it.

Sandra has no question that her story of survival is about God: "I could never have gone through what I went through," Sandra told me, "without my spirit having been fortified by God." It was as if her original spirit was transformed and then returned to her. "I was a shell that was filled with a super strong spirit—with a fortified version of my own spirit."

"What did it feel like to find that you had gifts?" I asked.

"The way I could compare it to is if you have embers," Sandra answered. "You have coals in the fire, but if you stoke those coals they begin to combust and they will really become quite brilliant. But if you leave them alone they are still there—they have the capacity, but they're not yet lit up yet—they're not manifesting that capacity. And that's how I felt. That that capacity, or those skills that I had—they opened up to me."

So as to fulfill her promise to God to live a life that mattered, Sandra decided she would volunteer to play the harp. She chose to do this for people who were close to death, and soon her harp (a serious professional instrument that is some seven feet tall) was housed in a local nursing home. Sandra told me that she had a wish to get close to death, not for any morbid reason, but rather for its spiritual value.

It is difficult enough to grasp Sandra's enhanced memory and heightened intelligence, but there were *other* sets of abilities that opened up to Sandra and which were explicitly spiritual in nature. My first hint of this came when Sandra told me that her intuition about what was going on with people around her had become so heightened that she was accused of being psychic.[9] Much of this played out during her volunteer work.

"With my nursing home patients," Sandra said, "it is like I could immediately know what was going on with them, and I knew when someone needed me. I'd be going down the hall and I would hear God in my head, telling me, 'Go in that room' or 'Go in there' or 'Go back.' I was definitely being directed—there were 65 rooms in the nursing home, and you could not visit them all."

And when Sandra played for the dying, she could sense changes on a spiritual level.

There was one resident for whom Sandra played for perhaps an hour and a half. "The woman was in great pain, just writhing in her bed, going back and forth, back and forth. And then when I played, I felt that Heaven was opening up—it was getting ready for her.... There was a light and a peace.... The music was taking me to a different plane."

"This is beautiful," I said, captivated by the imagery of it. "Were there other times as well?"

"There was this 84-year-old man who was my favorite at the nursing

The Spirit Transcendent

home, and I would make him brownies and cupcakes ... because they [the nursing home] didn't give treats out. I really loved him, and he was dying."

"I played for him for three hours, then when he was near the end he took on this rattle that people do as they are dying ... his family couldn't watch him because it was too hard, so they left the room ... and they called me—'Could you come in and play music for him?' Well, at first, I felt his soul was over there," Sandra pointed across the room, "but when he was within minutes of dying, I didn't feel his presence over there [by his body] anymore. I felt his presence on my side of the harp, by my right shoulder. And then I had a strong sense, a communication—he thanked me and left."

Hearing the totality of her story, I thought, "God must surely be a playwright." In the first scene, you are introduced to a beautiful, young, but somewhat conceited Ph.D. student who plays classical harp. In the next scene, she has a near-death experience and must reckon with God about what in life is important. Next, after being shown Heaven, she has to bargain with God, asking why she should be allowed to come back. An agreement with God is struck, and Sandra is returned. But this time her conceit has fallen away, and in exchange she is given special gifts. In the last scene, Sandra is playing her golden harp to individuals who themselves are dying and whose souls are about to go on journeys of their own.

To this day, Sandra plays her harp for the dying, and when she plays she feels her music opens up a channel to the spiritual world. She says of the feeling of the spirit that she gets during these times, "it is as if a scarf is fluttering in the wind."

Four

At the Bottom Rung of the Ladder

There is another class of events, besides coming close to death, that seems to have the power to bring about a spiritual event. These are circumstances where a person is in a personal crisis, at the very bottom of life, with nowhere to turn and no hope for the future.

Loretta, another of my pain clinic patients, brought this home to me. She was 45 years old, a Southerner who had just moved to Idaho from Atlanta. She had that genteel manner you associate with Southerners, and she spoke with that typical, soft Southern drawl. She was referred to me for help with pain management and the emotions that can sometimes act to make pain seem worse than it is. But Loretta's physical pain was real. It was the product of injuries sustained in an automobile accident about seven years prior.

Loretta came across as a conservative, middle-aged mother. I could image her ferrying kids back and forth to soccer practice, and it seemed out of character when I learned she had a history of drug abuse. And it was not a mild history either. She was an IV user of methamphetamine and heroin, was arrested and had spent time in jail. After court-ordered inpatient rehabilitation, lasting nine months, she emerged drug-free.

Along with the story of her drug addiction, Loretta told me about a spiritual awakening that transformed her life. In my third meeting with Loretta, I asked her permission to record the session. I began by simply asking Loretta how the addiction started. She told me that her life was going well, she was happily married, she and her husband both had good jobs that paid reasonably well.

"Everything is working great until I had my car wreck and that stopped everything. And then two and a half weeks later, Richard got laid off from his job, or fired from it. Fired, but they had to let him go because

The Spirit Transcendent

he had MS, and the car wreck stressed him out so bad that he was tripping and falling in his job ... and they had to let him go because he was such a liability for the company. So ... our bills are still coming in ... and they gave him some pay when they first laid him off, but things got really hard on us."

After the disaster of the accident, losing her job and then her husband losing his, Loretta was exposed to drugs. She told me how it happened. She had a birthday party, and "this guy came to the party, and after the party was over he said, 'Would you like to try something?' and he went out to the car ... and let us try some meth, and it was really good stuff. And I like—wow—and Richard [Loretta's husband] didn't try it but I did.... Because he liked us he left four ounces of drugs with us."

I'm not sure if Loretta understood that this was not so much a matter of "liking" as it was an attempt to get her hooked. Sometime later, the dealer came back with the proposal that Loretta and her husband deal drugs. They took him up on his offer. Richard became "the business man of it," Loretta explained, and unlike Loretta, he did not do any of the drugs himself. "It took the place of the money we were missing, because the business was so good.... We did ounces. People we sold to five-and-dimed it out. We stayed in business like that from 2003 'til 2006." By this time Richard was fed up with Loretta's accelerating drug use so he moved out of the home and was staying in an apartment.

Richard insisted that Loretta seek drug treatment. She agreed, and she and Richard had begun to reconcile. Then another tragedy struck. Just before Father's Day, Richard, who in addition to having MS, was diabetic, had a stroke. Loretta moved back to the apartment so she could care for him. One day, she went to the store to run an errand, but when she returned, she discovered his lifeless body lying on the bed.

The death was a terrible shock to Loretta. She didn't know how to cope with it, and besides, she was still heavily abusing drugs. Loretta was not a religious woman—she hardly ever attended church and she had no particular belief in God. But at this true nadir of her life, Loretta called out to God.

"I was sitting there on the toilet, you know, in the bathroom doing a shot [mixing meth in a spoon and then injecting it], and I asked the Lord, 'Lord, if there's a Lord out there, *I need to know it.*' I was desperate." In the weeks that followed, Loretta sensed a change within her that she did not understand. "I was so confused at this point. My son was with me and I kept on saying, 'Joe David, I can't *think*, there's something going on inside

Four—At the Bottom Rung of the Ladder

my *head*.' And I kept on referring to it as a war. There's a *war* going on inside of me."[1]

Loretta was profoundly depressed. She continued her drug use. And then she was driving along a back road. It happened to be near where a concert was being held, so the police were out with roadblocks trying to catch drunk drivers. Loretta was stopped and when the police found she had syringes, meth, heroin, and "a bunch of other pills" in her possession, she was arrested.

Loretta had a spiritual experience after she had been in jail for about four months. "When I got to jail," she told me, "I was tired of sitting in my cell all the time. So the girl said, 'Come and go to church.' 'Well,' I said, 'at least it gets me out of this cell.' And I got up there and the man was an ex–IV drug user. And he said, 'Do you know you have been saved by grace through faith, not of yourself, it's a gift of God?' So when I got back to my cell, I'm 'OK, now about this gift from God'—if He's really a God and He's out there and He's going to give me this gift of salvation, if all I do is receive it, then I'm going to receive it. I want a gift…. And He came alive—something happened to me."

"Something happened to you?" I asked.

"When I got back from church, I took the mat off of my little bed. Got it on the floor and I cried out. I asked Him to forgive me for the wrong that I had done. Selling the drugs and all that and everything that I had done. And if He was the Lord God of love and all this—well, I needed to know Him. I messed my life up, my husband's dead and gone, so if you're real, I need you, and I'll give you everything I have 'cause I have *nothing*. A desperation cry—'If there's somebody out there please come.'"

Loretta told me that after she was asleep, "God woke me up with two scriptures, Matthew 5, and the other was Revelation 22:13." (Revelation 22:13 states: "I am the Alpha and the Omega, the First and the Last, the Beginning and the End!")

I was surprised. "You were woken up, and with chapter and verse? Sounds pretty specific, but you told me you didn't know the Bible."

"Oh no, I never read the Bible," Loretta replied. "I never even picked one up, didn't have a reason to do so … the Bible never been cracked open before then because I didn't know how to read it."

Loretta had the option of leaving jail for a drug treatment program. This program, Damascus Way in Columbus, Georgia, had a spiritual orientation, and admission was based on guidance received through prayer.

The Spirit Transcendent

"I was with them, it was a trial thing, and God spoke to 'em and said I needed to be there."

Loretta's most crucial spiritual experience came three days after she was admitted. She was concerned about her husband and wanted to know what happened to him after death and if he was in Heaven. She was with a group of women in the program, silently praying about her husband's fate.

> I'm just sitting there with my head down and I'm saying [in prayer] I would like to know if my husband made it to You. This woman gets up and comes over there and taps me on the shoulder and says, "The person you're praying about is in Heaven and is with the Lord," is what she said. She didn't know I was praying because I wasn't even saying it, I was just thinking it, you know, in my mind. She says, "I don't know what this is supposed to mean, but the person you're praying about is with Him." And I fell apart, I fell apart.... It was super intense.... I guess it was Him manifesting in me or something because I changed, I never felt the same—I never viewed things the same way.... And, uh, the Holy Spirit fell. I mean, it's my third day there and I don't know *what* fell, but it was a *power*. It was something thick in that room that I had never seen or never experienced.... It was a thickness in that room and it was something that just changed. It's like.... *It turned me inside out.* I mean whatever was left of me in the world, it took that away from me. I mean—I don't know how to explain that, but I've never been the same since that day. I've never been the same.[2]

Loretta made some lasting friendships with other women who were thrown together in the rehabilitation program at Damascus Way. She kept in touch with several of them, and between our sessions, Loretta had been talking with a few of her friends, asking what they felt she should tell me about the spiritual experiences they all encountered at that time. Loretta especially wanted me to speak with her friend Linda. Before I had thought much about how best to contact Linda, Loretta had her cell phone out and was already making the call. I had been recording the session with Loretta, so I put the call on speakerphone, and Loretta and I spoke with her together.

Linda told me that prior to recovery she had a 17-year crack cocaine addiction, and *before that* she was an alcoholic for 16 years. "I had been on the streets for about 15 years," she said, "homeless. It was a horrible, horrible situation. And I was literally dying."

"Loretta was telling me that you and she were delivered at the same time," I said. "Do you remember what happened—what you felt?"

"No, mine was a few days earlier, when I was still in jail," Linda said.

"Well, were you there when Loretta says the spirit fell upon her?"

"Yeah, a lady just picked her out—picked Loretta out, didn't know

Four—At the Bottom Rung of the Ladder

Loretta from anybody, she wasn't there five minutes and she told Loretta that the one she was worried about was okay, and he wanted her to know that he was okay, that he was with God. Yeah, I was there for that."

"Linda, would you be willing to tell me about that spiritual experience you had in jail? What happened?"

Linda replied:

> Okay, I guess I can. Like I said, I had gotten into the Word and I was reading it, I don't know, I was never a Bible person. I didn't go to church as a child when I was young.... A lady handed me a Bible and said, 'Why don't you try this?' And I started to read in the Psalms, in the book of Psalms. And I realized there was hope, I found hope for someone like me 'cause I was totally hopeless. Been homeless for 10 years, I was just totally a drug addict. So in any words of survival I found hope. That got me interested, and I just wanted to read more, to read more, and I just got a hunger for the Bible and just couldn't get enough of it. And then one day, it was actually a physical feeling of warmth that came all over my body. And there was a lot of people in there and there was a lot of noise in there so—this is in jail—so I felt like I needed to get somewhere quiet. So we have a mop closet where they kept the things that we mopped the floor with. It was a mop closet. So I got in there and I just felt the power of God come over me, and a sense of peace, and knew that I had been delivered and that was five years ago. And I have never, I can't even remember what it [crack cocaine] tasted like or what it felt like, and I never relapsed. I never wanted it, never had any cravings. Nothing.[3]

Finding God in a mop closet. How remarkable. And the suddenness, depth, and transformative nature of the experience was very similar to what had happed to Loretta. So too was the feeling of being desperate and helpless, and of being at rock-bottom, before being saved.

Loretta and Linda had decided beforehand there were two events at the rehab that I ought to know about: one was a time when Loretta was healed, the other was the appearance of a dove. First, the healing: Loretta had a problem with her foot. It was frozen in a downward position, a consequence of her car accident and earlier extensive trauma to her leg. Because of it, she could hardly walk. Loretta told me about the healing.

> All these women were just sitting around seated, when the woman brushed my shoulder. She's saying to me, "The Lord wants me to take you for a walk." And I'm like, "Ma'am, I can't walk." And I said, "You know, I can't walk because of my foot." And then she said, "Well that's why the Lord wants me to take you for a walk." It was the first time that I had seen her being there because I had just been there a month, maybe. And she brushed my shoulder and told me that she needed to take me for a walk. I got up from the table and I showed her my foot. Around the table, and that's as far as I got. And she said, "Do you mind if me and my sister pray for you?" Well, I didn't mind anybody praying for me.... The woman got up

from the table, 'cause it was so intense and they made a circle around. These two women, one's on her knees holding my leg, the other one's holding my head and my stomach. As they prayed, my foot just receded down. And that was completely amazing. Because I could get it, get it in the shoe. They were praying in tongues. They started out just, you know, talking and thanking God, you know, for what He was doing, and they were already thanking Him for healing my foot, and I was like "That's pretty bold" for them to go in and start thanking Him even before anything happened. And as they were just giving thanks and everything, and they went off into the spirit.... It was just really amazing. And so now I could wear a shoe.[4]

Linda and Loretta had decided I also needed to hear about the dove. Loretta had already told me the story of the dove in an earlier session. Here is what she told me earlier:

> I am at the rehab, and I'm sitting there talking to an elderly woman, Judy, and we're sitting like this, and all of a sudden there is a dove and it is translucent, if you know what translucent is.... And it's amazingly bright. So I get up and I walk over to it. OK, when I get over to it, it was turning translucent. It was white, and it turned translucent. And I'm screaming, I'm making noise and you'd think it would scare the thing away.... And I want to tell you something—that place was in disarray. It was chaos amongst the women because you got 21 from all over the world, you know, at this place, different walks of life and there's no unity, not getting along. I mean it's really chaos amongst us. Well, when that dove came it brought unity, it brought peace, and it brought love to everybody. I mean, it was *amazing*.... I mean, loving people, you know, that you don't even *want* to love. It *stayed* that way.... That dove stayed in the yard for the rest of the afternoon.

Even though I was already familiar with the story, I asked Linda to tell me about it because I wanted to get her view, separate from Loretta's. "Linda, this dove, Loretta says it came, stayed, and went from white to translucent. By that I mean did you see it almost disappear?"

"No, I didn't see it," Linda said, "but I talked with a lady who said the tail went white to translucent." For Linda, what seemed most important was the way the dove changed the atmosphere at Damascus Way.

> OK, well, we were having a very bad day there. You know how it is when we get 12 or 15 women in a small area, and all these people had bad experiences in their lives. We were just having a bad day, where everybody was yelling at everybody else. They were arguing and there was just a lot of tension and a lot of stress. And it was really hard, because we had to get along. Like Loretta and I, we were court ordered—had we done something to get kicked out, we would have gone back to jail. Anyway, Loretta first saw it, and it was a huge white dove. And it was sitting out in the yard. And some of the girls walked by it and shooed it away and it would not leave. It was sitting there, and she took pictures of it. And then it eventually did leave. When it did leave there was a sense of peace that came over

Four—At the Bottom Rung of the Ladder

that building, and people were hugging each other, forgiving each other, and there were tears, and the whole climate of the place completely changed.

Learning about Loretta's spiritual experience, and the results that followed, make me think of Sandra. When Sandra told me her story of nearly dying and conversing with God, I was much taken with the fact that the spiritual part of the experience was not a one-time event. It was more like a door opened, and afterwards Sandra was left with a sensitivity she had not had before. When she was volunteering in the nursing home, God would tell her which of the residents she needed to speak to. It was like being clairvoyant and being impelled to obey God's will at the same time. I saw the same—call them spiritual after-effects—in Loretta.

"When He says move, I move—you know what I'm saying," Loretta said. "I'm not going to let anything hold me back from that. And so, I just can't. When He says, 'Go,' I go, and tells me to do things, I do it. I don't know how to explain that, but there's that inner thing in me, that inner spirit within me that is a guide to me. It's almost like a compass that's been built in."[5]

"Sounds like God is pretty immediate for you," I replied. "But lots of people have trouble finding God or even believing God exists and is not some sort of fiction."

"He's not far away; He's real close. Some people look at Him and think they have to pray to a God that's way out there. But really, He's not. He's within you if you just search. You'll find him. It's like that door." Loretta pointed at the door to my office. "Once you open it, He comes in and fills that area with a fullness and richness."

Loretta told me there was a time when she was concerned about not going to church, thinking this might be displeasing to God, so she prayed about it. "God told me that He didn't want me in church because it was like 'They're goin' put your light out. You're brighter outside the church.' It's not about religion," Loretta declared. "It's about a simple relationship with the Lord."

Loretta firmly believed in answered prayer. She gave me lots of examples, although I will admit that she seemed too ready to read God's will into common coincidence. For example, there was an ancient car at Damascus Way that stopped running when they most needed it. Rather than call a mechanic, the car was prayed over, the hood anointed with oil, and then, Loretta told me, with glee in her voice, "that sucker started right up!"

Loretta prayed for me too. After working with her for the space of perhaps six or eight sessions, I let her know about my designs for a book

The Spirit Transcendent

and especially my need to find a publisher. Not to worry! Between sessions, Loretta was on the Internet with more of her buddies from rehab, and they were on the job. "The Prayer Warrior Sisters have got your back," she told me.

But there were other examples of answered prayer that were not so easy to explain away.

> My dad saw how I would just pray and things would happen.[6] It was a cold winter in Georgia and we didn't have any firewood. We were going to buy some. It was real expensive. And I was in my room and I was specifically praying about firewood. You know, "Lord, that's what keeps us warm, you know you say ask and we shall receive, and we shall not lack in anything," and … I believed it. And I was already thanking Him for it. I was already thanking Him for it. I was like "Praise God. Thank you for the wood." And I come out from where I was praying, and I told my dad, "Put your money up, we're going to get some wood today." And he kinda laughed. But then we go to Walmart, do a little shopping around town and come back, and there is a dump truck with *eight cords of wood*, red oak, just as big as you can imagine, and, um, the guy didn't even charge us, just gave us the wood. It was amazing. It lasted my dad all that winter and into the next winter.

"Well, did your dad know the guy who delivered the wood?"

"Ah, yes—my dad knew him," Loretta replied, "and it's just like 'I came across this wood and I thought about you.' And I'm 'Yup, that's God, making him think about him.' He was clearing some land and he just happened to think about my dad, you know."

Like Loretta, Betty was at a point in her life where it seemed there was nowhere to turn. "It's when you are at the lowest rung of the ladder," Betty told me, "or when maybe there ain't no ladder at all, that God helps out." This is the story of Betty's marriage.

When Betty was just 16, two women in her Bible study group began to talk with her about "this preacher that was all crippled up and was looking for a wife." This is how Betty met Mr. Anderson. He was 31 at the time, a hunchback, with one leg shorter than the other. The women at church would set up opportunities for Betty to be with him after church, telling her that it was "God's will" that she should marry him. Betty brought him home, but her father objected severely, and being just 16, Betty felt she had to obey her parents' wishes. Just two weeks after she was 18, when she no longer needed her parents' permission, she married. The church put on the entire affair, even going so far as to purchase her dress. Then Betty left home and moved with Mr. Anderson to Bremerton, Washington, where, besides being a preacher in a small country church, he worked in the shipyards.

Four—At the Bottom Rung of the Ladder

Betty's marriage was a sham. She soon found out that she was basically a slave, doing the cooking, laundry, and being the ideal "preacher's wife." Her husband was domineering and abusive. Betty was not to talk with the parishioners about her own life. She should only speak about superficial things like the weather, or she was to listen patiently, passively to the parishioners' problems. In the true mold of an abusive husband, Mr. Anderson forbid her to have any contact with her family. She could not even write letters to them, and he kept her isolated for the next 15 years. When she didn't obey him, he would slap her around. He was dictatorial. "I couldn't even boil water," Betty said, "unless he told me when to boil it, how much to boil it, why it was boiling. Everything had to be just what he wanted." And if he was dissatisfied, he would take his unusually long arms, hold Betty by the back of her head, put her nose in the corner and make her stand there for hours. Betty could not even try to talk with him—he wore two hearing aids, one in each ear, and when Betty tried to get his attention he'd turn them off so that he would be "stone deaf." There was no affection in the relationship and sex was just an extension of the abuse.

Betty got to the point where she wanted a divorce. She confronted Mr. Anderson about her maltreatment, but he just told her that this was just the way it was, and anyway there was nothing she could do about it. He told her that if she divorced him, she would go to Hell. At the time Betty believed this, as, after all, this was the word of a (supposed) man of God.

Since for Betty divorce was not an option, she tried running away. Betty's property was about two or three miles from the highway. To reach the property, you had to take a one-lane bridge, one that she and Mr. Anderson had constructed out of logs and timber, to be able to cross a creek. Each time Betty tried to load up the car and run away, Mr. Anderson would block her way with his truck on this one-lane road. The fourth time Mr. Anderson found her trying to leave, he ordered her to stand in front of the shop door. Betty complied, not really knowing why he asked her to stand there, but then Mr. Anderson got in the car and backed it up, pinning her with the car bumper to the shop door. Betty couldn't stand because her legs were being crushed, but she could not fall either—she simply slumped over the car. She screamed with pain, and she was afraid that since she was trapped, Mr. Anderson would come over and beat her. But he didn't. He just looked over to see what he had done and left her there pinned to the wall, as he went inside the house. About 20 minutes later he reemerged. Then he stood there, with his hands on his hips, scolding: "Now what are

The Spirit Transcendent

you going to do? Are you going to run away again?" He demanded, "You are going to stay there until you promise you won't run away." Finally, after getting Betty to promise, he let her go, and Betty was able to crawl back into the house.

Betty had been telling me all of this in the comfort of my office. When she had finished telling me about the abuse, Betty pulled up both of her pants legs, drawing them over her knees, to show me the scars, still visible from that time decades ago. I was deeply moved seeing the marks of what she had been through.

Mr. Anderson could not make a living from his work as a minister, so over the next few years he built up a cabinet shop. He was the one who found the jobs, remodeling and such, while Betty did most of the actual work. This took its toll—over the next nine years Betty had nine miscarriages. Then, in her 10th year of marriage, Betty became pregnant with her second child, Rachel.

"I was fighting for my life," Betty summed it up. "I was drowning." When she got to her eighth month of pregnancy, Betty said to herself, "This is no type of life into which to bring a child." She stood on the edge of the bridge that crossed the creek. It was during a flood stage, so looking down she could see the muddy water and a swift current about 10 feet below. And then Betty said to herself, "Oh, God, I can't stand this no more, I'm going to end it. What's the use of living? Things cannot get any worse." But then Betty heard God's voice—and His words to Betty were, "If things can't get any worse, then they've got to get better." For Betty, this was the first time she had any hope, hope of anything getting any better.

Right at this moment, after deciding not to jump, a transformation began to take place. Within a few minutes, Betty's thinking had changed. God had told her things would get better, and she began to trust in this and to have confidence in it. She did not know how it would happen, but she believed her situation would change.

Soon after this, Betty began to have a series of visions. They began either that first night or a few nights after having heard God's voice, but they continued in a similar theme for years afterwards. In those first days, when Betty went to bed she would "lay there and cry. Cry and cry and cry. Cry myself to sleep." Mr. Anderson would be on the other side of the bed, separate from her, not talking to her, not touching Betty. After crying herself to sleep, Betty suddenly found herself in a tunnel.

"You had a dream?" I asked.

Four—At the Bottom Rung of the Ladder

"No, no," Betty replied. "Ah, it was too, too vivid, to have been a dream, you know what I mean?"

Betty paused, and then described her vision to me:

> I remember I was crying.... I was in this tunnel and I was standing in the tunnel kind of looking around as best I could in the very dark twilight and my eyes fell on this creature that was standing over on one side, and it was a hooded figure. He had one of these sweatshirts with the hood—I could not see his face, you see. I didn't know where I was or what was goin' on. And he looked over at me and he held out his hand toward me like this [Betty gestured with an opening motion of her hand], and he says, "Follow me." And I was desperate enough I would do anything. So I reached over and took his hand. I was behind him like a little kid taking his hand. I came up behind him—well, he kind of turned, you see, like we was goin' down this tunnel, and I was right up beside him like this [Betty again gestured] and I came right up behind him with his hand stretched out like this. And I took ahold his hand. Then I saw his face and I knew it was Jesus.

Even knowing Betty as I had come to know her, I was surprised, perhaps a bit like she herself had been at the time, to be meeting Jesus in the tunnel. Perhaps I should have anticipated the story would be about Jesus when I heard the words: "follow me."[7]

Betty continued, picking up from a point in the vision when Jesus had just turned his back to her.

"I realized He had this backpack on his back and He had these tools in it—funny, strange-looking tools. [At the time] ... He didn't mention about 'em, nothing, you see, but, He just said, 'Come follow me.'"

"Tools, Betty? He had a backpack with tools in it?"

"You might think," Betty replied, "there might be a hoe and a hammer, but these were strange-looking tools. They just weren't *earthly*."

Betty continued to walk down the tunnel with Jesus, and then the vision finally ended. Betty believed at this point she probably just went to sleep.

Betty returned to this vision again and again. "In a few days life would be Hell. And I would go to bed crying myself to sleep and I'd be in the tunnel again, and Jesus was with me. I was always hitting this point where I was desperate that something different would happen and things would not be so hard, so miserable for me."

But then, remarkably, Jesus provided specific solutions for Betty's problems. In her vision, Betty would be talking to Jesus, "telling him what Mr. Anderson was doing. And He was sympathetic ... and then He stopped, and He reached down and He pulled out one of them tools out of his backpack, and He says, 'This is a tool I want you to try.' And He says,

The Spirit Transcendent

'This is what you do with it ... when Mr. Anderson does this again, you use this tool against him, and see if it will work—maybe it will work for you."'

Betty called the use of these tools "spirit procedures." But the really interesting part of the story is that Betty's "spirit procedures" actually worked! For example, Betty could not speak to Mr. Anderson because he would turn off his hearing aids, and even if he was able to hear her, he would treat her as more of a slave than a wife. The spirit tool applied to this situation was to "read his mind and know what he was thinking."

"He would want a certain kind of meal, no matter what I had fixed for dinner, but then in the tunnel, the night before, Jesus would tell me what I was supposed to fix. Jesus told me the wood, what kind, how much, to buy for the cabinet shop. So when [Anderson] came home he found everything was fixed exactly as he wanted it, and the shop was supplied too."

Mr. Anderson found this pretty disturbing, and he became frightened of Betty. "This just blew his mind," Betty said. He began to accuse Betty of witchcraft and tell other people "that I was pulling witchcraft things on him."

Betty might have visions of being in the tunnel every few days, or six months or more might pass between visions. Toward the end of the series, many years later, there were signs of hope reflected in the vision itself.

"I began to see light at the end of the tunnel, and I wanted to hurry. [But Jesus said to me,] 'No, just follow me.' We went to the end of the tunnel ... [and] there was this great big iron grate. We couldn't get out of the tunnel. And Jesus was saying, 'We will find a way, we will find a way.'"

This was around the time that Betty finally obtained a divorce from Mr. Anderson. "And then," according to Betty, "the last thing I knew, the grate flew open at the same time I got the divorce ... it was kind of like God has delivered me from this terrible mess. Then I realized that I had the backpack on with all the tools [Jesus had given all of the tools to Betty]. And Jesus, in front of me, did not have the backpack anymore ...we rejoiced together, and He says, 'I have to go,' and all of a sudden He was just lifted up and was gone in the sky, and left me standing there with the backpack."

By this time, the ongoing physical abuse had stopped, but Betty was beaten up one more time, when she tried to obtain an attorney of her own for the divorce. In the end, she submitted and used her husband's attorney, but, predictably, the settlement was grossly unfair. She had to stay in Colorado for a year to pay off some debts, but then she loaded up her things, packed up her three children, and pulled a trailer house back to her property in Orofino. But at least then she was finally free.

Five

Theory of the Soul

If you ask someone who is religious what they believe in, usually it is God that comes first to mind. With the same breath, most would say they believe in the existence of the human soul.

The theory of the soul has two branches or subparts. The first has ancient roots and was captured best by Rene Descartes, who wrote that the soul is what explains free will and the fact that we are self-conscious human beings. This was part of Betty's philosophy too, and her explanation to me was right to the point: "The human soul is the boss of the human body—yeah, the soul is the boss. And it has a will and it has this ability to be independent.... The soul is the thing that says or makes the decisions and sets up his will to do or not to do." Descartes, and Betty too, would assume that the human soul—the boss, as it were—is not made of material and so therefore it is a genuine spiritual thing.[1]

The other branch of the theory says that, under certain conditions, the soul is able to defy material boundaries. It need not be confined to the body and, especially, it might be preserved after death. Betty tried to educate me about this also: "This soul is only the soul," she said, "and that soul was put in a human body. It's captured. It's not a free kind of thing. It's within this prison, like the human body is its prison. Until it [the human] dies, it cannot leave. And the only way that it can leave is to have a spirit body that it can leave in.... And that is the difference between being a Christian and not being a Christian. That is one of God's rules. Christ was before the foundation of the earth, that was his job, to set that up. And he did it beforehand and he did it afterwards. Jesus is the ticket. If you got your ticket to the party, you can go in. You ain't got your ticket, you ain't gonna get in there."

Well! Almost everyone today would assume that the idea of the soul is a religious belief with authority based upon Scripture and religious tradition. But I realized, after listing to my clients' stories, that they actually

The Spirit Transcendent

are capable of giving evidence about whether the soul is a real thing—let's call it evidence for the theory of the soul. I will start with James, an older gentleman who was another of my chronic pain patients. In the course of our work together, he let on that he had some spiritual experiences in the past. I suggested that we set aside some time to talk about them, and we scheduled another session. When we met again, the moment he sat down, the first words out of his mouth were, "The brain can't do nothin' on its own without the spirit.... Like I told you before, without Spirit all the brain can do is keep the body alive. Like I said, without the spirit the brain can't think, it can't see ... you need to have a Spirit to make things go."

What a way to open a session! Naturally, I wanted to know what it was, exactly, about the out-of-body experience that would lead to James' view that mind and body were so separable. Philosophers have been dealing with the mind-body problem for millennia. I wondered, could something be learned from direct experience?[2]

"How can you be so sure," I asked James, "that it is the spirit and not the brain that makes things go?"

"Like I said—just from my own experience, like when I was a little boy, I had that out-of-the-body experience." In an earlier session, James had told me that he was about five years old when suddenly the center of his consciousness was no longer in his body but in the trees, about 30 feet above. "Like I was telln' you, I was walking—actually, it was skipping—I come 'round the back of my house and the spirit jumped out of my body—came right out my back."

"How did you know it came out of your back?"

"Well.... I could see it coming out. When my mind left my body, I could see my body jerk real hard, and I was looking at my back. [The vantage point was no longer from his physical body.] And I just flew up by the trees, was hovering up there, and I was looking at my spirit-body, and, uh, then looked down at my physical body. It was just standin' there. It wasn't moving. Standin' there. I looked down and there was nothin' there; I wasn't connected to it at all. Cause my mind was with *my Spirit*. Looking down it's like, *he didn't have a brain at all*."[3]

I was taken aback. "Well, what was it like being up in the trees?" I finally managed to ask.

"I was up there just floating there," James said, "and when I looked down at my arm, it was kind of a whitish, transparent color."

A short time later James had a sense of traveling: "It was like my mind was going really fast forward, and I could see a big city." At the time James

Five—Theory of the Soul

was living in North Dakota, and he reasoned that from the vantage point of his Spirit he was now able to see either Grand Forks or perhaps Fargo.

The entire experience, from start to end, "seemed like about a half a minute," and then "I looked back down at my body, just standing there. And without even thinking about it, I just went back in my back, ... just like it [the spirit] had come out. I jerked really hard again as it went back in."

I know, and my colleagues would be eager to point out, that the perception of being separate from the body does not prove that consciousness or the soul actually separated from the body. Perception and reality are two different things, and besides, if James sees, it can only be through the action of his visual system, and obviously his eyes did not go with him, 30 feet above, into the trees.

But, mystery of mysteries, there are examples of "veridical" out-of-body experiences where the person in question has knowledge that simply could not be gained from normal operation of the senses in the physical body.[4] Another of my pain patients related just this kind experience to me: Beth developed serious back problems during pregnancy. She was to give birth to twins, but she lost one of them, and in the process her vertebrae shifted and shut off the spinal cord. Surgery was delayed until she had given birth to the remaining twin. Three months later she was in the operating room having an extensive operation, a laminectomy and fusion. Beth was lying on her stomach and then "I woke up during surgery. And when they discovered that, they really zapped me with medication. They started with morphine. Then I remember I was at the top of the ceiling looking down at them. My body was asleep on the table. There was a doctor, then a nurse, and another doctor, and they were trying to revive me. It was like cardiac arrest and they couldn't figure out what was wrong. And I'm up there trying to tell them, 'Quit giving me morphine, guys!' I remember thinking, 'I don't want to die; I have a three-month-old baby and I'm not leaving.' Then I felt a pulling sensation, and I thought, 'I'm going home with my daughter.' Then I started breathing, and I heard them say, 'She's breathing again.' And next I remember I'm in the recovery bed."

"So basically you are telling me that you think you were unconscious when you were watching the doctors work on you."

"That, and I had not seen the second doctor before that [before the operation]."

The other interesting part to the story is that Beth only knew she was allergic to morphine *after* the operation. It is as if, in addition to being able

The Spirit Transcendent

to see things she should not ordinarily have been able to see (being given morphine; seeing and being able to identify the second doctor), she also *knew things* she would not ordinarily be able to know.

Just in the way I was slow to come to a belief in God, I resisted the implications of what I was hearing. If souls exist—actually exist—then the material view of the world would have to be faulty. A supreme challenge to the scientific viewpoint! At the time, I probably would have argued that Beth must have been conscious even when she said she wasn't.[5] How else could she have known what she knew? Still, no one has ever been able to explain why a patient should feel they were up on the ceiling in the first place—it happens, but exactly *how* does such a thing happen, one has to wonder.

I was unable to simply dismiss what my clients were telling me, taken together with the reports I was reading that are out there in the literature, as some kind of illusion or trick of the mind. The theory of the soul was seeming more and more viable to me. While I pondered the problem, Betty continued to be my sounding board. One evening I put it to her directly.

"How, Betty, do you know that the human soul is a separate thing? How can you possibly be sure of that?"

"Because it came out of *this* body," Betty replied. "When I was 18, remember I was doing the relaxation thing—how that, uh, I was up by the ceiling?"

Yet another out-of-body experience! I have not yet gotten to tell this part of the story, but Betty became rather a virtuoso at going in and out of her body. Betty was reminding me of the very first time it had happened to her.

When Betty was a young woman, newly married and about the age of 18, she had problems with shooting pains in her legs and arms. She visited a doctor, but all of the tests were negative. There was a suspicion of leukemia. Then a visiting physician told her about a book he believed might help her, *Release from Nervous Tension* by David Harold Fink. Doing a bit of research, I found that Dr. Fink was a social worker turned psychiatrist. This book, which was basically one that gave mental health advice, was first published in 1943 and enjoyed a very wide circulation at the time. It seems to have been the granddaddy of relaxation techniques, which in their various incarnations psychologists practice even today. In my copy of Fink's book, I found him claiming great benefit from the serious practice of relaxation. The patient is to spend two half-hours per day in practice;

the first two weeks are devoted to learning how to relax the arms alone. Whole weeks are then assigned, one after the other, to the chest, then the back, legs, neck, face, scalp, eyes, and finally the speech muscles.

Evidently, Betty was making a dedicated practice of this form of relaxation, and she must have been following something close to Fink's sequence because she told me that she had gone as far as relaxing everything except her face, eyes, and tongue.

"Then one day," Betty explained, "I said to myself, 'I might as well relax them as well as everything else.' My tongue was tying up in knots in my mouth. I thought, 'Well, maybe it'd help it too.' So I was relaxing my mouth and my tongue, my mind, and my eyes. And when I come to my eyes—BOOM—I just came out of my body. And I was floating up by the ceiling, and I was looking down at my body, and I thought to myself, 'Oh my God, what have I done!' And then because I knew God, I just immediately said, 'Oh God, what do we do now?' or 'Jesus help me'—something of that nature. Then Jesus was right by my side."

"You mean Jesus was up there with you?"

"Then He was there," Betty told me, "and I was so thankful He was there. I says, 'I don't know what I did but *I've got to get back in my body.*' And He says, 'OK.' And He did something, and I went back in my body."

Betty's out-of-body experiences were even more interesting than those of James and Beth, because whereas the process was involuntary for them (and for most everybody who has had OBEs), Betty got to the point where she could go in and out of the body *at will*. Betty had not one but *three* separate near-death experiences, and it was probably these repeated brushes with death that gave her her talent.

Betty told me about the events that led up to her first near-death experience: "I was pregnant with Paula and really quite sick. And so I was having chest pains, lots of chest pains. And I was telling Mr. Anderson I needed to see the doctor and he was saying, 'No, you ain't goin' to see no doctor, 'cause they just stomach pains'—that was his excuse, just stomach pains. And this was a day or two before [Paula] was born."

Betty's maltreatment continued. Mr. Anderson forced her back to work, and besides, he was making her do heavy physical labor around the home: "He came home, and found me lying on the bed and I told him I was having chest pains. It didn't matter to him—it was 'Fix my supper' and so on. So I got up and took care of him, got him simmered down. Then went, went to bed. And during the night, once in a while, I get these sharp, sharp chest pains. And then the next day my labor pains started for having

The Spirit Transcendent

Paula. He took me to the hospital so the baby could be born. And I went into the hospital and while I was on the table having her I started having chest problems again. And I told 'em, I told the nurses that I was having chest pains and they started a cuff on my arm, and was taking my blood pressure. And they said my blood pressure was only 80 over 60 or something. The next reading was lower and the next reading was even lower. She [the nurse] says, 'Uh oh, we're going to lose her.' And so they kept taking my blood pressure and they started talking about giving me some medicine. From IV, you know..."

At this point, Betty's situation became critical: "I was lying there on the table and she says, 'We're losing her,' the nurse was saying." At that moment, Betty left her body: "I was gone; I was out of there, up by the ceiling looking down on them as they were working on me to get me back."

"You were up there watching them work on you?"

"Yeah, yeah. They says, 'You got to hurry because the baby's supposed to be born.' So then they lost no time and wasted no medications to get that baby out. And it only took them about an hour to—for the baby to be born."

At that instant, Betty felt herself go back into her body.

"After I went back in my body they said, 'She's back, she's back.' My blood pressure started going up again. But they gave me the medicine, the IV medicine to make my heart work."

Unfazed by her heart condition, Anderson immediately set about getting Betty out of the hospital and putting her back to work. Besides cooking and cleaning, he was arranging work for her as a caregiver, often having her work more than one shift a day. All during this time, Betty continued to have chest pains, but Anderson would not let her see a doctor.

One evening, exhausted, Betty went to bed and couldn't get up because any activity put pressure on her heart. Then she fell asleep.

"I went to sleep, I went to sleep, and then I woke up I wasn't in my body.... And I said, 'Uh oh, I'm gone.' I told God, I says, 'I can't leave these little kids, I've got to go back.'"

"You were with God again?" I asked.

"By my side. And so it was God who said, 'Well, take deep breaths, take a deep breath and grunt and blow.'" Betty showed me how she squeezed her diaphragm to make a grunting sound. "He was telling me what to do. Then I went back in my body and I started doing that.... I started breathing again and getting my heart working again."

I was amazed at the prospect that part of Betty—she would call it her soul—could have such a direct ability to affect her body. I mumbled something to her about biofeedback, with which I am familiar. But what Betty was telling me brought biofeedback to a whole new level: biofeedback is basically a technique where the mind learns to control body function, but Betty's control was on a spiritual level—it was her *soul*, separate from the body, that was doing the work.

Betty's excursions out of her body developed still further. "It was about a year or two years after that," Betty said, "that the third heart attack happened, and it was about the same kind of thing. And I realized that I had to do this all by myself ... of going in and out of my body. It was then, you see, that I learned this—that hey, I can do this! I can go in and I can come out of my body. I don't have to have God do this for me—I can do this myself."

"You learned to control it. You mean you didn't have to die to get there?" I asked.

"It was like I was going in and out of my house," Betty said, likening the soul to a person who might just be a visitor in the body/house. "It was a kind of a learning experience, because I learned how to go out of my body."

Not only could Betty leave her body when she wished, but once she left she was able to travel around at will. She thought of this as a phase of her spiritual development. The spirit had been her teacher for many years, but now she had become a kind of spiritual "graduate" and then she—or rather her soul—could go off on its own.[6]

Betty explained it to me. "This was after I had learned how to fly, and that was in '75, or '76.... And I was having so much fun going in and out of my body, you see, experiencing this spirit stuff, that I wanted to go and have fun, like a little kid, I suppose.... It was my spirit body that was able to come out of the human body and leave the human body behind and go out and have fun. I used to call it going 'planet hopping.' I would go to the moon, and from the moon I would go over to Mars, or to Jupiter. Jupiter and Saturn are just big moving bodies of ash because they've all been burnt up ... all they are is embers and they're burned out embers—that's all they are. I've landed on Jupiter and the ash stuff came up all over me, like I had fallen into a bed of ashes."

I tried to challenge Betty's belief—astronomically speaking, there are no burnt-out embers on Jupiter or Saturn—but she was dead certain about what she experienced. I tried a slightly different argument: "Well, how did you manage to get there?" I asked. "For example, an astronaut wants to get

The Spirit Transcendent

to the moon, it's a very complicated thing. You have to know exactly where to go, you know what I mean? There's a lot of technology involved. But, how would your soul *know* where it is? How would you literally get there, because the soul doesn't have a GPS system, right?"

Betty had no problem with this. "It's very easy to drive the spaceship," she said. "It's like getting in it and deciding that's where you want to go and you go. In the mind, you form a flight pattern like you would if you were in an airplane.... I remember I had to do that—you set that in your head as to where you want to go and what you're going to do. Like you're going to go to Mars first and then Jupiter and then to the moon and wherever else you wanted to go. And then you come back ... [meanwhile it is] like sitting here in this chair and my soul and my spirit would come out and it would leave the body in a comatose state, and you would come out and you go. It's kind of like projecting your mind somewhere else. It's kind of like that, only it's not only projecting your mind but it's projecting *your soul* and *your spirit* to do this kind of thing.... And it seems impossible, but it is possible because it is a spirit, a spirit energy and not a physical human [thing]."

By Betty's reckoning she had acquired a powerful tool. And the operation of that ability yielded a perception just as you would expect if we really do have a soul, which is separate from the body, and which can even be mobile. But we are back to the old problem of appearances versus reality: how do we know, if Betty perceived her soul going in and out of her body, that this was really the soul? It could be no more real than the ashes Betty thought came out of Jupiter's atmosphere. The same could be said of James—having the soul come out of the body seemed real to him, but was it? The experience of the soul as a separate thing could be an illusion. The only way to settle the issue is if we can somehow observe a single individual's experience objectively, from the outside.

The natural assumption is that this is not possible. After all, spiritual experience is a private matter, and it seems impossible to get into another person's head. I would have been able to rationalize that the perception of being out of the body was just an illusion but for the experience of another client whose story was destined to interrupt my comfortable materialist slumbers.

Lisa, when I met with her, was in her mid–40s. She had problems with low back and leg pain, and she had difficulty swallowing because of a narrowed esophagus—when she spoke she often had to pause so she could swallow. In the beginning of one of our sessions, Lisa brought up a profound spiritual connection she had just experienced with her sister. The weather had finally turned nice, so she was able to sit out on her patio.

"And," Lisa said, "I was really thinking about my sister a lot—and I was talking literally out loud…. I was just talking to her and I felt such a major, major, major connection with my sister, as I was talking. It was so intense. I mean, it's like she was right inside of me. She was—*with me*. It was so intense. I kept on talking. And then I also prayed for my sister. I was extremely worried about her."

"Well, did you have a reason to worry?"

"No, but when I was talking out loud, I had for some reason this fearfulness for her health. And I talked out loud to my sister. You know, 'I love you. I'm very concerned about you. I'm really praying that you're OK.' I prayed for you to not be an alcoholic anymore, for you not to be on pain medication, like you're not supposed to be on [other than] what's prescribed to you….' So I'm talking to her—just like we're talking right now—put everything in the past. Just let it all go…. And for some reason I felt something was very wrong with my sister—very, very wrong. So I probably talked for a good 15 to 20 minutes at least…"

After a pause, Lisa said, "What happened next was—she called me…. She called me immediately. Oh my God, you know, and guess what else? I was right. She had a heart failure. *That day*."

"Really. An actual heart attack?"

"My God, yes."

A few questions allowed me to establish that Lisa's sister, Cindy, did in fact have symptoms of a heart attack; the event was early in the morning, and the call to Lisa was later, at 6:52 in the evening (4:52 in Cindy's time zone).

The usual way of explaining co-occurrence of events like these is simple chance. Lots of people think—even very intensely—about their sisters; many sisters make telephone calls. Who among us, for example, has not picked up a phone, ready to call a friend, and they call us before we dial?

But there was a continuation of the story that made it exceedingly unlikely that the communication between Lisa and her sister could be passed off as mere coincidence. After the heart attack, Cindy was hospitalized for five days. Lisa picked up the story from the day after Cindy was released from the hospital.

"And here is where it gets really different…. So again, I go out on the patio, because I like to be in the warm, fresh air…. Now, when she got

The Spirit Transcendent

out of the hospital I was thinking of her again, 'course—because I was so scared that something was goin' to happen to her. And it [my feeling] was so strong that she was in me again. Oh my God! *She calls me* on the phone."

But this was not the strange part. "Get this. When Cindy was released from the hospital she went to stay with Penny [a cousin of theirs]. She was in bed, and directly in front of the TV is a picture of me and my mother. And I hadn't spoken to her that day. Well, all of a sudden—and Cindy is sitting up in an upright kind of position," Lisa gestured, "and my picture— not the picture—but *my face* came right up close to her face. I mean, *right this close,*" Lisa gestured again, placing her hand a few inches in front of her eyes, "at least."

"That's what she sees—your image coming from the picture to her?"

"Exactly. And I'm looking at her. And she can feel me thinking about her. And she felt the closeness of me—so strongly. And I was feeling the same feeling at the same exact time. Now get this ... she kept calling Penny [their cousin] to come into the room. Penny came in ... she went to the left side of my sister and she [Cindy] goes, 'What do you see right now? Do you see anything?' And Penny goes: 'Oh, my God, Lisa! What's going on?'"

"Penny and Cindy both see you," I said, still trying to grasp the strangeness of it, "they say 'Lisa—what's going on?' It's like they are *talking to you*?"

"Right. Yes. What's so weird.... I'm literally right there—literally right there ... it looked identical to me. It is as if I was right there with 'em. I was right there with 'em."

Lisa told me that the vision had to have been simultaneous with the point in time that she was thinking about her sister, earlier in the day, when she had the sense of "feeling she was in me again" while sitting on the patio. Here was her proof: when Cindy called, Lisa anticipated what the telephone call was to be about. Before Cindy was able to tell Lisa anything of the vision, she stopped her and asked her exactly *when* it happened—and it was exactly at the moment when Lisa had her feeling of union with Cindy.

So now we have a serious problem. Lisa is being visualized 2000 miles away at exactly the moment when she feels a strong union with her sister. And whatever happened, it cannot be entirely in the imagination of Lisa's sister Cindy, because her cousin was witness to the same vision. And if the vision is to be passed off as a mere hallucination, perhaps the product of pathology of some kind—who exactly is the patient? The supposed hallucination is not only part of Lisa's experience as would be expected of a hallucination; it is spread out among three women.[7]

It is as if the distance between Lisa and her sister did not matter; somehow that spatial boundary was crossed, despite the miles that separated them, and with the lack of any ordinary source of information that could explain the interaction. It is as if, in spiritual experience, spatial boundaries need not be respected in the way they obviously are in the material world. Betty would have explained this as the work of the soul that was no longer confined within the prison of Lisa's body.

The notion that Lisa's consciousness might not be bound up in her body but could actually travel brings to mind another paranormal phenomenon—remote viewing. I had already known of a program funded by the military, Stargate, which famously explored the possibility,[8] although at the time I was not familiar with the research that supported the possibility.[9] If it happens, even if only sometimes and with some individuals, it seems similar to what seemed like a "projection" of Lisa's mind. Betty gave me yet another example to ponder, one which perceptually seemed even more like "remote viewing." In any event, Betty believed she had this talent, and she even used it as a practical tool where her children were concerned.

"My daughter, when she was about 14, she began to be interested in some of the boys around, you know. This boy came and wanted to take her to the movie. He was a church boy and I thought, now, that's all right, if he wants to take her to the movie, it's just downtown there—I figured that's fine. Well, after they went…. I got this sensation—they didn't go to the movie."

Betty believed that her "sensations" were more than simple intuition. She distinguished among many varieties of sensations, all with unique meanings, that formed a kind of code she could use to communicate with God. "It's like playing 20 Questions with God," Betty said of her way of getting an answer about something she wanted to know.

Betty applied her tool to the problem of her daughter's whereabouts: "So I began throwing out the questions: 'Well, what did they do?' 'Well, where did they go?'"

Pretty soon Betty had her answer: "About from there [where the movie was] was Kamiah, and up at Kamiah they were having their bar-b-que days, or something like that. And they had taken off, up along the river, you see, to Kamiah, to the bar-b-que. And I was seeing what they were

The Spirit Transcendent

doing in the spirit; I was getting visions of what they were doing—that this is what they were doing."

Like any mother, she had questions for her when she came home. "So after a while, by and by, my daughter comes home. And I says, 'Well, how was the movie?'"

"Oh, it was fine."

Betty played it cool. "And I ask them about the movie. 'And then in this movie,' I say, 'did they have some barbequed ribs?'"

"Yes, Mother, yes, Mother."

"And in this movie, did they have some corn on the cob?"

Betty, it seems, could have gone to a movie herself, except it was as if she attended the private showing of her vision as it was displayed to her. Eventually, the point of Betty's questions began to hit home to her daughter.

"And I came right out and said, 'You didn't go to no movie. You went there to Kamiah to the bar-b-que!'"

"And I didn't have to worry about her when she would go out on dates," Betty said, laughing with that cackle of hers. "I knew where she would go and what she would be doing. Because the spirit would tell me. It is a wonderful feeling to not have to worry about your kids."

Betty's ability to sense events from afar only scratches the surface of what she seemed capable of. The story is complex enough that it deserves a chapter of its own.

Six

Travels to the Collective Unconscious

I kept on meeting with Betty, week after week, but there came a point when there was a turn for the worse, and it seemed her many illnesses were getting the better of her. It began with kidney problems. Betty's ureters had become blocked, and a procedure was performed to open them. Unfortunately, a biopsy of her abscess showed that her cancer had spread and was now invading her kidneys. This was bad news.

The operation was successful, and Betty went into a nursing home because she needed a higher level of care than she could receive at home. The situation was dire enough that during a staffing her oncologist told everyone that Betty had from just a few weeks to at most a few months to live. Betty complained to me about the nursing home, telling me everyone was "just waiting for me to die."

I was by Betty's bedside more as a friend than as a psychologist. It struck me, Betty's protests to the contrary, that her end might be near. I felt awkward, seeing her sitting in bed, hooked up to an IV. But Betty was glad to see me. She was alert, her one eye was bright, and soon we were back on track talking about God's plan and the nature of the spirit. I addressed the elephant in the room: "Betty, I know you have beat this twice before when prospects were dim, but what do you think is going to happen this time? You know the cancer is spreading."

"God is not about to leave me in the lurch," she said.

"I'm glad you are so sure. Me—I'd have a hard time believing it."

"Well," Betty replied, "many of those things Jesus told me in the garden haven't come to pass, so I'll be around some more, I think."

One of Betty's unfulfilled visions was that she was going to be a teacher in front of a class of students, telling them about the spirit and how the spirit works. Her vision surprised her because she was shy talking

The Spirit Transcendent

in groups, yet here was God showing her she would be instructing everyone. Another of Betty's visions was that there would be planeloads of young children who would be sent to her so she could start them on their own spiritual journeys.

Maybe it was a bit crass to bring it up, given the comfort that a belief in God might give someone in Betty's condition, but I could not help myself: "If God is so powerful," I asked, "that He could help cure you of the cancer, why give you cancer in the first place?" And then, remembering my manners, I offered a possible answer: "Well, maybe cancer is part of the human condition. You know, being human means being frail and all, so having something like cancer is just one of those things that happens to us."

But Betty was able to answer my first question directly. "I think God is trying to show Himself," Betty said after thinking a moment. "He has no human body, so He has to show himself through our human body—our human ability to talk and act and so on and so forth. Yeah, I know that God has to do something, God has to do something, for me to get completely well to be able to be a teacher and do the things [all of the things in the vision], but sometimes God has to create these problems for us to live through so other people can see that something else is really going on there, you see."

Betty had great confidence. "You know, Dr. P [Betty's oncologist], I know she's just sitting there on needles and pins, waiting for me to die of this cancer, and I keep on going in and saying, I'm doing fine." Betty laughed in her usual infectious way, and after some final small talk about our families, I took my leave.

Defying the odds yet again, Betty recovered, partially, at least, and she was able to return home to live with one of her daughters. My next visit was at her daughter's home. By now Betty was hooked up to an external pain pump that was running morphine, and she was hardly even able to sit up in bed. Still, not yet defeated by the illness that seemed to be taking over her body, Betty had enough energy to talk with me. Pretty soon we got to talking about Betty's past. Summing up that long, well-traveled road, Betty said, "I have had an extraordinary life."

"Extraordinary," I nodded in agreement. After a pause, I asked, "Looking back, what do you think was the most remarkable thing?"

"It was when God Jehovah took me to meet His parents and to show me around Palora."

We were back to another of Betty's spiritual experiences. This was

Six—Travels to the Collective Unconscious

a trip she had taken—a trip to Heaven. And when Betty had the experience, it was not like a product of the imagination. For her, it was real and direct. For all the world it might be as if you or I lived in Kansas and had never, in all of our lives, seen a mountain, but then literally, and not in the imagination, were driven to see the Grand Canyon. Afterwards we might say, "What a great trip!" and then thanked the person who took us. This is just how Betty viewed her visit to Palora and her relationship to the God Jehovah who took her there.

The trip to Palora happened in that phase of Betty's life when she had just escaped her abusive husband and had moved with her children back to her home in Orofino. It was also around the time of her third heart attack and her third out-of-body experience. By now, Betty was an expert at going in and out of the body—she reminded me, to her it was just like "a person going in and out of a house." It was also around this time that Betty had made the further discovery that not only could her soul go in and out of the body, but it could also travel other places too.

Betty was in the habit of hiking in the mountains. "One day while lying on a grassy hillside I watched the white clouds floating by overhead. As I watched, a voice called my name. I sat up and looked around, saw no one, so I laid back down, then heard my name again. I looked up in the clouds. I saw my friend there."

When she was much younger, at about the age of 13, instead of attending school her father decided Betty should be a goat shepherd tending his flock in the mountains. It was then that she had an important vision. A young man whom she called "God Jehovah" came floating over to her. As she described it, He was a young man with blue eyes and short blond curly hair. During that first visit, God Jehovah placed His hands on either side of Betty's head and then, miraculously, gave Betty visions of Bible stories "as they actually happened." God Jehovah visited Betty in the mountains for several years. He became a kind of companion to her, someone to whom Betty could talk about her problems, and there was more than one occasion where He would warn Betty—about a rattlesnake, for instance—or He might alert her to the whereabouts of a lost goat. Then, to Betty's dismay, he disappeared.

Now, many years later, when she was in her mid–30s, God Jehovah was back and Betty was overjoyed to see her friend again. "He held out a hand and I reached up to Him. He grabbed my hand and drew me up into the cloud with Him. We hugged and rejoiced to see each other. Then He took me for a flight up and about, returned me to my place, and we parted."

The Spirit Transcendent

There were more voyages. Betty told me that God "was teaching me to fly." Still, Betty knew that whatever was happening on these trips, it was not her *body* that was flying. When I asked what someone else would see during one of these voyages, she told me they would see nothing other than her body lying there on the hillside, presumably in a trance state. The following is the most important of Betty's visits with God Jehovah. I quote it in detail because of its importance not just to Betty but to our story.

> One day we left Earth and went into outer space. I looked back and saw Earth get smaller and smaller until it was but a star in the sky. I was scared I would get lost, but my friend [God Jehovah] held me firmly. Then I saw a yellow line of cubes and knew that this was a map of the outer-space world. Looking ahead of me there was a huge throne with a robe draped over one arm and a jeweled crown hung on one side of the back. All were a beautiful silver color. I thought, "Where is God? He should be on His throne." But then I saw Him by my side and felt better …
> [God] was showing me a huge wheel under the throne. On the spokes there were people of many nationalities walking about. God explained to me these were the "Creatores" [Betty spelled the word out for me] who were busy at work.
> We flew through space again, going very fast. In a short while we came upon a large tent floating in space. It was kinda like a big circus tent. It was round. The place is called the Palora. That is God Allie's home—that is His abode—the Palora. [God Allie is God Jehovah's *father*.] The door had a breeze where it just kind of blew. And I went in. And the floor was carpeted. And it was purple and different variations of the purple color. And more or less I floated on it.… You see in the center it had His throne, which was more like a couch than a throne. Next to God Allie was seated God Jehovah's mother whose name is Sophia. And when they got up [to greet me] they were joined at the hip—like Siamese twins.

I could not be more surprised. Taken aback by the bizarre complexity of it all, I asked Betty, "You got all of this in that one vision?"

"Well," Betty replied, "God Jehovah told me or mentioned different things, [in previous visions] you see, but it wasn't put together like when I was up there and we was in this tent, and they explained things to me."

"Was this real? I mean," I said correcting myself, "*did it seem* really real to you?"

"Yeah, when I was there it was real. Even today, when I think about it, it was real. It was as real as anything here on Earth."

"It was kind of like," Betty said, "I was His girlfriend and He wanted me to meet His parents. I had come that far, spiritually, that He came to that point where God and I had this union[1] and He wanted me to meet His parents. That's the way it came out," Betty laughed, "but I needed to know all these different things about the gods and Palora, and, well—they were telling me about them."

84

Six—Travels to the Collective Unconscious

"So you were having this little family talk," I offered, beginning to get caught up in the humor of the scene.

"Yeah, a family talk," Betty replied with a chuckle of her own. "So much like that, but it was words being put into my head rather than they were talking. And God Allie was putting up His hand like this," Betty raised her hand high, "like He had more to say, and wanted to talk about it, and Sophia was telling me about Plain Error [their first born child; God Jehovah's older brother] and that She had made this terrible error and did not teach the child [Plain Error] to stay out of some of the rooms."

Betty explained to me that Palora was made up of many rooms "like tents within a tent, but without doors." Each room was an emotion. "God Jehovah was taking me into the different rooms and explaining what was going on in each of the little rooms. The very first one was love, because love is so important. And we went in there, and He [God Jehovah] grabbed me and we hugged each other and you felt love. And we went to the room that was anger. He wouldn't go into that room—He said, 'This one is anger and you don't want to go in there.'"

Betty amplified on the problem with God Allie and Sophia's son "Plain Error." Betty learned that the problem with Plain Error was that he was allowed to roam freely throughout Palora; he was not disciplined in the way that a child should be. Because of this (to Sophia's regret) he turned out to be a bad god, stirring up trouble for all of the other gods, and playing "practical jokes" on everyone.

"He was creating a heck of a world for the other gods to live in," Betty said. "That's why they declared war on him; they wanted to put a stop to it."

"They declared war on him?"

"Yes, they declared war on Plain Error and his demon buddies. They said, 'We have to do something with this fella. He can't just run loose here and create havoc for everybody.' So they captured him and all his other angels and demons—his family, you might say—he had a flock of angels or spirits to help him."

"Captured, you say?"

"Well, they captured him and put him in a place where he couldn't get away. This place was Earth. That was their prison, but it was like God was the warden."

I loved it. Earth—what we think of as our home—was in fact but a prison for the demons with God as warden. But Betty's vision was about to

The Spirit Transcendent

take a new twist and to become an alternative version of the Bible's story of creation. "Here they [the demons] are in this prison, and they had no one to play practical jokes on. So they wanted a doll to play with, and that is why they created Adam."

"You mean Adam, as in the Bible's Adam?"

"The Bible says that Adam was formed by God. But God Jehovah told me that He didn't do it. He said He didn't do it. I says, 'Well, who did?' And He told me that evil demons made this doll, and not one of them could make the doll work. They filled it with water, and they filled it with gas and air, gases, many of the gases in the air like oxygen, and they tried all kinds of different things to make the doll walk and talk like the animals—they couldn't do it. So they got disgusted with the doll and put it aside. And then God Jehovah comes around, and they [the demons] ask Him about it. They dug the doll out and showed it to God Jehovah and He was, ah, overwhelmed that these demons could put together such a thing. [Such a wonderful creation.] So He took the doll and created a soul for it. And then He did not bring the doll back. The doll was His, then He figures. He made this beautiful garden for the doll to live in, and gave the doll different things to do, like naming all of the animals and all of the plants. God gave that job to Adam."

"But these demons could not keep quiet. They kept going to God and saying, 'We want our doll back; the doll is ours.'" Betty said, as an aside, "God really did an underhanded sort of thing. He had taken the doll and he hadn't brought it back. So He thought, 'Well, I have to do something to be fair and honest, you see.' So He created the tree in the garden that was good and evil. And when people ate the fruit of the tree, their minds would open and they would be able to know good and evil ... if they were going to disobey God or obey the demons."

"Yeah, even today you can choose to go God's way or [humans] can choose what they themselves want to do, or what the demons whisper into their heads. But that's where it all came from.... And people on this earth, for the most part, just automatically follow the demons rather than choosing to go God's way.... And every choice you make all day long—'Am I going to do this God's way, or the demon's way?'—every day, until you get rid of the God dang demons and get rid of the root."

"You're telling me when something evil happens today, it is because Adam was a doll?"

"The plaything of the demons, yeah, but God says, 'It's not going to be their choice forever.' He says, 'Plain Error and that crew can only have

Six—Travels to the Collective Unconscious

this human doll for seven kingdoms.' And when the Seventh Kingdom has come to an end, God is going to take His turn. He's going to take control of the dolls again, for 1000 years. That's the deal God made with the demons. The demons will be put in a dungeon. Like solitary confinement, they would be tied down with great big chains so they can't do anything. And the only way that is going to happen is for people to realize that they want to go God's way, rather than the demon's way."

I was greatly entertained by Betty's alternative story of Adam. True, it was revealed to her in a vision, but that by itself did not mean it was spiritual per se. Why not just call it an amazing creative product that was unique to Betty and that was called up from somewhere inside of her?[2] And that was just how I first conceived of Betty's story of Adam and the pantheon she discovered in Palora. Later, when Betty had a chance to talk about the events in her life that followed, I was forced to change my mind.

"I got to thinking," Betty said, "that something so important would have to be written down somewhere.... It's not in the Bible," she reasoned, "there are old scholars—there has to be something somewhere about this kind of religion. And so I think I hear about it first in some magazine."

Betty had her vision around 1974 or 1975. She remembered where she was living when she first heard about something that seemed remotely like her vision and was able to place the date as 1991. The magazine in question was at the checkout stand at a grocery store and was probably the *National Enquirer*. This only gave her a hint, however, and she continued her search for some record of what she had seen. In 1997 she happened to be talking with a librarian in her local community college library. He said her vision reminded him of something written by the Gnostics. The librarian dug up a volume for Betty, a book from a scholar of comparative religion, and there, in a chapter titled "The Creation of Man," Betty discovered what she was looking for.[3]

Between our meetings, Betty checked the volume out from the library again so I could read it too. She opened it to "The Creation of Man." "There—there it is," Betty said, pointing, "it says here what was told to me by God Allie."

Important parts of Betty's vision *were* found in "The Creation of Man." The scripture tells of a group of spirits who attempt and fail to create a soul for Adam. This was exactly what God had told Betty. And it was only when the chief among these spirits obtained Manna from a higher

The Spirit Transcendent

source that Adam's soul could finally be created—a striking parallel to the way God Allie was the one to finally give Adam a soul.

A session or two later, Betty showed me another place where her vision was confirmed. This turned out to be in *The Secret Book of John*,[4] one of the Gnostic Gospels. The discovery of the Gnostic Gospels is itself a story of great drama and intrigue. Most were discovered in 1945 when an Egyptian peasant was digging for fertilizer at the base of a cliff near the village of Nag Hammadi. Instead of fertilizer, he found a large sealed jar buried in the sand. Smashing it open, he found it filled with ancient texts—the famous Nag Hammadi library, which dates from the fourth century. They were probably buried by monks from a local monastery, hiding their sacred texts so they would not fall in the hands of the church, which thought of them as heresy and would have them destroyed.[5]

It turned out that there was indeed much in common between Betty's vision and the concept of God found in the Nag Hammadi library. But why? It was natural for me to question whether Betty could have picked up the Gnostic theology prior to her vision, as this would have been the easiest explanation for the similarity. But Betty was very definite about the time and place that she first learned of the Gnostics, and her memory seemed clear. I put it to her directly.

"What kind of exposure to the Gnostics did you have prior to your vision?"

"I didn't even know that there was such a group of people," Betty replied.

"Maybe you were exposed to it but forgot that you were?"

"But what I told you," Betty replied, "what I picked up when I was there [in Pelora] in the '70s, but I got to thinking that, hey, it must be written down in history about these people. And so it was [in] my researching different groups of people that I heard about the Gnostics."

"But Betty, what about Sophia? Why would the god you saw, Sophia, have the same name as in the Gnostic scripture?"

"That's because that's *who she is*."

Betty never quite grasped my question. Sophia, God Allie, and God Jehovah were so real to her they were like actual people. I could just as well have asked Betty, "Why is your Uncle Ralph called Ralph?" Because that is *who he is*, obviously.

In the back of my mind, it seemed likely that the name Sophia was discovered later by Betty and that Betty then identified the name with her vision from the '70s. The same could be said of Betty's Palora—it sounds so close to *Plemora*, which is the Gnostic term for the heavens. But even if Betty later filled in the name "Sophia" to represent the god she met (an interpretation which she pointedly refused), or had transplanted the actual Greek term Pleroma into her earlier vision, calling it Palora instead, I still had to contend with all of the similarities between her experience and what is in the Gnostic Gospels.

Whatever the true source of Betty's discovered mythology, it was plain she was recalling events from her own memory and not making up a story for my benefit or entertainment. We talked about Palora often enough, her and I, and the story Betty told was always the same—even when the tellings were more than a year apart. And after all, back in the mid–'70s, how would Betty have obtained information about the Gnostics? It wasn't until much later that Gnosticism became a popular topic. (Although the book *The Gnostic Gospels*, by Elaine Pagels, published in 1979, would be an early exception.) Betty, with her limited education, was definitely not a religious scholar, so how could she possibly know?

There simply seemed no way to account for the match between the unique features of Betty's vision and what Betty discovered in the library in the 1990s. Sophia and God Allie have male and female aspects—"like Siamese twins." That image is straight out of Gnosticism. So too is the idea that there is not one God, as in the traditional Bible, but generations of gods—just like the emanations of divinity in Gnosticism.

And, thinking about it, the near-misses between Gnostic myth and Betty's vision were as interesting to me as the correspondences, because it was as if she was somehow receiving an underlying message, and it was being transmuted by Betty as if she were a kind of receiver, one that involved her own creative conscious. There is the fact that Sophia made a mistake—in Betty's vision it was by not setting down rules for Plain Error, so that he became a chief among demons, creating all manner of havoc. By comparison, in the Gnostic literature, Sophia makes an *error* out of ignorance—she creates a god the Gnostics call Yaldabaoth, but since he was created without Sophia's male counterpart, this god was defective and egocentrically thought he was the only deity.

The Gnostic Gospels also agree with Betty's vision in that Yaldabaoth was a kind of chief demon, who with a host of lessor demons tried to create Adam, but Adam remained lifeless. According to the Secret Book of John, unknown to Yaldabaoth, Adam is given a spark of divine power from his mother Sophia, and with this divine spark, Adam begins to live. So the

The Spirit Transcendent

Gnostic version ends up in a way very close to the end of Betty's vision, where God Allie agrees to breathe a soul into Adam.

Betty's vision is convoluted and bizarre. *But so is the Gnostic scripture.* When I looked at Betty's vision by itself, it seemed too outlandish to be called real. (God has parents? His parents are half male, half female? And joined at the hip?) "This had to be a fantasy," I thought. Yet, all along, Betty was trying to tell me that these things "really happened" and that was why she went searching to see if they were written down somewhere. Well, these things did not happen in our material world, but what if Betty and the Gnostics shared a reality in some spiritual world?

Many years ago, C.G. Jung had to contend with exactly the kind of data Betty presented to me. Even as a young psychiatry resident working in a Swiss sanatorium, Jung realized that the images produced by his psychotic patients mirrored those found in primitive myths. There was a point in his career when Jung disagreed with and then broke with Freud. Right afterwards, between 1913 and 1916, he had his own descent into the unconscious.[6] Jung himself had visions and hallucinations that were right out of myths the world over. His visions, the hallucinations of his psychotics, and religious and mythological images all seemed to be cut from the same cloth. To Jung, it meant there had to be a level of the unconscious that was deeper than the individual, a level that was "collective." He called it the Collective Unconscious. If Jung were still around, he would see the match between Betty's vision and Gnostic scripture as proof of a connection that goes beyond the personal psyche.[7]

I had read Jung because I teach the history of psychology, and I thought I understood his idea of the Collective Unconscious. What I hadn't appreciated was that the Collective Unconscious is also a statement about reality—alternative realities, that is. It's more than just saying myths and visions are connected at a level deeper than the individual. It implies there is something separate from us that is floating around out there. Whatever that thing is, it was realized in the Gnostic scriptures buried in the sands of Egypt. Betty, in her vision, tapped into the same source.

After my meeting with Betty when we reviewed the highpoint of her life, her cancer progressed still further. Soon it was clear to me that she was close to death. In my next to last meeting with her I was shocked and saddened to see Betty reduced to a kind of elementary existence. She was too sick to talk with me, and all she could do was grunt and moan in pain. She was past the point of conversation, and the character of our relationship had changed yet again. Hospice had provided a hospital bed for her room, but there remained the problem of getting Betty from her own make-shift bed into the new one. Betty's daughter asked for my help, and as impotent as I felt, at least I was able to do one thing—perhaps my last thing—that could be helpful: by grabbing the sheets she lay upon, Betty's daughter and I were able to move Betty over to the new bed, hoping she would be more comfortable.

By now, in my mind, I thought Betty was surely only days from death. But I was wrong, and I was surprised when, a bit more than a week later, Betty's daughter called to tell me that Betty was doing well enough for another visit. I stopped by after my day in the clinic, as was my custom, and was encouraged to see her stronger and more verbal. Perhaps God would intervene yet again? But this was not to be, and a few days later, Betty's daughter called me a second time with the news that Betty had passed away. In the end, she did finally succumb to her cancer, in March of 2012, at age 75.

Up to the very end, Betty was convinced it was not time for her to die. What about her revelation when Jesus had given Betty her life's plan? There were still parts of the vision that never were fulfilled—there was to be that time in her future when children would be sent by the planeload so Betty could initiate them in the spirit and begin the growth of the spirit inside of each. And one of Betty's last images was that of her as teacher, addressing a class and instructing everyone about the spirit. This last part of the vision surprised Betty, because she had no doubt it would come to pass, but she knew she was not good with words—"everything always comes out wrong," she told me. Besides, Betty told me, she was extraordinarily shy about being in front of a group.

Each semester I give one special lecture on my research interests to a class of about 60 students. That time had come around again, only a few days after Betty's death, and I found myself talking about her—although with some trepidation that what I was trying to say would be seen as soft-minded and not at all what you would expect from a professor and psychologist. But still, I just had to argue in front of that class that there is much real evidence—facts that simply cannot be explained away—that tell us our view of the world is incomplete. Betty, I told everyone, might just be our best evidence for a spiritual reality, even if that notion seems like a modern heresy.

In the quiet of the classroom, after everyone left, I had a chance to reflect. The topic of my lecture lingered in my mind. I was still feeling sadness for Betty's passing, but then, I thought, perhaps Betty was still

The Spirit Transcendent

present in a kind of strange way. Maybe, I thought, that last part of Betty's vision was correct after all—but with the difference that it was me, not Betty, who was facing all of the students, and that it was me, not she, who was taking about the spirit. It was almost as if Betty was still with me. Lost in these thoughts, I packed up my notes and left the room, and returned to the ordinary life of a professor.

Seven

The Gates of Heaven

I met Carol for the first time less than three months after Betty's passing. Just as it had been with Betty, our association began most innocently. Carol was another pain patient who was referred to me ostensibly for pain control. She had many physical problems. Most importantly, she had advanced breast cancer that had metastasized so that it was invading her spine and hip. Carol was on medication that had succeeded in slowing the cancer's advance, but it was probably only going to provide a temporary respite, and she had poor prospects for survival. If the cancer was not enough of a physical challenge, Carol had heart disease, and because of it she was wearing a pacemaker and a defibrillator. She was a diabetic, and she had kidney disease. Her stomach was failing, and she would have been a candidate for a gastric bypass operation except it was determined that she would be unlikely to survive the procedure. Despite all of her conditions, Carol did not appear ill if you were to look at her. When we first met, she appeared as a vibrant woman in her early 50s, with straw-colored hair that contrasted with her blue eyes.

With so much going wrong physically it would be natural to expect, on a first meeting with a psychologist, that the main topic at hand would be the prospect of facing one's own death, or, if not that, how to handle chronic illness. It turned out that Carol did not perceive these to be problems the same way most of us would. My first hint of this came to me in our first session when I asked her what it meant to know she was going to die. Carol casually brushed this off, telling me that impending death was the *least* of her worries. Rather, what caused her distress was worry over how her children and husband would manage without her. At the time, in that first session, I simply expressed my curiosity at how it was she came to feel that death was nothing to be frightened of. Carol casually mentioned that she once had died and the experience had freed her of her fear.[1]

"Ah—another near-death experience," I thought to myself. By now

The Spirit Transcendent

I was quite in the thick of these, and they deeply fascinated me—but I struggled during the session to contain my interest, and even enthusiasm, mostly because it seemed inappropriate: how could I be sure that talking about Carol's near-death experience would be important or therapeutic? After all, there were so many challenges that she was faced with in the present, and maybe they needed our attention. Despite my hesitancy, it turned out that to have Carol tell her near-death experience to someone who could receive and try to understand it, without rejecting it out of hand, was the best therapy I could provide.

To tell this story properly, background is important: Carol grew up on the west side of Washington, near Seattle. When she was 11, her parents divorced, and she moved with her mother to the east side of the state to a small farming community with a population of around 600. In this small town, everyone knew everyone else's business, but in Carol's case, she felt even more scrutinized because members of her family were prominent, long-standing members of the community. Her grandfather owned the town's hardware store and another large business. He was highly respected and was once the mayor.

When Carol was a freshman in high school, she had a secret relationship with a young man who was 25. She got pregnant when she was just 15 but managed to keep the entire pregnancy secret.

Carol explained her need to keep the secret. "I was scared people would find out. There was only 76 kids in the high school. There was 13 kids in my class…. I had fear of my parents; fear of the kids finding out; fear of being shunned by the town. My worst fear was my father would come and get me." This last possibility was the most horrible for Carol to contemplate because it meant being taken away from her grandparents, whom she loved, as well as her friends and her home.

About three months into the pregnancy, Carol was spotting and she began to have acute pain. She was taken to the doctor, but she did not let on that she was pregnant, and she was misdiagnosed with acute appendicitis. After being admitted to the hospital, Carol thought, with a mixture of dread and relief, that at least now she would be found out and the charade would be over. But she was still not discovered. The doctor who performed the surgery had just returned from lunch smelling of alcohol, so perhaps this explains how the pregnancy was missed. With the appendix out, Carol returned home. Her bleeding stopped, and no one was the wiser.

Carol continued to hold on to her secret out of fear and shame.

Seven—The Gates of Heaven

"Surely, the signs of the pregnancy would have to be noticed sooner or later," I said. "How could you disguise it?"

"I was small," Carol answered. "I was about 130 or 140 pounds, and that was the day of smock tops where your shirts were flared." Listening to Carol tell the story, I anticipated that the secret had to come out, eventually. Soon Carol began to describe the inevitable. She began to have cramping pains, the bleeding became severe, and then everything came to a head.

"I don't think I would have remembered a time in my life I was more afraid. I was really hurting by that time. I waited until the middle of the night—the pain was so bad. My sister heard me crying and got up and told my mom."

Carol *still* did not own up to being pregnant, but it was obvious she needed to see the doctor. This time, the physician could not possibly miss what was going on, and the long-held secret was finally revealed.

"But why not," I had to ask, "simply have told your mother? You knew you would have to have done so eventually."

"I just couldn't."

By the time Carol had finally been seen by the doctor, she had been bleeding for two days, her blood pressure was low, and her life was in danger. There was a hospital only 18 miles distant, but rather than be taken there by ambulance, the doctor arranged for Carol to be driven to a hospital in Spokane, a full hour's drive away, and to be admitted under an assumed name—Winifred. Protecting her family's reputation seemed to have a higher priority than anything else, including her safety.

When Carol finally arrived in Spokane, she required seven units of blood. Her blood type was rare, so her mother was enlisted as a donor. Still, there was not enough, and in a scene that seems more than unlikely in today's medical world, a nurse called out into the waiting room seeking a volunteer with the correct blood type. An African American gentleman probably saved Carol's life. Lying in a gurney next to hers, and hooked up with a direct line, he gave her two pints of his blood.

Carol was taken to the operating room. "I had IV's in my neck, ankle, and arm. And leads everywhere. They told me not to push yet … the pain was unbearable. I was exhausted [she had already been awake for 48 hours]. I kept going in and out." And in a final insult, "they kept calling me Whinnie."

Carol's next memory was of being given an epidural. She could not feel anything from the waist down. She was told to push.

The Spirit Transcendent

"All of a sudden I heard that noise you hear when they give you an anesthetic, and you hear a kind of humming noise." The pain was completely gone, and in its place was a warmth. At this point Carol could no longer feel anything in her body.

"All of a sudden I saw a bright, bright light. Like the sun. It was warm, but not burning like the sun.... You could look into it and it didn't bother my eyes. And then I remember just traveling fast."

Carol had a sensation of a tunnel. But the tunnel was not like a cylinder. "At one end it was narrow," Carol illustrated with a gesture of her hands, "and at the other, it was wide spread out here."

Carol's experience of a light and a tunnel are cardinal features of the near-death experience, certainly experienced by many patients.[2] However, Carol was only 16 at the time—she had never heard of the phenomenon of a near-death experience, let alone features like a light and a tunnel. Despite the fact that she had no prior expectations going into her experience, it followed exactly the same pattern seen in so many other individuals who have had been near death and returned.

"I was floating, and I had this warm feeling. Before the pain was so intense, but now no pain, none at all. I couldn't see my body, so I must have been a spirit or in spirit-form. I couldn't wait to get further to see what was ahead. There was no [sense of] time; I just kept going forward into the light." And then something new happened: Carol had an awareness of "an unbelievable feeling of joy, of love—complete love."

"It was like stages. I call them 'realms,'" Carol said. Each realm was deeper than the next. "First was the realm of color—it was like bright stars, only every color, bright colors, purples, bright blues, reds, oranges, greens—it was so beautiful, glorious." The light became brighter as she continued to travel, still without the sense of having a body.

Then the tunnel seemed to fall away, and Carol entered a realm of sound. "A combination of what I would call heavenly sounds," Carol explained. "Choirs, instruments, like every kind of music you could imagine all playing at the same time, but it all went together in harmony.... It was just floating music. And I remember that it just kept making me want to go further. And that at this point I felt ... *glee*."

At the time, while Carol was telling her story, I was much taken with her sense of the absolute beauty of her experience. It was like my other patient who, when in a coma, saw a locomotive and railroad cars made of Indian headdresses and was overwhelmed by the "take-your-breath-away colors," as she put it. And what kind of music is it that can go so far beyond the beauty of an individual sound? Listening to Carol, I was reminded of Plato's ideal forms. Perhaps this is what Plato was proposing—that when we talk about beauty on the earthly plane, it is just an imperfect instance of the perfect version that exists in an Ideal Realm.[3] Plato's Ideal Realm truly is transcendent, beyond the human perception of space and time. Perhaps in his writing Plato was expressing what Carol experienced directly: to Carol, the colors she saw, and the heavenly music she heard, really were divine because they were beyond human experience. And then there was Carol's perception of complete love. Perhaps, I thought—still remembering Plato—if we could only go past human love to its ideal counterpart, then we would at last have managed to be close to God.

Carol was not done with her story. She told me how she traveled even further yet to a deeper realm. "This brought me to the next point where I saw spirit forms. I came first to the form of a person. A spirit who was to be my guide…. It looked like a woman. She was radiant with light all around her. I couldn't make out her face, she was so bright."

"Could you communicate with them?" I asked. "If so, how?"

"It was not verbal like talking, but a knowing, like telepathy," Carol said. "And as I went further into the light, I encountered the spirit forms of more people, all covered with light. They knew me somehow, and I felt their love…. It was like they were gathering to meet me…. There were angels with wings…. I had knowledge I didn't have before. It was like they wanted me to know certain things, and I was recording this inside me."[4]

By now, Carol anticipated that she was going to see God, the endpoint and the deepest part of the entire experience. "I had to go to the place where you are judged. The light was even brighter, and the angels were covered in gold. The spirits were gathering in one place." Now Carol was filled with anticipation. "I knew this is where I would go through the Gates of Heaven…. My soul was being pulled to this place. It was the last stop."

In my office, at this point in the story, Carol was overcome with emotion. She could no longer speak.

"What is it that makes you cry?" I asked, after a pause.

"I don't know if I can explain the feeling," she replied. "I wanted to stay there. I felt like something told me it was Heaven … and that there was a place for me there."

This was a surprise. I had thought Carol's tears would have been because of coming close to death or perhaps because of being young, pregnant and alone. But that was only a minor element of what she was feeling. Her tears were mostly tears of happiness.

"In that place there was no judgement," Carol said. "It's just ... like you gave yourself up.... You know, like you surrendered yourself, and you were going to accept anything ahead that was going to happen to you. That you couldn't wait to get to where you were going.... It was like," Carol paused to find a comparison, "you were going to open a birthday present and it was, like—'wow'—the excitement of knowing what's inside."

But just as Carol was about to "walk through to get to the other side" she heard a name—Whinnie, Whinnie, Whinnie. It repeated over and over and over again.

Carol looked at her spirit guide. "She said I had to go back, that I was needed there.... She lifted her hands and touched me. I didn't hear her voice coming from her mouth. I just knew what she was saying. I started moving again, but it was not toward the light. It was away from it." Carol heard her name being called, louder and louder. "Then I woke up—just like popped up, opened my eyes. I was very incoherent; I didn't at first know where I was or what was happening. And they were calling my name over and over, and apparently they had done the paddles, and they were stabilizing me, and they got a heartbeat again."

At first, although she was aware of her surroundings, Carol felt frozen; she could not move. A nurse told her that she had delivered the baby, but when she looked over at the incubator, she could not see it. Carol was moved to intensive care, and eventually the doctor came in with her mother to break the news to her that her baby did not survive. "They told me it had internal bleeding." Carol sobbed as she continued her story. "I asked if I could see him, and they said they did not think that was a good idea."

Carol remembered being left in a dark room. Her mother had to return to work, so she was alone with her grief. Three days later, her mother checked her out of the hospital and bluntly informed her that she had to go to the funeral home. Carol wanted to have her son buried, but her mother insisted on cremation.

"And it was a 'total cremation,'" Carol said, "so not even the ashes would be left. There was no name either on the birth or death certificate." Carol was left feeling totally defeated. "It was like my baby was nonexistent. Like it never happened, and no one would ever know except me, my boyfriend, and my mother."

In our next few sessions, more of Carol's life story emerged, piece by

Seven—The Gates of Heaven

piece. After the birth, Carol's fears were confirmed: when her father found out about the pregnancy, she was plucked away from her grandparents and friends to live with him in Seattle. Her boyfriend was given a job in her father's business, but this did not work out, and so the couple escaped together to live on a homestead just south of the Canadian border. These were very primitive surroundings—no running water, heat came from a wood stove, and during winter, the snow would be as high as the eaves of the roof. This was hard living, but Carol felt that she was able to attain some peace of mind. She fashioned a small memorial for her baby at the ranch where only she knew where it was. But then, her boyfriend got in trouble for drugs. With no alternative, Carol called her father and asked if she could go back to Seattle to live with him. At first, her stepmother was against it, but she relented, and after a long bus ride Carol arrived sick and malnourished, having lost about 30 pounds. Although she was again with family, Carol never felt welcomed.

All this time, Carol held onto the secret that she had gone to Heaven. She felt, and rightfully so, that if she told her family, they would simply think she was crazy. Yet she wanted to tell them, and she wanted them to know that Heaven "really and truly is real." She had discovered that there was no reason to fear death, but no one understood. Even her pastor, when she tried to tell the story, did not take it seriously. His response was simply to pray for her.

Carol finished high school and then began taking courses in horticulture. By then, she was living in the "U District" of Seattle, a full-time student and working full time besides. Carol discovered that she had a gift. A client might talk about a flower arrangement and Carol found that she could sense the pattern immediately and intuitively. Then there were the demands of her program—there were literally hundreds upon hundreds of species of plants to memorize. Carol believed that prior to her near-death experience she never would have been capable of such a feat, but that somehow her near-death experience had unlocked abilities that she never knew she had.[5]

What I found most interesting, as Carol related her history, were signs of other gifts, even more pronounced, and which were more clearly of a spiritual nature. Carol began to see auras.[6] Now, I have talked with many of my clients about auras, and most of the time when they spoke about them, I found the experience was subjective, maybe something along the lines of a feeling or an intuition rather than direct perception. But in Carol's case, when she saw an aura, it was so pronounced that at first she believed

The Spirit Transcendent

"there was something wrong with my eyes." Rather than assuming the aura was spiritual, Carol thought she needed to see an ophthalmologist!

Carol also discovered she had the newfound ability to sense spirits. "I became a sensitive," she said. "I *see* spirits."[7] Once, Carol began one of our sessions with an example. That past Sunday she was at church, and a woman walked in late. The woman seemed out of place because of what she was wearing—a flowered dress that seemed of another era, perhaps the 1800s. Carol said to one of her daughters, "Look at the woman; look at what she is wearing," only to discover that no one could see the woman but her. A hallucination in our world, but to Carol it must have been a spirit.

Fascinated, I asked Carol to tell me more about her spirit sightings. Sometimes they would appear when Carol was simply walking down the street.

"There may be a person coming towards me," she said, "and then I'll see a form behind that person, not of the person that is coming at me, but a different form of someone else—looks like a person, but not in the flesh. It's in a spirit form."

"It's not like the image of a person?" I asked.

"Right. I want to say it's like white and may have yellow on it. Usually two colors, but there could be three, like yellow, green, and another color, and with the yellow they are like—lit up. And it can be a man or a woman-form."

"So this form is not in the figure of a human, but you can tell the sex?"

"Right. Almost like an angel-form—I have seen angels." And Carol began to describe a different category of perception, not of a spirit, but of an angel: "Angels I see in different forms. I have seen them in angel-form and in human-form [angels that look just like humans]."

"Well, if it looks like a human, how do you know it is an angel?"

"I just know."

By the mid–1990s, Carol had quite a business built up. Her father had bought a 25-acre farm in Brush Prairie, Washington, half of which was planted in blueberries. There was a large nursery where Carol was growing 400 varieties of herbs, plus greenhouses where customers could come and pick their own flowers and vegetables. There were 17,000 square feet of interconnected barns, and then she expanded the business with a gift and floral shop, "The Country Heart," a short way down the road. And like a human dynamo, all the while Carol was driving a truck, "a 28-foot truck, a 1900 International," back and forth to Canada to make deliveries and pick up supplies.

Seven—The Gates of Heaven

In the midst of this hubbub of activity, Carol developed ovarian cancer. With her illness she could not possibly keep the business going, but by providence or by God, her childhood sweetheart, Dave, rediscovered her. He was a Navy man, stationed in Bremerton, Washington, and soon he was commuting three hours each way to help out at the farm. Dave overcame Carol's considerable resistance to marrying again. Finally, and at last, she had someone in her life she could count on.

"A number of psychic things happened at Brush Prairie," Carol told me in another of our sessions. She rummaged around in her purse to show me a photograph she had just discovered at home. "Let's see, where is it?" More rummaging. "Ah, here it is. I came across it the other day and it reminded me—that's where I saw my grandfather."

The picture in question, which is now on my desk, is a four-by-six photograph, an unremarkable scene of a field with a trailer in the foreground. But, Carol explained, it was the *spot* approximately in front of the trailer that was significant. Probably around 1997, toward sunset, Carol was looking out from her porch. At first, she thought she was seeing a shadow, but soon Carol saw that it was her grandfather who was standing in that exact spot.

"He was wearing his straw hat," Carol exclaimed, "in his overalls, right there in the field of blueberries. I freaked, and it was like my heart leaped, and I was trembling, and I called Dave who was upstairs. I said to him, 'I just saw my grandfather out there!' So I'm screaming and I'm running out the door, out through the kitchen, out to the porch, and as I went down the steps—it disappeared. And I was so upset, and I didn't even know why.... I had a really bad feeling about it then, because he had shot himself."

"Shot himself?"

"Well, I understand why," Carol continued. "He was in such pain. He was 87 and at that point he had prostate cancer." Carol went on to tell me of how he had to use a catheter to urinate, which he hated. One evening while he was asleep, he rolled over, which pulled the catheter out. "There was blood all over the place and so much infection ... and my grandma had died two years before." Clearly, her grandfather felt life was no longer worth living. "They had been married 65 years and had never been apart—they were basically my parents."

In fact, Carol's grandfather and grandmother were the real parental figures in her life—much more so than her actual mother and father, who divorced when she was around 11. By Carol's thinking, this explained her grandfather's appearance. She would say that those who die, especially in

The Spirit Transcendent

unusual or unexpected circumstances, sometimes stick around in the form of a spirit. And if you do see a spirit—or ghost, as some would say—it may be of someone who loved and cared about you in real life.[8]

I didn't doubt that Carol had a vision of her grandfather, but in the back of my mind I realized that I was back to our old problem: that precious little separates a vision from a garden-variety hallucination. Carol believed her vision to be a spiritual product, but the spiritual claim is not necessary if it was a simple hallucination. Carol, ever tolerant, listened when I posed the problem I was having accepting her vision.

"But it was confirmed," she insisted. "Afterwards."

Maybe a week after her grandfather's suicide, a stranger stopped by the farm. "So he starts talking to me about herbs," Carol explained, "and the conversation wanders over to, you know—do you have a family? He talked about going to his church, which was a Quaker church, and all of a sudden he says, 'Something told me to pull in here. I can't tell you what.'"

"I was standing at the door of my greenhouse, probably putting plants in or out. It was kind of towards the end of the day and he said, 'You saw someone, recently.'"

"What do you mean?"

"'You saw someone out in the field.' And he says, 'Show me where it was.'"

With tears running down her face, Carol exclaimed, "How would you know that?"

"I don't know," the man said. "Something made turn in here and something is telling me this."

By now, Carol's husband Dave saw her walking with this visitor out in the field, so he came out to join them, wondering what was going on. The stranger stopped at the exact spot of the vision and then he said, "Here, right here, is where you saw your grandfather."

"When he said that," Carol said, "Dave's hair stood up on his head. We stood out there for quite a while and talked about it."

The stranger's name was Dave Garcia, and he became a friend of the family. "He would show up at our place all the time, and he was always doing something for us. He would come in and have dinner with us and he'd come to the store all the time.... He had his own business, a Hawaiian restaurant business-type thing, where you could sit at the counter and he'd make food." Carol suspected there was more to Dave Garcia than met the eye: "When he showed up things became more calm and everything seemed to work out. He was just kind of a mentor that showed up—which was really weird. He was good to the kids, and the kids loved him." At the time, Carol's daughter had a boyfriend who was living with the family. "He was 18, and he had a lot of things happen in his life, and Dave [Garcia] just kind of took him under his wing. They had a relationship and John [the boyfriend] would go and have lunch with him all the time and talk, and a lot of John's problems went away. Today John is married and has a really stable family, and is doing really good, but before that he was on a really bad path—before he met Dave."

There were a few weeks when Dave Garcia didn't show up. Being so busy with her own business, Carol did not stop to worry about it at the time, but then some people from Dave Garcia's church happened by and she found out he had had a heart attack and died. "He walked into our lives," Carol summed it up, "and walked out, and that's where I feel God sent someone to us. He served his purpose and then he left. I don't know if he was an angel in human form. I can't explain it."

For me, it was easy enough to assume that Dave Garcia was simply a good person, religious, for sure, but he did not have to be sent from God or be an angel in the form of a human to have such a beneficial influence. My main problem, personally speaking, was to reason within the confines of ordinary logic how this Dave Garcia, who was a stranger to Carol, would know she was visited by her grandfather, let alone be able to mark the exact spot of the apparition.

Carol and I talked directly about the problem of the reality of a vision. In one of our sessions our discussion turned to Betty and her many visions and the problem many of us would have in believing many of Betty's stories.

"It's too bad," Carol offered, "that when you were with her [Betty] you didn't experience some of the things that did happen. That's what is hard—these things happen to us and it's not always in front of someone. Now, in my experience of my family, they experienced some of those things *with* me. You know, for example."

"You mean there were times when both you and Dave experienced something paranormal together?"

"The one that comes to mind right away was when his mom was in the nursing home and dying with severe emphysema. She had an hour or so to live. This was in 1997, the day after Christmas."

"Dave's mom was in the hospital dying—lingering, lingering, just gasping for air all the time. All of the kids were in the room—*all* of the kids—and it was like Shirley was just hanging on. And I could feel it, feel it in the room, that she was just going to stay there. She was afraid that her kids would not be okay. So I prayed that the kids would walk out of the room and I could spend a few minutes with Shirley. And then, *all of a sudden*, they walk out—every one of them. And I went up to Shirley. 'Shirley, you can go—your kids are going to be fine, they're okay, they're going to be okay.' The one she was most worried about was Dave because he's the youngest. I said, 'I'll be with him; I'll take care of him.'"

"Right over here," Carol gestured toward the wall of my office with her hand, "at that moment came a light, and there was this area here—opened up like a big square. I looked up and I said to Dave, 'Oh, there is an older lady here,' and I describe what she was wearing, what her hair was like, and I could see it just as clear as day. There was a younger guy there, in his 20s, blond hair, plaid shirt, mustache. And I was telling Dave there was an older gentleman, and I described him too. Dave goes, 'That's my nephew who was killed in a plane crash.' And I never met these people; I never seen them before; I hadn't seen pictures or anything. And yet Dave knew exactly who they were. And I said, 'Shirley, Shirley, your family is here. They came to get you, you can go.' And she *died*, right at that moment. All of a sudden, she just went peaceful. It was like she had been gasping for air," Carol made gasping sounds to show what it was like, "and all of a sudden, she just went peaceful. And I looked at Dave and I said, 'She's gone.'"[9]

"Of course, his family would never have believed that, and they would've thought I was a nut case, but I had confirmation from Dave of what I had seen."

"When we got home Dave said, 'I've got a picture.' And sure enough, it was his grandparents and his nephew, Michael, who was killed in a plane crash."

"You could recognize them from the picture?" I asked. "They looked exactly as what you had seen in the vision?"

"I did not recognize the clothes so much—details like that. It was mostly in the face." Carol picked up most of the details in the faces. "She had a specific hairdo. Her hair was up in a bun. I described them in detail to Dave, and I had never met nor seen his grandmother, his nephew, and his grandpa."

It is not that I doubted what Carol said she saw, but I always have been intellectually troubled with the idea that a spirit—which presumably is spiritual and not material—should show up as a particular human. I tried to translate what was bothering me into a question.

Seven—The Gates of Heaven

"I mean, I can understand the soul part, and even maybe the bit about the soul going to Heaven and coming back. But why should Grandma's soul look like Grandma? Why should you see her as a woman of a particular age, actually looking just like when that particular picture was taken, and with her hair in a bun?"

"Because, it even says it [in the Bible], it talks about people in Heaven; you're going to recognize the soul as the person you knew in life.... I think I told you in my death experience I didn't recognize anyone as I knew them, but they all recognized *me*. Everyone acted like they knew me, and we communicated on the same level. We didn't have to talk, but we knew what each other was saying. I didn't know anyone who had died [yet, in real life]. I didn't have anyone in my family or friends that had died. I didn't know my great-grandparents, or many of my ancestors. So I think it was that I did not recognize them as people I knew, but yet they knew me. So who's to say that my spirit guide person is not a great-great-grandparent?"

"So we're supposing that the remnants of the person, or the soul from the person, retains some identity of the person?"[10]

"That's what I believe."

"Well, okay," I replied, thinking that, after all, Carol had just given me pretty good evidence for some form of survival after death. Little did I know at the time that there was still more evidence to come, and that it would be a drama that was to involve me directly.

Carol and I became close. The general model for psychotherapy is that there should be a distance between therapist and client, and it is argued that this keeps things objective. But I think that this sought-after objectivity is mostly fiction and, really, a distance is advocated and kept just because it would be impossible to become personally involved with everyone—and maybe no therapist would *want* to be. But I *did* become involved. It was like it was for Betty: I counted Carol as a friend, not just a client. Perhaps this is why I did not feel I needed to be confined within the sterile boundaries of traditional psychotherapy. As a therapist I knew that I had helped Carol with the challenge of her illness, and she relied on me greatly for this. But after all, much of our work together was a mutual investigation, and of issues that were as deep as could be, issues that involved both of us, equally. Is death the end? Is the material world all there is? What about God. Is God real?

Yet, despite everything I had been exposed to, I could not relax my inherent skepticism.

The Spirit Transcendent

And so we would argue, Carol and I, in the friendliest of ways. "Well, why *should* I believe? What is the *evidence*?"

"Because I constantly have answered prayer," Carol told me.

Here she cited Paul in 1 Corinthians, chapter 12, that we are given different gifts by the Spirit. Some have the gift of prophecy, some discernment. "My gift," Carol said, "was answered prayer." There were many examples. She prayed that her daughter would manage to find a job, and about a minute later the phone rang with an employer on the line. Then her other daughter had Vista come to the door to shut off the power for unpaid bills. Carol suggests that she too pray, and at that very moment, with the serviceman still in the house, *her grandmother calls* asking if she needs help. Carol prayed that a friend would be healed of a mysterious illness—and he was, literally, in front of Carol's eyes. We could spend hours discussing examples, each one as unlikely a chance occurrence as the other.

"Like the time the car broke down. It was going to cost $500—$503 was the exact bill to repair it. Well, we don't have that kind of money. I told Dave, how are we going to get $500? So *I decided to go direct*—I prayed and prayed. *Three days later*, I open the screen door and there's this envelope with $503 in it—*the exact same amount*. And then there's a slip of paper with money, the paper has no name on it, nothing. 'God says,' that's what it says—'God says,' and nothing else."

"Well, where do you think it came from? Someone from your church?" I speculated.

"Well, yes—but nobody knew. I didn't tell anyone. I asked Dave. *He* didn't tell anyone. Nobody knew."

Just in the way Carol believed in God and Heaven, she had an equal belief in the demonic, and this too came from her direct experience. Our conversation turned to some of the weird events Carol experienced on her farm in Brush Prairie, a few years prior to the time Carol saw her grandfather.

"Renee brought into our house what I will call the Wiccan faith, and she believed it." Renee was Dave's daughter who came to live on the farm when she had just turned 14, soon after Carol had married Dave. "There are Mother Earth Wiccans and Dark Side Wiccans. And Dave's old girlfriend was a Dark Side Wiccan and she got Renee into it."

"When she first came to the farm, she did not want to live there. She did not want to go to school in dumb Battleground, to live on a dumb farm. She fought me on everything, she even fought *me*. Because we had moved her from her hometown. Before she came into the house, it was fairly calm before that. We didn't have these periods of total outbursts, anger, meanness from her being with everybody. She just brought it on. And we could tell the minute she walked in the house she was bringing it in with her."

"But a presence?" My thoughts were that this might be ordinary family turmoil, with no necessity to invoke spirits. "You think she brings in actual spirits?"

"Yeah."

"So then there would be an actual entity of some kind. That implies that there is something out there that has a will of its own. How do you think it got there?"

"It got pulled in, in some way."

"But an actual evil spirit?"

"Things happened, haunting-type things, like the piano playing."

"The piano playing?"

"Playing. By itself. With nobody there."[11] The piano in question was heard—and seen—playing a scale all by itself. This happened several times, and it was witnessed not just by Carol alone, but Dave and the rest of the family. Neither were the keystrokes random; a scale was played. Inspection of the *inside* of the piano did not explain anything. One time, Carol's father was alone in the house and "when it played for him," he was so frightened that "the next thing I knew there were four men at the door, movers, to take my piano away—*my piano*, the piano that was given to me when I was five."

Our conversation returned to Carol's stepdaughter. "Renee came in the house one day. She was very agitated. Dave had talked to her about getting rid of her books and all of her Wiccan stuff. And she was *mad*, so she said she is going to conjure up something against us. I mean, she was evil at that time, you could see it, you could feel it in her. And then she spoke in a different voice."

"A different voice? You mean like of a different person? What did it sound like?"

"Ah, gravelly. Like it would be a man, but it was her voice, but it was a really lower voice, a gravelly voice."[12]

"Dave is there too? I take it you're seeing all of this together?"

"Right. Next thing Dave says, 'I'm taking your books and taking your things and I'm going to put them in the burn barrel.' So we picked up four or five books, took them to the burn barrel. She was sitting there screaming at us, swearing at us, and it wasn't even her, it just wasn't her…. You

The Spirit Transcendent

can't believe what's out there," Carol added, "there's a lot of evil as well—and it's all around you."[13]

I had a hard time believing there could be evil spirits floating about. "You said they are all around. Could there be a bad spirit in this building," I gestured at our own space in my consulting room, "for example, right now?"

"Absolutely!"

"Absolutely?"

"And I tell you what, doctor's offices, hospitals, they are the worst."

"That's very comforting," I said and began to laugh, maybe too heartily.

"Honestly, I could take you with me—and I have a lot of witnesses on this—I used to go to take demons out of rooms, hospital rooms. I get a call, 'Can you come clear a demon out of a room?' And I'd go."

"Well, it's hard for me to accept that there are independent entities that we can't see, can't touch, that are present around us."

"Sick people are coming in here [meaning my clinic] and they could have a bad spirit with them."

"But why would a sick person have a bad spirit with them?" I asked, confused.

"Illness can be caused by evil spirits, not in everybody, but sometimes. Or evil spirits can make it worse. So that's what happened with John James. He was in the hospital, he went in, but he went downhill fast and they couldn't find anything necessarily wrong with him. So when we went in and cleared the room, all his vitals jumped right back to where they were supposed to be. And he walked out of the hospital the next day. You can call it coincidental, but he could feel it, and we could feel it when we entered the room. I'll tell you one of the places I hate going are hospitals because that is where they show me their presence. People die there all the time. Spirits are left there all the time."

Carol had no question about the reality of God or spirit. But an aspect of her near-death experience from so many years ago still troubled her: she still couldn't talk about her visions freely because she felt no one would understand. This was particularly true when she tried to tell her mother, who Carol felt would simply think that she was crazy. "It's too bad we can't talk to others with the experience," Carol told me, "someone who would understand."

I thought if I could not be much help with Carol's terminal illness, I could at least fulfill this one wish of hers. I knew that Richard, the janitor at the pain clinic, was right at hand, and his experience was every bit as profound as Carol's. The only real difference I could see was that whereas Carol was thoroughly Christian, Richard was not. His spiritual practice developed within the Native American tradition. Despite this, I thought it would be therapeutic to bring the two together, so I made some preparations, explaining the plan first to Carol, then to Richard, getting permission from each, and then finally arranging a meeting.

It turned out to be the beginning of a great friendship. Common friendships develop based on mutual interests, likes and dislikes. But in the case of Carol and Richard, it was as if their relationship proceeded at another level in addition to the first, a true spiritual level, one that escaped definition in human terms.

Eight

The Christian God Meets the Great Spirit

Our plan was to have Richard meet with Carol in the pain clinic, right after my session with Carol. At this point, Carol and Richard knew about each other through me, and they knew that each had had important near-death experiences. They had never met face to face before.

As soon as Carol and I were finished, I found Richard down the hallway and invited him into the office. After we were all seated, and after a bit of small talk, I chose to break the ice: "It's striking to me that both of you have said almost the same exact thing to me about being near death."

"Both of our experiences," Richard said, "were before anybody had heard anything about them. My son had just turned three, so it was 40 years ago that it happened to me."

"And I'm sure," I said to Carol, "that this was true for you too. Here you were, only 16 years old—"

"Just *turned* 16 years old," Carol replied.

"It was just an incredible experience," Richard began. "And to me, the light flowed through me. I felt the light was *alive*. I don't know how else to describe it."

"I do," Carol said. Carol looked at me and gestured toward Richard. "You see, he's feeling the same way I am right now. Just the thought of going there triggers, like I said, it triggers this feeling right here in my chest and, I don't know where you are religiously, but being around it just confirms my belief strongly."

"Oh, absolutely," Richard agreed.

Richard and Carol shared the graphic details of how each physically encountered death. For Carol, it was the story of her hiding the entire term of her pregnancy, until she hemorrhaged and lost so much blood that her heart stopped. For Richard, his injury was a chunk of bone that went

Eight—The Christian God Meets the Great Spirit

through the artery at the back of his sinus cavity. It went undiagnosed and he almost bled to death.

I began to sum up the physical parts of the stories, hoping to move on the essentials. "That's a pretty good description of some terrible physical events, but—"

"I think God did it to me," Richard interrupted, "because I questioned whether He was still alive or not. So I think what He did was to knock me in the head to wake me up."

"Seriously?"

"Yeah," Richard replied, "I think *He set me up*. And I don't regret it for a minute."

"Well let me follow up," I said. "You take for granted, both of you, that what you experienced was God. But how do you know that? Someone could say, these two people, they lost all that blood, they were semi-conscious, maybe things weren't so clear. How would you know that it was *God*?"

"To me," Carol said, "it was clear as the nose on your face."

Richard joined in. "It's the light. As soon as that light came and started going through me—"

"Yeah, the feeling," Carol completed his thought.

"So incredible," Richard finished.

"That's why I know," Carol said, "experiences I have now, when the Holy Spirit moves I have the same feelings. I still have those feelings coming back to me. It's confirmation that it was—that God was involved in that."

"True for you too?" I asked Richard.

"Oh, absolutely! That feeling of comfort, love. Best way I could describe it is *there's not a word to describe it*. Take every word in the dictionary, put them all together, and nothing can compare."

"It's heavenly," Carol added, "because there's nothing on earth to compare to it."

"Ever since that happened," Richard said, "there is one word that has always been there for me. It's *harmonics*. Everything in existence is based on harmonics. The vibration of the molecule—the very tiniest speck of God's creation vibrates at a given harmonic. It's alive. God created it all, and underlying it all is harmonics."

"You mean, you have an ongoing perception? But of what?"

"Everything is connected. To me, God created it all."[1]

"And this is after your experience?

"Yeah, before I was kind of dead to it. And—the Native Americans—

The Spirit Transcendent

this is where I could never find a church where I was comfortable. I never accepted some man standing there shaking his finger at me, telling me I was going to go to Hell. Who is he to tell me that? I told you I went to powwows? The Native Americans introduced me to their god. To the Lakota, the Wakan Tanka, translated in English that is 'The Great Mystery.' It's kind of all-encompassing; they're not trying to say it's a man, or what he is. It is The Great Mystery. Jesus, Takashowa, was his son. It's the same god, it's the same belief, just from a different perspective.... They woke me up."

"I believe," Carol agreed, "if you believe in God, you believe in the Holy Spirit, whether it's Native American does not matter."

"Yeah, it's the same spirit." Richard agreed.

"I believe," Carol continued, "if you're Native American, you're going to see in the Native American way."

"The way I put it," Richard explained, "my truths are not necessarily your truths. What's right for me may not be right for anyone of you. But it's right for me. But there's absolutely no doubt that God exists."

After their near-death experiences, Richard and Carol developed their faith in different traditions, although here they were together, with a mutual understanding that the core of it, call it God or the Holy Spirit, was the same. It seemed obvious to me that having a deep spiritual experience cut across all denominations.[2] Richard told me about his initiation into Native American spirituality.

"After I died it was a time of confusion. It's as if someone gives you a gift but you don't know what to do with it. I was in limbo. It was profound, but I couldn't figure out why—I knew there had to be a reason behind it. Ah, it was three or four months later Steven and Sarah stopped over. They were on their way to a powwow and Anna [Richard's wife] and my son decided to go along for the experience. That's when Anna heard the heartbeat." Richard explained that the heartbeat came with listening to Native American drumming. "When they came back, Anna and Jerry were just beaming. It brought something out in Anna that she wasn't aware of. Anna says to me, 'You have just got to experience this.'"

When Steven and Sarah returned from the powwow, they asked if they could set up a sweat lodge on Richard's farm. "And that's when I saw the spirit of the stone." Richard described what being in a sweat lodge was like: "When you're in a sweat lodge, it's you and God. You talk to God. The sweat lodge becomes the center of the universe for those people that are in the lodge. And as many as I've been, I've never yet been

Eight—The Christian God Meets the Great Spirit

in one that didn't expand. I don't know how else to explain it. This little confined space, we're almost shoulder to shoulder with people, and yet it expands."[3]

His first time participating in the ceremony, Richard had an awakening. He explained to me that it's completely dark within the lodge, so dark that you would not be able to see your hand in front of your face. And on the inside of the lodge it is *hot*. At intervals, a flap is opened, and the fire keeper brings in hot rocks. Water is added to create steam, steam that cleanses body and spirit.

"There was this little thing, about the size of a pea, that came out of the stone. It looked like a little blue sparkler. It rises slowly, maybe for a second—but a second is a long time—it rises slowly and sits right in front of my face. Then it went 'poof,' and went out. When I came out of there I told Tom, I seen that. He says, 'That's the spirit from that stone.'" Richard reached over from his chair and fingered the leaves of the plant in my office. "God created everything in the universe—that plant is *alive*. Everything has some kind of spirit to it."

"Even the stone?" I asked.

"Even the stone. I guess that was my baptism, when I accepted God completely. That little sparkler. From then on things started happening again. Totally a lot stronger than it was than before."

"Stronger?"

"It was like an overpowering urge, a drive. I don't know, you know what it's like to be driven to focus on something? That was the feeling. I *had* to do this. I realized in that first sweat lodge that it was given to me that I was here to help people. He let me come back. It's like something really unbelievable had happened to me, but I didn't know what to do with it. Say I give you a hammer and you never seen a hammer and there's a nail there you don't know what to do with it yet—it's like that." But now Richard could put the two together, and he understood the purpose of his gift was to help people.

Richard became a follower of Steven and Sarah. Steven and Sarah, in turn, had been sent by Wallace Black Elk[4] to find other people to join the Morning Star Society, so named because the sweat lodge lasts all night and into the next morning. When it finally concludes, and you emerge, you might well see Venus, the morning star, rising before the dawn.

"I began making pipes, doing pipe ceremonies. The original pipe—I'm being pretty loose with it here—it's a Lakota tradition. It's their birthright, I guess you'd call it. White Buffalo Calf Woman brought them that.

The Spirit Transcendent

She was what you would have to refer to as an angel. God sent her down to help, to give them the pipe so they could use it to carry their prayers to the Creator."[5]

"Did she really, literally appear, or was it a mythical-type thing—a legend?" I asked.

"I think White Buffalo Calf Woman is an angel. It appeared to them and gave them the pipe. At that point she had to be a person because the spirit can't do something physical like delivering a pipe, you know what I mean. That pipe still exists, it's in South Dakota somewhere. The tobacco that's smoked in it, the smoke sends the prayers. In any person that accepts the pipe—if you touch the pipe, you're honor-bound to tell the truth. If you hold the pipe and lie you're in deep trouble. And all subsequent pipes that were made were made in its image."

"It's like an angel in human form," Carol said. "It's like Dave Garcia who I told you about, who I feel, I believe, was an angel in human form."

"Like Ralph Red Fox," Richard added. "He was the holy man of the Cheyenne nation, an elevated being—just being around him you *knew*. Ralph Red Fox was one of the three keepers of the Beaver Bundle, the most sacred object of the Cheyenne. He took me under his wing."

"I made my second pipe for Kenneth and Paula. Paula was ill with metastatic cancer, nearly at stage IV; I made it for them to help. This was in the late '70s at the Four Horsemen Ceremony."

Richard talked about the Four Horsemen Ceremony. He held a place of honor: at the opening of the ceremony there were four horses, each representing the four sacred colors—black, red, white, and yellow. Richard was mounted on a black horse; his son was on one that was deep chestnut; someone else rode on a white horse; and the yellow color was represented by a Palomino.

Later, Richard went about a dedication of the pipe. First came a purification: Richard and Kenneth made a fire using sage and sweet grass so that the smoke would cleanse the pipe and drive away any evil spirits. "We no more start doing the prayers," Richard said, "and as soon as I began to ask the spirits from those four directions to attend, and to come and lend us their energy, and share with us, that's when the butterflies begin to appear."

"Wait, this prayer, I guess it is to heal Paula, right? What kind of prayer?" I asked.

"The prayer just comes out at the time."

"Well, were you conscious of what you were saying?"

Eight—The Christian God Meets the Great Spirit

"Somewhat. But in any ceremony I'm simply the voice; I'm the tool. I let them speak through me as much as possible."

"Okay, so tell me about these butterflies."

"At that point I think there's maybe one or two landed on the pipe, because I was asking for the spirits to come to Paula and Kenneth. We're focusing on them. And then at some point I look up and I notice, 'My gosh, they are really covered with them.'"

"How many?"

"Hundreds. On each of them."

"How about elsewhere, like on you?" I wanted to know if the butterflies were specific to the couple being blessed.

"Well, maybe two or three on me; maybe two or three on J.R. [Richard's friend]. *All of them* on Paula and Kenneth.[6] And the butterflies just stayed. You lose track of time. It might've been there for one hour, or two or three."

"What happened to Paula?" Carol asked.

"She recovered. She's still alive to this day, I assume."

"Do you think it was because of your work in the ceremony?" I asked.

With his typical modesty, Richard replied, "I can't say we had a hand in it, but maybe we did."

And then Richard returned to the main thread of his story: "It was shortly after that when the spirits came to me and brought me that dream and told me to shut up and listen."

"Oh, great story," I said in anticipation, because I knew what was coming.

"In the middle of the night, I wake up to go pee at three in the morning. So I go to the bathroom and crawl back into bed. Then there is this guy that starts talking to me—I swear to God himself a man was standing in that room, the voice was so clear and distinct. I'm reaching in the nightstand for my pistol, because this guy is in the house. What is he doing in my house at three in the morning? And then he starts *laughing* at me."

"I love it—being mocked by a hallucination. Maybe he is amused," I offered, "with the idea that you could shoot a spirit with your gun, you think?" I was humored by the absurdity of it all.

Richard returned to the scene in his bedroom. "I'm going crazy," Richard said aloud.

"No, you're not," the spirit said.

"I am; I've lost my mind."

The Spirit Transcendent

"Shut up and *listen*. I am here to take you on a journey and you have to go with me."

"So he took my spirit out of my body, I'm assuming, because all of a sudden here's this meadow. He shows me the ceremony, he said, 'You will construct the altar and the pillar of the four directions,' and he showed me how he wanted the altar built, the colors of the flags for the four directions—because they represent the spirits of all those directions—the four corners of God's creation."

"Of course, by this time I have learned to shut up and we get back [to the bedroom]. He says, 'Now you will perform this when the time is right.'"

"Perform what?" Richard asked.

"The ceremony."

"What ceremony?"

"You have done this twice before." To hear Richard tell it, by now the spirit was exasperated with him. "You already *know* and have but to remember. You will know when it is time because I will tell you and you will listen. *You* have the ceremony and *your sister has the song*."

"So we begin arguing again. 'I don't have a sister.'"

"Shut up and listen. Your *spirit sister*. She has the song."

"Well, this spirit sister of yours, I presume she is a real person?" I asked.

"Yes, it's hard to describe, but there's these people you are connected to. When you find a spirit sister, or a spirit brother, it's just something that you know. You could meet that person for the first time, and just sit down and talk for hours, as if you had known them forever. My spirit sister is Maddy."

"Two or three days after that night Maddy calls me, and she says, 'There's this song I can't get out of my head.' Maddy and me—one of our totems is the same, the red-tailed hawk—Maddy says, 'I had the weirdest dream, this eagle tore my breast open, and I began to bleed. But when I bled, a song came out. I did not cry out in pain, but in song.' That's when I told her about what I had been given."

At this point in his life, Richard was living in the small, very rural town of Salmon, Idaho, and working as a janitor at the high school. It was a few months after Richard's visit by the spirit who gave him the ceremony, around November of 1996. "It is cold out, subzero cold. I had just finished at the high school, about 11 p.m. I'm driving through downtown; that's the way I go to get back home. That time at night, in Salmon, everything is closed up. Well, walking down the street is a man—you've seen all the

Eight—The Christian God Meets the Great Spirit

pictures of Jesus and the flowing robes—it was like that, some kind of white linen, very coarse cloth. And he has a walking stick, and he's wearing *sandals*, and it's like *five below*. Well, when I get up to him, he looks at me. I mean he *looked at ME*. We made eye contact, and I knew at that instant I had to talk to him—it was just overpowering. So I drove home—its only maybe two minutes away—thinking I've got to get Anna; she's just got to see this. But he was gone. I drove all over looking for him. The only place open in all of Salmon is a coffee shop, the Dog House, but he wasn't there either."

Naturally, a psychologist like myself, at the time I heard the story, was thinking in terms of a simple hallucination. But developments did not fit this simple explanation. The next day, Richard spoke with two women at work.

"One of them says to me, 'Did you see that weird guy walking up the street wearing the Jesus robes? I thought I was hallucinating.' 'I don't think you're crazy,' I told her, 'because I seen him too.' Then the second woman pipes up and says, 'Well, you guys are not going to believe this, but right after I saw him, my husband was coming home from Missoula and he is in North Fork, and he sees this man walking alongside the road dressed exactly the same way.' North Fork is 26 miles away from Salmon, and it's maybe five minutes after we seen him. Well, *there's no way* you can get from Salmon to North Fork in five minutes."

Richard's wife, Anna, ran a gift store in Salmon. Perhaps three weeks later two women came into the store saying their husbands were looking for a pipe. "And it just so happens that I make pipes for ceremonies. My wife told them, 'OK, my husband makes them, but he would need to meet your husbands before he would *even consider* making a pipe.'"

"So Sunday we go to meet the husbands, Paul and Steven. Paul invites us into the trailer, and I go in. I turned around. Here is this wall covered in portraits. It's in pencil, and the artist is fantastic, I mean, they are all full of life. And guess whose picture was hanging over the door? *The guy who I had seen walking down the street.* Wow! Something was happening here."

Richard found out that these two men were natives living on the Hopi reservation in Arizona. "They were told by the spirits that they had to travel to Salmon, Idaho, to talk to two people. This was a trip of 1500 miles, and they had no idea who they were to seek out."

"That's it?" I asked, incredulous. "Find two people?"

"They were just told, 'They'll find you; you'll find them.' So they took jobs in the gold mines just so they could eat, until they could fulfill the will of the spirits."

Carol gave out a chuckle. "People show up with me all the time. They might not even know why—'Something told me I ought be here' or 'For some reason I just turned into your road,' and so on. Happens all the time. And then they tell me about a spirit, or a problem, so it's 'Ah, now I see why...'"

Richard found out that Paul and Steven had stories of their own. Steven was a healer; Paul, who was to figure more importantly in Richard's story, was a medium. Paul was given his gift after his own personal crisis.

"We get acquainted and that is when Paul told me about his experience. He's sitting in the trailer, so depressed. His wife has left him, and the kids are gone, and he wanted to commit suicide. He has the gun to his head and the gun is cocked, [he's] trying to pull the trigger. And the door flies open, and a blue light comes in and his life was changed. He committed himself to the mental hospital three different times after that because these voices started talking to him."

"That is interesting," I simply replied. But that was not half of it, I thought at the time. Here was yet another example of an experience that from one perspective is mental illness but from another is a spiritual event. And I was beginning to think it could even be both, at the same time.[7]

"Let me ask you more about it," I said. "He wanted to commit suicide and then there's this blue light. How did the blue light prevent him from pulling the trigger?"

"The pure shock of it and the blue light was so intense that it just blew into the room and just overpowered him. He was helpless, and he said he broke down, started crying, a total breakdown."

"Well, I see it would be appropriate to go the mental hospital when you are suicidal and you have a gun to your head, but you said that he was thinking he was going crazy because of the visions he was seeing?"

"Yes, the voices."

"What voices?" I asked.

"It started after that happened [the suicide attempt], when things calmed down. These voices started talking to him.... That is when he decided something was seriously wrong with him. He commits himself in Arizona; I think it was Phoenix or someplace like that."

"So you think the voices are not mental illness, but he was getting messages from what you would call spirits?"

"Yes, probably from his guide, or maybe someone way more powerful

Eight—The Christian God Meets the Great Spirit

than a guide. They came to him. Each time he thought he was crazy, but he absorbed something [from the encounter] each time. Finally, after the third time they came to him, he accepted it."

"Accepted what?" I was still a bit confused.

"That he was not nuts. That he had been given a second chance. But this was a responsibility. Paul says it is a gift and he was told he could not sell it, could not collect a penny for it, or else they would come back and they would punish him a thousand fold. After me arguing with that one spirit I told you came to me, if I were in his shoes, with this much more powerful spirit, I do not think I would argue with him at all. I would accept what he had to say."

Richard picked up the thread of the main story. "So we get there, and we are having our cup of coffee, and Paul is explaining what he does, how they were compelled to come here and meet somebody they did not know to deliver a message."

But first, Paul had a test that Richard had to pass. If he did not pass the test he would go no further. "Two questions, no clues. Paul asked me, 'What is the truth?' 'Unconditional love,' I answered. That is the first truth." Richard leaned back and elaborated. "Love beyond everything. God loves, and he expects it in return, I assume—at least I try to give it to Him in return."

"Then he asked me the second question: 'Are you of the light?' I answered, 'Of course I am.' He who rules the darkness, I absolutely *refuse* to acknowledge that he exists—not in my world. I have a wall and he cannot penetrate it, and my wall is the light.... Those are the two basic truths that God gave me."

"Paul asked me to answer those two questions—no clues. The first one has to be love, unconditional love, and the second one has got to be light, because God is the light."

Richard passed the test, and now it was time to get down to business. "Normally they set up a camera and a tape recorder whenever he [Paul] has done a communication for whoever. They would make copies of both the video and the tape for the people and just give it to them, so they wouldn't forget, you know. But here Paul goes into a trance—he starts to raise his hands and he starts talking, and the others, they were like, 'We're not ready!' They're wondering, 'What is going on here? They [the spirits] are coming and we are not ready!'"

"About that time the one who stepped into his [Paul's] body said, 'This is not for you people to record. This is for the ones we came to talk

The Spirit Transcendent

to.' The voice that came through Paul, the name he gave me was Akalian.... That was the picture of the man over the door. That was the man we seen in the Jesus robes.'"

"Well, how did you know that picture was the spirit?" I wanted to know.

"He told us. And he introduced himself first [he was the first of many spirits to introduce himself] and it was just conversation like we are talking right now. But yet Paul is sitting there, and you can just see virtually the change come over him and see that person."

"Wait—who did you see exactly?" I did not yet understand the nature of the possession/mediumship experience.[8]

"Maybe that is the image they [the spirits] give you, I don't know, but I did not see Paul, I saw Akalian[9] ... and Akalian spoke," Richard explained as he leaned forward, "and pretty soon he says, 'I have to step out because so-and-so wants in.' They were like magpies—they wouldn't shut up. They had so much to tell us. 'Can you step aside so I can use him?' For seven hours, it was *nonstop*. And Paul, the poor guy, he's just sitting there—he's exhausted. Physically exhausted, and obviously, I'm sure, mentally exhausted. So Steven asks the spirits if they could stop and we have dinner. Well, there's one place to eat in Salmon, the Salmon River Truck Stop. So we go to the truck stop, everyone orders a meal, and no sooner we sit down, *they come back*—they had so much information to give us, to share with us. Poor guy didn't get a chance to eat, and we all ate our meals while they were chattering through him. Finally, his wife said, 'It's going to kill him, *we have got to stop*.' So we got up and excused ourselves."

"They called the next day and said, 'Well, we think our job is done.' They had already resigned their jobs at the mines and they are going back to Arizona on Wednesday morning. Well, Wednesday morning comes along and we get *another* call. They said, 'You have to come over because they did not finish telling you what they needed.' We go over there, and they have already hooked up their fifth wheel to their trucks. Paul sits down and the person that steps in, he tells me his name is White Cloud. He says, 'I am the one who brought you your vision. To show you who I am, I will tell you enough that you know, because no one else can know what I am telling you.' Well, he did. It was White Cloud that gave me the ceremony."

At the time, Richard was having trouble accepting that that the spirits would single him out in such a powerful way. "It was like, why me? I'm nobody; I'm a janitor at the high school." A week later, Richard visited his

Eight—The Christian God Meets the Great Spirit

daughter in Boise. "No sooner I get in the door, it's Ralph Red Fox on the phone. Telling me to get over to his place. Well, it's midnight. 'I don't care what time of day it is, get over here.' So I get there—this is on the other side of Boise—and he says, 'About time.' I thought he was talking about how long it took to get to his house, but he meant 'It's about time the spirits came and spoke to me.' He wanted to know why I was having trouble accepting what I was told. And *he knew* everything that had transpired, and he's 250 miles away."

"Well, it sure seems like you were being singled out," I said. "Why, do you think?"

"I don't perceive me as being special," Richard replied. "They're working through me. I am the tool. They are working through me, because I will not brag about it."

Thinking to myself, I realized that the story of Paul, the medium, posed a tremendous challenge to traditional psychiatry. If a medium is taken over by spirits, the standard interpretation is that it is a form of dissociation and it is not expected to have any validity *outside* of the person.[10] Those personages cannot be real, by definition. But in Richard's case, there is confirmation all over the place for an independent reality, because there are lots of people, normal people, who experienced the same spirit. And the implication—the reality of a spirit—is almost impossible to fathom, because, after all—*it is a spirit*. Spirits and the material explanation of the world simply don't mix.

Now, the problem with showing that there really is a spiritual reality is that we are dealing with perceptions of a privileged few, unlike our material reality, which everyone agrees on. This was one of the reasons—besides the fact that I thought it would be therapeutic—that I wanted to get Carol and Richard together. I personally may not have had the spiritual eyes to see it, but I wanted to know if there would be agreement between two spiritually sensitive people. And there was—Carol and Richard agreed on everything that was essential. I made a point of it in the session.

"You both are on the same wavelength," I said, "but that does not mean everyone sees what you see, understands what you understand. What is the message for everyone else?"

"Even people who believe," Carol offered, "they still have the question of what is it like to die. The fear of it."

"Yeah, fear," Richard agreed.

"Fear of the unknown."

"We don't have that."

121

The Spirit Transcendent

"No."

"I'm not going to go stand in the middle of the street in front of a Mack truck—"

"Especially for that one minute where it does hurt, you know," Carol added with a laugh.

And Richard summed it up: "It's trying to make Mark and all the others understand just how beautiful an experience it is. It's simply—death is a doorway. It's just a door from this world to a much more beautiful world. It's like a graduation. With what we've experienced, it's so incredible. And everybody gets to experience it. Everybody *has to* experience it."

"Wait," I objected. "You think *everybody* who dies experiences it?"

"Absolutely!" Richard and Carol exclaimed in unison and then laughed that they should speak as if in one voice.

"But that's not necessarily given." I would not let it rest. "Maybe you both have a spiritual sensitivity that others don't have. Maybe it's a gift."[11]

"There's times," Richard replied, "where I don't look at it as a gift but as a burden, but I don't say that out loud, because maybe they'll knock me in the head again."

Carol chimed in with an example. "That's what's frustrating. Well, here is an example from last week. There's a guy that worked for Les Schwab in Colfax. Well, the one area that I have happen a lot is I can feel illness on people—not all the time, not all the time—but when it's strong, I can feel that something's going to happen. But this guy, his name's Roger, we went in there the other day and normally he says hi to us. He's cordial.... So I went up to him and I said, 'Hi, Roger. How's it going?' And he didn't really answer me; he didn't really say anything. And I thought, 'My, that's weird, he usually would talk to us.' And when I was in there, something made me watch him. And when I was in there, I felt pain. You know, like chest pain, physical pain. Well, I didn't say anything. I didn't know how he would react, and anyway they might think I was a little touched in the head. Well, he was life-flighted out yesterday to Sacred Heart. They can't find out what it is wrong with him. They put him in induced coma. Every time he comes out he has massive seizures. There's not any known reason why, so they have to keep him in this coma. And they've done brain scans, every test in the world, and it's coming not just from the chest area, where I felt pain, but it's coming from his head. I didn't get that—I got the chest. Then you're in this spot where [you say to yourself,] 'Why didn't I say something? What have I got to lose?' They can either believe it or not. The question is, is it going to help the person?"

Eight—The Christian God Meets the Great Spirit

"Yeah," Richard agreed. "For a number of years, traveling down the highway, a car would pass me, I would know who was going to be in a wreck. A mile, 10 miles up the road—there they were. That went on a long time. It got bad, nobody wanted to travel with me, it was happening *all the time*.... I asked them [the spirits], 'Don't show me this anymore—I can't handle it.' This had gone on for 10 years. What do you say? If you run them down, you may be the cause of the wreck. Or you may *get shot*, you know. Who knows what the consequences are. Why are you showing me this? I could never put my finger on it."

After a moment, Richard added, speaking to Carol, "I think the same reason the spirits come to people like you is because they know we can pass that on, you know, or we can be the voice for that. I really do. And there are times when we don't really want to say anything."

"My family gets it," Carol said. "They know what I experience. How they were raised. If I say, 'You're not getting in the car now,' there's not a doubt in their minds—they know."

"God brings people together for a purpose." Carol turned to me and said, "The first time I met you, I knew that God brought us together for a purpose. Otherwise, I would not be here, because I was more skeptical about you—the psychologist—than you were of me."

Richard had a similar feeling about our meeting: "When was it that we first talked?" he asked.

"It was nine—no, nine and a half years ago," I replied. It was then that Richard first told me about his near-death experience. I remembered it clearly: it was early evening; he had taken some trash out to the dumpster and we lingered for a while, chatting beside my truck before I left for the day.

"I had the extreme feeling that I had to talk to someone here. There was someone here that I had to share that with. At first, I thought it was Ellen, but it wasn't Ellen."

"You were told to search out someone? And you think that someone was *me*?"

Richard thought he knew why the spirits were working through him and Carol. "They sent us to wake you up, that's probably what it's all about. Because it's there in everyone—all they have to do—it's like if you look at a person, you see there is this keyhole. It's like you're putting in a key and unlocking the door. We all have spirits. Whether people accept it or not, it's true."

Maybe out of modesty—that I should be so special that Richard was

The Spirit Transcendent

sent to seek me out—or perhaps because of my skepticism, it was hard for me to accept what Richard was telling me. I didn't know what to say. Rather than respond directly, I thought I would buy some time. "Well, Carol, what do you think?"

"Yeah, we talked about this." I was not to be let off so easily. "You have to surrender, you have to totally surrender. It was easier for me because I've been there [Heaven] and back. I have the knowledge. You've been trained to *learn* the knowledge. Learning the knowledge is harder than it just being given to you. But what you have to do is totally to be able to surrender your total life. So that means you have to give up *control*. Like Job. He was a rich man; God said you have to be willing to give everything away and come follow me."

Richard learned the same lesson outside of the Christian tradition. He nodded in agreement. "'God made it simple; man complicated it.' That was nearly the first thing out of Akalian's mouth. It's about giving yourself up.... Look, all these material things, the entire material world, makes it hard. Like my pickup, say, for instance. I like my pickup, but I could live without it. I could give everything up. It's not what's important."

"Well, to tell the truth, I've been trying to unlock that door," I said, "but I don't have the ability to sense what both of you can sense."

"I see where you're coming from. It's not easy. I don't think you can do it consciously. It's almost a subconscious thing. It's accepting here," Richard pointed to his heart, "not here," he said, pointing to his head. "That's the problem. You can't think yourself into it."

"What Richard and I have is the spirit," Carol said. "Whether in Christianity or the Native American, it's the same." And after a pause, Carol added, "Together like this, I can feel the spirit move. There's a lot of spiritual force in the room."

"Well, you both seem almost like lightning rods for spiritual things," I said.

"Sometimes I just need a rest," Carol laughed.

Richard had the same sense. "I asked them to leave me alone for awhile. As long as you're willing to keep accepting, they're ganging up on you. Because you're the one that can communicate it."

"I didn't figure that out for awhile," Carol replied. "For years. When I was younger, it was more frequent; later I could control it better. The thing I couldn't control was people that would randomly come to me and start asking questions. I just have had the strangest, strangest situations."

"It's *your aura*," Richard joked, and Carol laughed. But turning more

Eight—The Christian God Meets the Great Spirit

serious, Richard said to Carol, "You have a blue aura right now, just a lovely blue."

"He's got a green one, did you know?" Carol was talking about my aura.

"Mine is green?"

"You're *sick*," Richard joked again, drawing out the word "sick" to give it emphasis.

What about Richard? I asked Carol, "What is *his* color?"

"What I see around Richard each time is light. Without color. He just has light around him. Usually white light to me symbolizes spirit acknowledgment." A few weeks later, Carol said to me of her impression during that meeting. "When I saw Richard, it was like, 'Yikes.' With Richard there is always light.... It means the spirit is always with him."

I always loved talking about auras. It was part of a pleasant banter between Carol and me in our sessions. It was almost a game between us, where I would ask, hopefully, "Well, what color is my aura?" Once, just once, it was a yellow that projected a distance from my body. Carol announced that yellow was my natural color, but usually, when I asked the question, she would tell me in a disappointed tone of voice that I was blue, still blue—as if my true color could not come out, because my mood was low or my energy was depleted.

By now, the three of us had been talking together for a solid two and a half hours. I was exhausted, and I certainly had a lot to think about. "Well, I have to go home sometime."

"We wore you out," Carol said, playfully.

"We're just getting started," Richard replied, and then he suggested, "We'll have to do this again."

The meeting was a great success. And we did do it again, several times. A special bond had developed between Carol and Richard. Our meeting told me that the spirit was a great unifying force, and I thought perhaps this was the real core of religion, and if you can only get at the core, differences among particular faiths become irrelevant.

Things worked out so well, I decided I should have Sandra meet Richard too. Sandra already told me she identified with her Cherokee heritage, and I knew there was another part of her vision that involved the spirit of her Cherokee grandmother, although she and I had not talked much about it. When the three of us got together, Sandra talked about her accident.

"On the mountain where I was hurt, I woke up in the snow red with blood. In that little tiny bit of time, when I was just coming to my senses,

The Spirit Transcendent

I felt the presence there. It was almost as if she was there making sure; she knew what happened to me, and she was there to protect me and get me help. In the spiritual world she was right there. That's the first time I became aware [of my grandmother]. I have not seen my grandmother [in actual life], I have not heard her.... I knew it was her."

"How long ago did this happen?" Richard asked.

"This happened on Christmas Day, 2000. And then—in that period of time—I've had five surgeries. I was in a lot of pain when I came back from a near-death experience. I had a strength that was not mine. Like I was telling Dr. Yama, I was fortified—you've heard of fortified milk—I was fortified with a strength I did not have."

Richard looked at Sandra. "Every person has a spirit guide," he said. "Your spirit—your soul—elected to come here. Okay. Then another soul agreed to come along to be your guide, to protect you. You know that feeling you get every once in a while—you shouldn't take that step? That's the guide, trying to manage without interfering. That could very well be your grandmother who chose to come back with you. Maybe, can't be sure."

"Ever since then I feel she is with me," Sandra said. "Her situation was like mine. If I died, my son would be an orphan. And when she died, that's how she left my father. And when I look at that I can see such hurt, for her to leave this baby."

"And she didn't have any choice, did she?" Richard said.

"I realize she cares deeply, and I want to be connected.... Obviously she is real."

"Absolutely."

• • •

By now, I was no longer working like a traditional psychologist. By now, I was convinced that there really was a spiritual world, even if it was beyond my own senses. I began to act more and more, in my practice, as if this were true. And since I had little direct access to the spiritual world itself, it made more sense to bring people who knew about it directly together. Pretty soon, we were meeting as a group of four: Carol, Richard, Sandra, and me.

Nine

Hallucinations of the Demonic Variety

At the beginning of the session, just as soon as she slowly shifted herself from her walker to sit in my chair, Monica announced, "Weird things have been happening to me lately."

Monica lived in a small town in eastern Washington. The first of her weird events took place when she was shopping at the town's one grocery store, a Rosauer's. "So then I walk into this store and there was this lady there—an older gal with gray hair, very sweet. She had a display set up right inside the entrance. You know, she was giving away samples of gummy bears, gummy worms, and sour gummies. I just took the gummy bears ... she held out her arms and hands, and I'm kind of looking around, thinking, 'What is she doing?' you know. And she came over and hugged me, and said, 'I've been waiting for you.'"

"Really, she said that?" I asked. "I've been waiting for you?'"

"And I said, 'For what?'"

"'To pray for you.'"

"I just didn't really say anything and she said, 'You are very sick, aren't you?' And I said, 'Yes,' and she says, 'You have liver disease, don't you?' And I said, 'Yes,' and she said that she knew about my hip also, and that I was thin."

"How did you find me?" Monica asked.

"I was told to look for you by my higher power."

"And anyways," Monica said, "she put her hand on my forehead and started praying. She said a beautiful prayer for me, and it was like we were praying together. And then she was saying Jesus' name, amen. Then I went on, and I just felt it was a little weird."

This was new to me. Previously, I had never heard anything like this from Monica. Defaulting to my psychologist mode, I wondered if the strange experience was, at root, a hallucination. "So here you are. Did you have the sense that you were in your normal mental state?" I asked.

"Sure."

"Was it like your mind was hazy?"

"No."

"So you were aware of everything around you?"

"Yes."

"Were you taking any kind of medication or anything like that recently?"

"Well, I took my normal morning medications, and the nightly medications are the only ones that would have hazed my mind, but I've been on it for a long time, and it's a low dose."

Listening to Monica, I began to wonder if the older woman with gray hair might be real. But Monica herself made the discovery that this could not be the case. Her first clue came as she was shopping. Monica took the sample of gummy bears, which were in a small cup, and set them on top of her purse. "And so I was reaching in to get one every once in a while, and I reached in after I left her, and I couldn't find my gummy bears. So I looked and there wasn't even the container there. And I thought, 'Oh, they're at the bottom.' But they weren't there either."

Then Monica met her neighbors in the store, and as she was checking out, she struck up polite conversation, asking them, "So what did you guys pick—the sour gummy bears or the worms?" The woman Monica encountered would have been standing where anyone who entered would have to have seen her, but her neighbors knew nothing of this. Nor could they have missed her, because, driving to the store, they were right behind Monica's car, and they entered the front door right after her.

The next day, Monica was killing time before a dentist appointment. She didn't like having her teeth worked on and was nervous; she wandered into a thrift shop where she used to volunteer. "So I got a basket and wasn't looking for anything special. I was going down an aisle and I got a tap on the back on my shoulder, and I turned around and it was a little Hispanic woman, real pretty. And she had a boy with her who was about three. And he was very well behaved and did whatever his mother told him to—not like one of my boys," Monica laughed. "She put her hand on my head."

"May I pray for you?" the woman asked.

"I said, 'Sure,' and [she] did almost the same prayer as the lady from the day before did. At the end I said to her, 'Why did you pray for me?'"

"Because you're very ill."

Nine—Hallucinations of the Demonic Variety

"How do you know that?"

"Because my higher power told me that."

"So I turned around and thought, 'I'm going to ask her one more thing.' I turned around real quick—but she was gone." Monica knew the check-out ladies, since she had been a volunteer at the store herself, so she asked them: "That small woman, real pretty, that Hispanic woman with the boy? Did she leave the store?"

The women looked at each other. "We didn't see her."

"Are you sure she didn't slip past you?"

"No, we have been here for the last two hours."

Monica folded her hands in front of her and said to me, "That just blew me away."

Then there was yet a *third* event, soon after these first two. Monica had just returned home, and she walked into her bedroom. "I was just in so much pain that I just leaned over and started crying. Then I had this tap on my shoulder again, and I looked and it was this plain average guy."

"This was in your bedroom?" I asked.

"Yes, in my bedroom. And he was sitting on my bed and he did about the same thing. He said, 'I've been waiting for you.'"

"Why are you in my house? You're trespassing!"

"No, I am not. I was sent to give you a message and pray with you," he replied.

"What message?"

"Be strong and things will work out in the end, one way or another."

"And then he prayed the same kind of prayer," Monica said, "to give me strength and to know how to go through this."

Putting myself in Monica's situation, I asked, "Did you have any question in your mind if this guy was real?"

Monica's response surprised me. "Of course I thought he was real! I said, 'What is your name? Why are you in my house? I'm going to call the police.'"

But then Monica went to touch him, and whereas with the women in the other encounters their touch was solid, in this case Monica found "I am touching nobody.... But he was still sitting there ... and that's when I freaked out."

"'No!' I told him. 'You're not going to do this to me. Please leave my house.'"

"I am very sorry. I just hope that you listen to what I have told you. I'll be going for now," he said.

The Spirit Transcendent

"And then he just walked right through the door [the *closed* door], and I didn't see him at all."

A few weeks later, when I met Monica again, she had no more visitations to report. But there was a new development. Whenever Monica was distressed, she would feel a tapping, usually on her left shoulder. "It's just a light tap but it happens a lot when I am in the bedroom trying to decide what to wear for the day, and I get kind of depressed because of my stomach area [her stomach is bloated because of retained fluid] ... it will happen some if I am on a phone call and I am really irritated with the insurance or a customer service person or whatever. Like, I am ready to explode, and it will happen all of a sudden and bring you back down to reality, I guess.... When I get it, I feel chills, because I know it's her."

Naturally, I again pursued the psychological angle. These visitations of Monica's were hallucinations, after all. "Monica," I asked, "in the past, have you ever heard voices?"

"No, I know it's not schizophrenic."

"Well, okay—"

"I know it's not schizophrenia; they are not telling me to do anything; they are not taking over my mind; they visit and it's always been positive. Usually in schizophrenia, in what I have heard and read, it's a very tough life with all these demons and fighting things internally. It's usually not a positive experience."

I thought Monica's response was well reasoned, but schizophrenia is not the only cause of hallucinations, and there was a terrible lot going on with her medically. Monica's difficulties began 16 years ago when her mother passed away. She was overcome with grief and coped with drinking, maybe as much as a bottle of wine per day. Alcoholic drinking is a risk factor for all kinds of problems, and in Monica's case, she developed esophageal varicosities. At one point these weakened blood vessels ruptured; one evening she began to vomit blood and nearly died. She was rushed to the hospital and, after being infused with eight units of blood, survived. But after she was patched up and recovered, Monica's liver became diseased, and she told me that, unless she could receive a liver transplant, her prospects were not good. On top of all of this, Monica has severe osteoporosis—she fractured her pelvis in multiple places once and leg bones on multiple occasions—and chronic pain has been a constant problem. And *then*, in one of our sessions, Monica told me that the physicians discovered a lesion in her frontal lobe, and this turned out to be due

Nine—Hallucinations of the Demonic Variety

to a parasitic infection, possibly contracted when she had visited Brazil during her senior year in high school.

Knowing her medical history, it was easy for me to assume that Monica's visitations were garden-variety hallucinations, even though I did not know the exact cause. Well, if they *were* symptoms, it would be natural to ask: When did they begin? (Monica had earlier told me about her near-death experience—she is the same Monica featured in Chapter Three—but she never mentioned hallucinations or spirits before.) I finally got around to asking her, "Have you seen spirits before this?"

"Oh, I have seen spirits and had other things like that happen all my life."

"Well, why didn't you tell me?"

"I was afraid of how you might feel about it."

"By now you should know I'm not going to go making assumptions."

"Okay ... there was my mom—I saw my mom a couple of times after she died. She was in my house up north. She walked from the kitchen out to the fireplace and then she just disappeared out the front window.... She was walking, and she never talked. She was just checking things out."

Then Monica brought up another vision, from much earlier in her life, of her father-in-law, Shiro. Monica and Shiro were deeply connected. "He told me I was the daughter he never had." Monica gave me some background about him: he was a Japanese gentleman who was a teenager during World War II and spent time in an internment camp. After the war, he settled in Los Angeles, and he and his wife ran a grocery store. Tragically, one day a gunman held up the store. He was shot twice, in the head and in the abdomen, and died.

Shiro's first visit as a spirit was memorable. Monica explained that her husband, Philip, had a fishing boat parked in the backyard. One day he sat in the boat and was practicing casting. "I looked up," Monica laughed, "and Philip was sitting in the seat and his dad was sitting in the front seat, plain as day. I watched for a long time, and his dad spun his seat around and was talking to him." As Monica called her husband Philip's name, Shiro started to disappear, then vanished.

But Shiro continued to visit. This seemed to be always when Monica would be doing the dishes. She would look up and catch his reflection in the glass window. There he would be, behind Monica; sometimes she would move her head to one side so she could get a better glimpse of him.

I knew from working with her that Monica had problems with depression, so I asked about her mental state at the time. She was not depressed back then, nor did she seem to suffer from any kind of mental disorder. She was working full time and had four small children. It was a stressful time in Monica's life, and her husband was not treating her well. Once Monica got over the initial shock of seeing him, she came to find comfort in Shiro's visits. "He was looking out for me."

There was an even earlier episode, involving a "ghost," about two years after Monica's first child was born (and therefore after her near-death experience). "We were living in Cruz Bay and Philip had gone hunting. I was real homesick, and I begged him not to go, but here I was home with Ursula, which kind of creeped me out. I was doing dishes, and it was dark out, and I looked up, and there was this guy standing right there looking at me through the window. I thought it was a peeping Tom. And there was this presence behind me—real cold, the room felt, and my body felt real cold—and all of a sudden, he smiled at me. He was like a 25-year-old guy I had never seen, but he seemed familiar."

"Where was this fellow you were looking at? Was he in front of you, or behind you?" I asked, confused.

"Through the window; I thought he was actually there. I was scared but … it was like gradually disappearing. It was getting dimmer and dimmer. I thought I was using too much hot water [doing dishes] and the windows got steamed up, so that was making it go dimmer. But I wiped the window to make sure it wasn't steam from my dishwasher."

"But why behind you?"

"Well, I felt this really cold chill and I could feel someone almost, you know, you can feel someone behind you, you know, breathing on your neck."

"Behind you? But no one was there?"

"But there was a reflecting in the window."

"Oh, now I see—you think there was a reflection in the window and the actual physical being was behind you."

"Yes, and it was just *weird*. And when we moved back to Palouse, and we lived there for a time, and I never said anything to anyone. One time we went over to my parents' over in Palouse … she [Monica's mother] had gotten this box and was going though all these pictures and she was organizing them. And she was saying, 'This was your great-grandmother,' and anyways, it turns out that the reflection was so familiar because [from the picture in the album I discovered that] it was my dad's brother who had died at age 25. He had been drinking and he had a sports car, and was driving too fast between Palouse and Potlach, and there is a Grange Hall

Nine—Hallucinations of the Demonic Variety

on that hill.... That is where he rolled his car, and landed on a boulder, and crunched the entire thing. He was still alive for a few hours but he was never conscious. But that was before I was born."

I began to ask Monica about earlier experiences. There was still the medical question about a possible parasite she may have picked up that could have affected her brain, and I wanted to go back before this was a possibility. And there *were* earlier stories.

When Monica was 14 or 15, about three times a week, she and her mother would get in the car and go visit Monica's grandmother, who lived about 10 miles away on a rural road. On one of their trips it began to rain, then pour, so Monica's mother pulled off of the road at a grange.

"Mom said, 'This is almost the spot where your uncle Ned went off the road and flipped his car.' So we pulled over because we couldn't see, and because the window wipers couldn't keep up."

"Your uncle Ned died over there?" (In the interview, when I first heard this story it had not yet occurred to me that Ned was the same presence Monica felt behind her, years before, when she was doing dishes.)

"Yes—Dad's only sibling, but it was before I was even born. Well, all a sudden, out of the sky, there was this huge spotlight and it came down and lit up the whole car, and the grange and a house on the left side. Mom starts shaking because she is nervous, and I start freaking out, and I go, 'Mom, what is it?'"

At first, Monica and her mother considered that it might be the moon, because the light appeared when the clouds had parted. But it was not the moon, and besides, it was *huge*. "It was kind of like an eye, because it had this thing that came down, like an eyelid, and when it shut, the light went out. And then it closed."

I still held to the theory that it could be the moon, although as Monica told the story this began to seem less and less likely.

"But my mom was shook up real bad," Monica said. "And whenever I tried to talk with her about it, she would just go 'Shush.' She never wanted to talk about it."

I wondered how far back these experiences would go. "The very first time you saw something that was like a ghost or a spirit—how old were you?"

"About 12." This surprised me.

"So there's a story that goes back even further?"

"There is one other thing, but a thing me and my dad saw, but he won't ever talk about it."

The Spirit Transcendent

"You remember it and are sure there was something there he never wanted to talk about?"

"Yeah."

"All right. Tell me what it was."

Monica told me that the house where she grew up—in a small town in eastern Washington—had a view of the cemetery. "I don't know if you've ever been to the cemetery in Palouse or not, but it has this huge oak tree in the very middle, and I'd go on walks there, like on a spring day when all the cottonwoods are blooming."

"Mom canned a lot and us girls we were always helping. Dad and I were sitting there snapping beans on the backdoor steps that faced right up to the cemetery. It was a dark night, there was no moon out, and we were talking a little bit, because he goes so slow on snapping beans. We'd talk about how slow he was."

"And I look up at the cemetery and I see a couple of lights blinking. And Dad goes, 'Wonder what's going on up there, I didn't hear any cars.' And all of a sudden there's lights everywhere, thousands of them, blinking in the cemetery. Like a flashlight going off and on, at different times. It was here and there, up in the trees, and on the ground. And Dad and I both sat there, and I was scared to death, and I knew he was too."

"Fireflies?" I wondered.

"No, these were big lights."

And anyway, I realized there aren't fireflies in this part of the country. "How far away is the cemetery from your porch?" I asked.

"Well, we have five acres of land, so maybe a football field away.... And every time we talked about it, he said, 'Don't mention it to your mom, it would scare her.'"

There was no easy explanation that I could think of. At the time, I passed Monica's story off as perhaps the product of an overactive imagination in a 12- or 13-year-old. With hindsight, I realized that every one of Monica's unusual experiences was connected with death—the death of Monica's mother; the murder of her father-in-law; the uncle who had the fatal car crash ... even the last story fits the pattern because the lights were in a cemetery. It was as if found myself within the movie *The Sixth Sense*, where Bruce Willis plays the psychologist, and he hears his client, the child protagonist, whisper, "I see dead people."

But where I had been sitting patiently with Monica, listening to her stories of spirits and the paranormal session after session, there was a subsequent event that was to soon lend an urgency to our meetings: after

Nine—Hallucinations of the Demonic Variety

a space of about a month, Monica called me on the telephone. With a tremor in her voice, she pleaded, "Dr. Yama, please help me—I don't want to go to Hell."

The day before, Monica had fallen and re-injured her hip. She called her hip doctor and he suggested using a cream that had been given to her on a previous visit, however, the cream was 10 percent ketamine, and when Monica applied it, she suffered an overdose. Normally, Monica wakes up at 4 a.m. because her husband works early, but he was unable to wake her. Eventually he got hold of a neighbor who was an EMT, the EMT called an ambulance, and Monica was taken to the local hospital and then airlifted to a larger hospital in Spokane.

Monica was very confused. When she got to the hospital she was diagnosed with acute liver failure, acute kidney failure, and acute encephalopathy. She was intubated, and in the process, three of her teeth were knocked out. From her point of view, Monica felt suffocated, then she remembered hearing her teeth being ripped out, and then she lost consciousness and went into a coma.

Frightening images followed. Her father was with her, and Monica was telling him, "I'm sorry," but when she held up her hand, all of the skin fell off and her father would not take her hand. And then she saw one of her sons standing there smiling. He changed in front of her eyes to a Mexican, and then into an African American man with a ponytail—"a real scary person." Her son pushed her into an elevator and sent her to the seventh floor "where they take people who are expected to die."

"When the elevator opened," Monica said, "I was in Hell. I was in this dark place with all of these demons around me. And I kept on saying, 'God, please let me wake up, this is a dream, let me wake up.' And He wasn't listening to me. And it went on and on and on.... The devil was there. I couldn't wake up. I knew I was in Hell."[1]

Monica found herself in a swamp-like place that was filling up with water. She had the image of being in a tank where she had to swim to the top for air, but at the top there was fire. There were evil, witch-like people in the water with her. The devil was there, and he forced everyone to look directly at the sun. Monica felt her eyes burning up. "Every second seemed like a year."

There seemed no escape, but then Monica heard, "If you put your driver's license on your back, then you can get out of Hell." Finally, after what seemed like an eternity, Monica began to regain consciousness. She could not open her eyes because they hurt so bad. And, in actual fact,

The Spirit Transcendent

Monica's eyes *were* swollen and red. When she did open them, they were exceedingly light-sensitive, so much so that she tried wearing dark glasses, but even this was not enough, and she had to drape a cloth over her head. Her light-sensitivity lasted for days.

Now that she was finally conscious, Monica went to get something out of her purse and discovered that her driver's license was in a separate bag instead of in her wallet. She reasoned that, even though she was not conscious of it, at some point she must have reached into her purse to grab it herself. This, and the fact that her eyes were so sensitive to light and hurt so badly, added to Monica's belief that she was really in Hell.

When we managed to meet, a few days after her telephone call to me, Monica remained convinced that she had been in Hell. She was shaken by it, just as if she had been someplace real. Did this mean, she wondered, that she was a sinner—that when she dies, Hell will be there waiting for her? Monica became afraid of going to sleep, because she feared she might slip into a coma again, return to Hell, or, even worse, be trapped there forever.

I tried psychotherapy by reason: "Monica, here you were in a delirious state. You're trapped, somebody is shoving a tube down your throat and knocking out teeth, you're helpless. Doesn't it make sense that, like a dream, you would feel that you are in Hell?"

"But it was so real."

"But a hallucination can seem every bit as real as reality, so why couldn't it be that?"

"But what about my driver's license, how did it get outside my purse?"

"You could've been in a delirious state, not aware of your own actions."

"But what about my eyes? My eyes—the devil had me staring at the sun for hours and hours, and then when I came to I could not even see."

"Well, of course they would *seem* sensitive after what you'd been through."

I suppose I would have prattled on at length about the power of the imagination, but Monica stopped me short. "But they were swollen and I couldn't see for days. And the doctor diagnosed me with sunburned eyes."

"Wait—you say sunburned? You mean an actual doctor diagnosed you with *sunburned eyes*?"

"Yes, a what you call it—ophthalmologist—diagnosed me with sunburned eyes."

Now, I began to feel a bit foolish. All this time I was talking with Monica under the assumption that her experience was the product of a delirium, and, in my defense, that is just what would be expected with a diagnosis of acute encephalitis—she *was* delirious. But I had ignored the fact that there is no actual way for a hallucination, even in the setting of a delirium, to produce light-sensitive, red and swollen, and *sunburned* eyes.

Much later I realized that something like this has happened to others before, but rarely. It sounded exactly like a report of stigmata. There is a tradition in the Catholic Church that goes back to St. Francis of Assisi, the very first stigmatic. On September 14, 1224, St. Francis was contemplating the Passion of Christ. He had a vision of a seraph with six fiery wings descended from Heaven, and when the vision faded, St. Francis' body bore the imprint of the Passion—his hands and feet showed the marks of the nails of the Crucifixion. This, mind you, was observed by others and recorded in writing by a fellow monk.[2]

Since that time, over the centuries, and even into current times, there have been other cases of stigmata, probably in excess of 400 of them. Many have been thoroughly investigated. In some cases, the wounds were physically produced by the individual himself or herself, consciously and sometimes unconsciously. But there are many other cases where deception cannot have played a role.[3] A recent case, painstakingly documented, shows that the phenomena is real, although unexplained.[4] Here, an elderly Italian Catholic woman showed stigmata in the form of painful, round red marks on the palms of both hands. They began on the first Friday of May, in 1990, after she saw Jesus in a vision. The same marks appeared on the first Friday of each and every month thereafter, and in this particular case, were examined 96 times. Physically, they appeared closest to a mark caused by a burn, but, unlike an actual burn, the marks disappeared without a trace each and every time.

There are related phenomena where it seems the mind can affect the body in mysterious ways: blisters can sometimes be produced by suggestion in hypnosis,[5] and there are even "somatic repetitions of previous experiences" where marks made by ropes, or weals as if from a whip, appear on the body years later.[6]

Monica's red, swollen, and sunburned eyes seemed to me to be yet another example of stigmata but of a negative rather than positive variety. Rather than a mark of Christ's crucifixion, she was bearing a sign of being tortured by the devil!

A close experience with Hell was bad enough, but in our next session Monica began to tell me of recent events that were even more disturbing, if that could be imagined. Now she was being plagued by demons.

The Spirit Transcendent

They were ghoul-like figures in black robes, sometimes with blood dripping from their faces. Sometimes Monica would only glimpse part of the figure, an arm or a leg, the rest of the boy being behind a wall or around a corner in her house.

"I am in the kitchen loading the dishwasher and I hear footsteps, and I hear laughing, and I looked around and it is one of those people. And I see the black pant leg [as if the rest of the demon is in the living room], and so I thought, 'I am not going to go in there.'" More footsteps, and then "it sounds like two or three people, and they were laughing, and all of a sudden I hear something break." Monica rushed into the next room, found no one there, but on the floor in front of her curio cabinet, she found a smashed glass figurine of a dog given to her by her husband.

"Well, could it have *rolled* off of the cabinet?" I asked.

"No, it was heavy; it was pure glass, and sitting in the back."

And there was still more evidence of spirit activity. "I have this cabinet in the living room, it is round and beautiful, where I hold all my Japanese-like china and dishes—all the Japanese stuff. I haven't dusted it, and Philip doesn't do it. My china closet—the key has been lost for years. So you have to take a table knife and put it between the doors and open it that way. That's the only way to get it open. On one shelf I have these four little pewter figurines. They're really cute, one for each of my kids when they were born. I have them in order from the first baby to the last. So when the laughing stopped, I looked in my cabinet and one of them was gone. And there's two fingerprints in the dust, like two fingers went behind them."[7]

Back to reality: Monica was always alone when the spirits were active. No one else saw a figurine crash to the floor. And it was odd she should see just glimpses of the demons—like a pant leg, or just a hand, emerging from around the corner. And while probably no one else could have gotten into the china cabinet, Monica could, and it is possible she could have removed the figurines herself in some kind of alternative state so that memory of her actions was not available to her conscious mind.

"The other day, I turned my head and I saw one in the kitchen, dressed in black, almost like a Ku Klux Klan robe, but black. The face was real, and it was dripping blood. I said, 'Get away from this house!' I was so scared, so I ran into the bedroom. When I came out, I saw on the floor two drops of blood; one in the kitchen, one in the dining room, on the hardwood floor. I left it there, so I could show Philip when he got home from work."

"Did your husband see the blood too?"

Nine—Hallucinations of the Demonic Variety

"Yeah, he said it was the dogs in heat—but it couldn't be that. He just said, 'You're so crazy you probably put it there yourself.'"

I was at a loss for how to help Monica. I argued with her, in one way or another, that her experiences with Hell and with the demons were not real. It may have been that my arguments rang hollow—after all, I was perfectly happy to claim that there was something real that lay behind a trip to Heaven. So if I could accept God as real, why stop short at the devil?

Toward the end of my session with Monica, she said to me, "Dr. Yama, do you know someone who can exorcise a demon? I am so frightened." I thought to myself, "Well, why not?' Logical argument was not helping Monica. If she simply were brought to *believe* the demons were exorcised, wouldn't that be the best therapy? I was not beyond making practical use of suggestion or a placebo, if it were possible to do so. And, returning to the hypothesis of spirit activity, I realized too that I knew someone who actually had experience in this area—Carol! Coincidentally, she even lived in the same small town as Monica, although it turned out the two of them had never met.

It was worth a try. "I think I know someone who can help you, and actually she doesn't live that far away. But she is very sick, with cancer, actually, and I'll have to call and see if she would be up to it."

Monica was sympathetic. She chided me a bit. "Well, you went to college; you should have the answer. Didn't they teach you that in school?"

"No, I never had that class."

"No Ghostbuster class?" Monica said, teasingly.

"No, I've never had a course on dispelling a spirit. But like I said, 'I've got just the *referral* for you.'"

Monica laughed. "Okay, so, your friend. Would it be best if I called her, or maybe you should talk to her? You said she was sick."

"I had better call. But I need your permission."

In my next meeting with Carol, I laid out the problem—Monica's physical condition; her earlier trip to Heaven; the positive spirits she first saw; her delirium and her trip to Hell; and, last, being plagued by demons. At the very least, I thought there were grounds for a bond to form between Carol and Monica, because their near-death experiences—and their glimpses of Heaven—happened during the delivery of their first-born.

I didn't know if Carol was up for the task. She was about in the middle of her latest round of chemotherapy, which was on hold because her bloodwork showed her immune system was being compromised. And the chemo was arduous. There were long trips to the cancer treatment

The Spirit Transcendent

center, daily treatment by IV. She had great fatigue. Her hair—strawberry blonde—by now had all fallen out.

I need not have worried about imposing on Carol. She told me, "I feel that God has a purpose for the people I encounter, why it is in my life—that's my mission. And anyway, it's not what I want, it's what *God wants* me to do."

Carol and I talked about possible explanations for what was happening to Monica on a spiritual level. She thought it was hilarious when I named her as "my referral," but in lots of ways the problem I had given her *was* just like a referral—and she looked at it that way too, considering the possibilities like any diagnostician, just that in this case she was trying to make a diagnosis in the spiritual realm.

"There's always this fear people have of Hell when they're dying," Carol said. "I think it's possibly her that's bringing them [the demons] in with her doubt. So her faith right now may not be quite as strong.... Do you get the sense that she is giving up, that she does not want to do this [continue to live; cope with illness] anymore?"

"I think she feels guilty for things in the past and for getting cirrhosis of the liver. She thinks, 'What I did was wrong,' and she feels guilty—so, yes, that is possible."

"Spirits in the form of demons will do things to get your attention," Carol said. "Knock over glasses, shadows, all kinds of things can happen. Most likely she is in a negative or more of a doubt mode, thinking, 'Am I worthy?' That just opens up the door, the Pandora's box, for the demons. Because they're strong. Not as strong as God, but they're strong if you're in that negative frame of mind. So possibly she is making this occurrence happen herself."

Diagnostically, Carol was thinking that Monica's negative frame of mind had unwittingly invited the demons in. The alternative—here we would be talking about a kind of *differential diagnosis*, but on a spiritual level—was that the bad spirits already were in the home. "I've gone into homes where they were already there," Carol said. "But there's usually a story that went with it, [which told] the reason they were there."

"You know," I said, "all of this is pretty much at right angles to a psychiatric diagnosis."

"And there's probably some delusion there," Carol acknowledged. "But I also would say that if she is in a stage where she is going down [physically; mentally], that she is being visited. Because usually that's when angels are around you, when spirits are around you."

Nine—Hallucinations of the Demonic Variety

"And the shattered glass, the missing figurines, the blood on the floor?"

"Well, it is possible she could have done those things herself," Carol replied.

"Speaking of the spirit possibility, I am trying to get straight these different forms of spirits. To hear you talk about it, it's like a taxonomy, I might say."

Carol filled me in. "Well, first there is spirit form, which we have talked about, which is a spirit can talk to you, and you don't always see 'em, but you can feel their presence. A lot of times if you have a relative that dies, a lot of times you can feel the spirit form if you know what to look for, and tune into it. They usually make themselves known to you to protect you, to tell you, 'I care about you; I love you; I'm fine'—that's usually why they come back."

"What about Monica's other experiences, the earlier ones—you know the story with the gummy bears?"

"I think that's definitely angel form. That's an angel that has gone to her. You may be thinking of the Bible where there are angels with wings, but they usually come in a form that we can relate to. Meaning human form. So they can look like a person."

"Well, how do you know it's not a human in human form?"

"Because of the circumstances. I have walked down the street and have seen angels around other people. Let's say you're walking down the street and you have two of them with you."

"Okay, it looks real. So in the psychiatry world, it is a hallucination."

"Except that when I'm around it, I know it. Someone like me, what I would be called in the world is a sensitive. I'm sensitive to spirits, demons, angels, so I have a gift to see it, or understand it. I went through a near-death experience so I consider that a gift that I came back with. And I didn't expect it. And over the years, I discovered things that I was capable of doing. Now in my fatigue, interestingly enough, I'm not as sharp tuned as before."

"Fatigue from the chemo?"

"Yeah, and I have chemo-brain. I've decided I'm going to go by a new name: I'm going to have everyone call me 'Chemo-Sabe.'" Carol gave a belly laugh. "But something else is happening, like in church I feel the Holy Spirit. I feel it *strong*. And I hope it's not a sign [of being close to death], because I feel ... like I am being guarded now."

The next step in our plans—when I was with Carol, we began to call

The Spirit Transcendent

it "Our Project"—was to stage a visit with Monica. By now I had wandered considerably away from traditional psychotherapy. I called Monica, we set a date, and, feeling amused at the path I was going down, penciled in "demon expulsion" in my planner, set for Monday, June 6. When the date approached, I called Carol and she suggested we reconnoiter about a half-hour beforehand to form a "game plan," as she called it. She suggested a coffee shop in Colfax.

"How's your fear level?" Carol said to me on the phone.

"Well, it was okay *up until just now*." "What had I gotten myself into?" I thought. "But I tell you what," I said into the telephone, "we get in there and something starts moving around, I'm the first one outta there."

"Before I go in a situation like that I pray a lot beforehand," Carol said.

"What kind of prayer?"

"To ask God to protect you; to give you strength."

When the appointed time came around, I drove to Colfax to meet Carol. It was the most beautiful of early summer days, crisp, with the bluest of skies. The coffee shop was small, with space enough for just four tables. In this small town, everyone knows everyone. When I arrived, Carol was talking shop with the owner. Carol's daughter dropped in for a moment. I was introduced, and soon she left, off on some errand or other. We got down to the task at hand.

"Spirits—ah, they're easy."

I laughed. "Glad you can be so casual."

"Hospitals are the worst. With Monica being in ill health, she might be weak, and in the frame of mind of giving up. It's in a low moment like that a spirit can come."

"The idea, I take it, is that the origin of these spirit things was in the hospital."

"It's like it was with Matthew." Matthew was a friend of Carol's who had been diagnosed with cancer, perhaps 20 years ago. "Matthew's girlfriend thought something spiritual was going on. I go in the hospital room and right away I feel a bad, bad presence. Joyce walks in there and feels the same. I'll tell you what it was like: what it felt like was like someone shoving us, like in the shoulder, catching you off balance. And both of us felt the same thing ... we sat on either side of Matthew, and were each of us holding his hands. We prayed, prayed it would go away—'You need *to go*.' All of a sudden, he starts to squeeze our hands with a lot of strength. Now, mind you, Matthew had been in a mini-coma for two days. And he had been given just a day or two to live—but he opens his eyes. He says, 'Hi,

Nine—Hallucinations of the Demonic Variety

guys!' We asked how he feels. He says, 'Fine, other than I've been on this oddest journey.' Well, Matthew had left his body. We didn't feel anything in the room after that, and Matthew—this man was predicted to soon *die*—was discharged the next day."

"Well, what happened to him after that? You mean he was cured?" I asked.

"Matthew did eventually pass away of cancer, but not 'til a year later.... Now the question for Monica is going to be if the spirits were already there in the house."

"For what it's worth," I said, "Monica told me about them when she was traveling around, I mean away from home. Just the other day she told me she was driving in the car. Then she looks in the rearview mirror and she sees one of her ghoul-figures. She was so frightened she had her husband stop the car. She actually vomited out of fright. 'Dr. Yama,' she told me, 'I don't want a demon to take me over.'"

"Poor thing."

"Back to the hospital thesis," I said. "It's kind of like you're telling me demons can be sticky, like you pick one up and it sticks to you."

"That's why it's so important, when you get rid of them, that you tell them, 'Go back where you came from.'"

"Oh my, so you could expel one and it could stick somewhere else, as in *on me*?"

"Don't worry, I'm powerful enough for the both of us. When I come in the room, watch out! I'm like a lightning bolt."

Carol and I hopped into my truck. I had Monica's address. Carol directed me through the sideroads she knew so well, and we got there quickly. Monica's house is modest but well kept. The front yard and porch made for an inviting, shaded space. The original home was built in 1910; later other rooms were built on, and later expanded even more. The front door opened into a dining room and parlor; the kitchen and a bedroom were on the ground floor; and several other bedrooms were tucked away downstairs.

Monica greeted us. She was getting around better than when I last saw her and had traded in her walker for a cane. "Oh, I'll have to let them in too," Monica said of her three dachshunds who were busy barking and scratching at the door.

Monica and Carol had never met, but they shared many common connections. They had the same family doctor; there was talk of who was getting married to whom; they agreed that a knick-knack shop was no lon-

The Spirit Transcendent

ger as inviting now that new owners have taken it over. Monica discovered that Carol was the one who put together the floral displays in a storefront, and she was all compliments.

This was Carol's show, so I mostly kept quiet. I was seated a little distance from the two of them, scribbling down what was said on a piece of paper. Eventually, we got down to business.

"How did it begin?" Carol asked.

Monica began by taking Carol back to the morning, now six weeks ago, that she was found unresponsive. She told Carol about being taken to the local hospital, being intubated, having three of her teeth knocked out—and then the trip to Hell.

"How can I go to Hell," Monica asked, "when I'm a Christian and I love the Lord?"

Monica told Carol about everything she had seen. It was completely consistent with what Monica had told me earlier, in private. There was the beginning of the vision where she saw her son turn into an African-American with a ponytail. Then he took her hospital bed into the elevator. "I feel the drop.... I hear these doors opening.... I was in this dark space. There were other people there too. Scary, scary people.... Everything was black. I was in this round tank.... All of a sudden, I see the Devil and his eyes were red. Everyone down there had this evil voice.... The tank was filling with water. He said look directly at the sun and you won't drown.... All of a sudden, I'm out of there; I was into this space with all these evil people.... For *days* this went on and I am saying, 'Help, help.' And then I found this girl who said, 'The only way to get out of Hell is to take your driver's license and put it on the back of your shirt.' And when I woke up my eyes hurt so bad, I had to wear dark glasses, and then a cloth over my head. It was like I had really looked at the sun."

Monica talked about the demons plaguing her: their black robes and ghoul-like faces; the demonic laughter; the smashed glass and the missing figurines. Even yesterday something else frightening happened: "I was looking at George when he turned into one of the demons. I kept saying, 'I hate you, I hate you—*go away*.' I was hitting him again and again. He thinks I'm nuts."

"Do you see the animals react?" Carol asked.

"They look at it and growl. Or they go to the same spot and growl."

Carol gave me a knowing look. The attention of the dogs might indicate there really was an evil spirit present in the house. "How strong is your faith?" she asked. "Do you pray when it happens?"

Nine—Hallucinations of the Demonic Variety

"I don't want to live anymore, when it comes to visit. I'm scared to death and my own husband doesn't even listen to me."

"Do you mind if we look around a little?"

I followed Carol as we walked through the first floor of the house. I knew that because of her sensitivity, she was on alert for signals; Carol had already told me, "From the time I walk in, I would know right away." Monica showed us the curio cabinet that was now missing two of her figurines and the place on top from which the small glass sculpture had fallen and shattered. There was a study off to the side, and Monica told us that sometimes she would come in and find all of the chairs—heavy chairs—gathered in the middle of the room. She showed us the kitchen window where she might be looking out and see the reflection of a spirit behind her. A set of steps right off the kitchen led to the basement.

"Do you feel there might be something negative in the basement?"

"Maybe."

"Mind if we take a look?"

"Yes. I can't come with you, because I'm afraid of falling."

Carol and I walked down the stairs. I could tell that her senses were on alert. She walked slowly, stopping for a moment, then moving on, now inclining her head one way, now another, as if in deep concentration. A short while later, she drew near me. In a low, confidential tone she said, "I'm not picking up anything." In fact, Carol could only pick up positive feelings from the environment of the house. "I feel it's from *her*," Carol said softly.

After Carol and I emerged from the basement, all three of us sat down together. "I think what you did," Carol said, "is you brought it in with you. It started at the hospital. In my experience, when we are sick and in a down state, then defenses are low. That's when Satan can move in."

"Well, what can I do?" Monica was tearful.

"Well, I'm going to pray for you before I leave. You have to be very strong now in your faith, to keep it away. It's fairly simple: God is stronger. If you spend as much time in prayer as in seeing the demon side of it, then they will eventually go away. Just spend time giving Him praise, being joyful. Know that God has more power than Satan has. You can get rid of them on your very own. If your faith is strong enough, they have no power over you. When you see them, realize you are manifesting them—they are not in the house.... I can come back later, and we can pray about it together."

After a space, our talk turned to more human concerns. Carol gave

The Spirit Transcendent

encouragement to Monica about enduring physical illness. When she stood, as we were getting ready to leave, Carol faced Monica and said, brightly, "Look at me—no boobs!" It was so like Carol: illness, cancer, a double mastectomy—none of it mattered if you had faith and put your trust in God.

And what of our diagnostic experiment? On the ordinary, psychiatric level, Monica was being plagued by delusions—and Carol *agreed* with this. Even what seemed like concrete evidence of demon activity—the broken glass; the blood; the moved furniture—could have been produced by Monica herself. Afterwards, Carol spoke to Monica as if a demon could have been at work, but one she picked up at the hospital. To me, at this point, it seemed to be an unnecessary complication: everything could be accounted for by mental illness. Even Carol herself believed it was Monica who was creating the demons, which to me meant they were not independent things, although, in truth, I was still disturbed by Monica's sunburned eyes—how can the mind affect the body so?

On the practical level, I thought that perhaps my plan of bringing these two women together had a chance of success, after all. If Monica could pray away her demons, what did it matter if their status was real or imaginary? But as to that most sticky problem of reality—of what is real and what is not—Monica was to hold still more surprises for me, only to be discovered later.

Ten

Through a Glass Darkly

> For now we see only a reflection as in a mirror; then we shall see face to face. Now I know in part; then I shall know fully, even as I am fully known.
> —1 Corinthians 13:12

Carol's health was fast declining. For a time she lost her sight, possibly because of her diabetes. By the time of our next meeting, Carol, thankfully, was responding to treatment and had gotten back vision in one eye. Carol put a bright face on it—first she insisted they change her name from "Chemo-Sabe to "Chemo-Sabe No See 'Um," and lately it was "One-Eyed Chemo-Sabe." But the joking was on the surface, and everyone knew what was going on, although no one wanted to admit it. I had news that her cancer had moved from her spine and was now invading her stomach. This was bad news, because cancer can spread more rapidly in soft tissue. Carol's options were running out. She had already suffered through a combination of chemotherapy and radiation. The next step would be a more radical form of chemo. Carol thought long and hard about it, but to her it meant trading quality of life for, what it now seemed, was simply living just a little bit longer. The new treatment just didn't seem worth it.

Richard was as concerned about her as I was. I lingered one evening after my work was done at the clinic and walked over to the other side of the building to find him as he was cleaning one of the surgery suites. We talked about Carol, and finally I asked, "Do you think there is something we could do for her, a prayer or something?" In the back of my mind I hoped that Richard had some power that he could use to help Carol. I knew he had once prayed for a friend with metastatic cancer and she had survived, although Richard refused to take credit, saying simply that maybe he had a hand in it, maybe not.

The Spirit Transcendent

After thinking a bit, Richard said, "Maybe we can put something together ... to help her. I'll look into it." At the time, I took Richard's "we" to be another way of saying "you and I," but later I realized Richard's "we" really meant "the spirits—my spirit guides, and *me*." Fourteen years ago, Richard was feeling the press of his relationships with the spirits: "They were so demanding. So I asked them to stop coming." And they did. Richard's wishes were obeyed, and they stopped. Now that Richard needed their help, it was first necessary that he inform the spirits that it was okay to return.

"All right, Richard," I asked another evening, "let's say we get it all together. What's the plan? How would this work to help Carol? I assume you are marshaling some kind of spiritual force."

"The objective is to draw a spirit in," Richard said. "The objective is to get our guides and Carol's guide together."

"Our guides?"

"Everyone has a spirit guide, at least one, and often more than one. We want to bring them all to the focal point of the ceremony. I learned this in the sweat lodge. See, the lodge, it became the center of the universe for those people involved in that lodge. That was now our center of the universe. We were attracting—or attempting to attract—those spirits and guides to come forward and meet and strengthen that ceremony."

"Well, I'm on board for that, but—"

"It depends on the individuals involved. For some people, it's a pipe and a tobacco offering drawing the spirit. The drumming does the same thing. I'll set up a circle with the four cardinal points. And everything revolves in a circle. That works so well, like when I was doing that ceremony for that couple down in Stanley."

I already knew something about this story—Richard had performed a wedding ceremony for a couple who worked for the forest service around Stanley, Idaho, sometime in the late '80s. Richard filled in the details for me. "The couple were friends of ours, both working in the rangers' station. One was stationed right there in Stanley—Stanley Basin is a beautiful place. We've commonly went and did sweat lodges at Elk Creek there, because it's so remote, people won't walk in and bother you."

"That was probably the most powerful ceremony I had ever conducted. We had 50 people. When I set the circle up, it was probably 30 feet across in diameter, and we set stones at the cardinal points, and we put in flags—each direction has a color that is associated with it. Those 50 people, I had all of them hold hands, and lend their hearts, and clear their mind ... and that brought all of that energy from all of those people together in that single focal point."

"I started with the east. In the east, that's where life begins. East symbolizes life. Life begins in the east. I asked them [the spirits] to come and attend and to share and to show us a sign. I think that's when there were cranes, if I remember right—a formation of cranes flew straight over us. Probably 30 feet in the air, right over us. And it was kind of a blustery day."

"So I turn to the south and ask for the spirit that was in the south—which is the Sun Spirit—to bring us its warmth. That is where the sun dwells that gives us life. Some would call it the Life-Giver. And lo and behold, a ray of sunshine comes right through the clouds, down unto our ceremony."

"Then I turn to the west and asked the Thunder People. And right then we had a flash of lightning and a clap of thunder. By now, why, everyone had their hands joined and had given their hearts—but let's say now they was getting a bit *nervous*."

"So I turn to the north. That's where you go to rest, so I asked for the cleansing wind from the north, and a good strong wind blows through the ceremony. 'Course I honored Grandfather, Mother Earth, Father Sky, Grandmother Moon, all those, but the four cardinals were the most important part of that."

"After that ceremony," Richard laughed, "those people could not get away *fast enough*. There was this big wedding dinner set up. When I approached the table where the line was, everyone makes this big space. I sit down on a log, or a stump, or whatever—and they get up and go someplace else. Finally, after hours of this, a couple of women—and they are about 30 feet away—they won't come close—they shout to me, '*How did you do this?*' Well, I didn't do this, it was the spirits that did it. I'm just the conduit. That's why in the sweat lodge I am the door mat. The door mat is the one you walk on. It's the spirits that have the power."

Richard and I decided we had better arrange Carol's ceremony soon, since by now it was already fall, and soon the weather would turn. Richard talked about what he would need: he had to find some white sage, not the common sage from around where we live, but a fragrant variety whose nearest source is about 300 miles south. He also had to find a source of sweet grass. Our prayer circle was to be made up of Carol, her husband Dave, Richard, Sandra, and me. We decided to set up on my property, because I live in the country and there is a bit of distance between neighbors.

I spoke with Richard two days ahead of time, at the end of the day in

The Spirit Transcendent

the pain clinic. "The spirits have returned," he told me. They had been silent for the past 14 years, ever since he had told them to "let me alone." But Richard had invited them back in, and he was awakened by them at 2:30 a.m. They spoke to him until dawn, about how to go about the ceremony. Richard was optimistic. "I believe there is a good chance at least one of them will attend," he said.

The five of us met at 10 a.m. on an unseasonably mild morning in early October. At first the visit was social. Richard showed us some prayer drums he had brought along. Then he opened a cloth bag and brought out his sacred pipe, the first pipe he had ever made. The bowl was made of red stone, a special kind of stone that is found on only one hill in Minnesota. The stem was made from a strong wood, the kind natives use to make a bow. And the bowl had four ridges around its outside. Richard explained that these represented the four races of man—black, red, white, and yellow.

Richard and I slipped out of the house to make further preparations. I watched Richard as he walked about my backyard, directed by the spirits, looking for a powerful spot. He settled on a place bounded toward the south by a group of pine trees. I made a small fire while Richard set up the prayer circle. Everything was laid out as a square with the four corners pointing to the cardinal directions—east, west, north, and south—each marked by stones and markers with their own color. Last, Richard placed a post in the middle that had six colors, all the colors of the cardinal directions plus green for Mother Earth and blue for Father Sky.

Carol, Dave, and Sandra joined Richard and me in the backyard. Richard gave out the prayer drums and soon we set up a loose rhythm. Next, Richard took the sage and sweet grass from the fire and began the feathering—purification by smoke. Sandra held out her arms as Richard went about covering her body in the sweet smell. Carol, Dave, and I were next. Last, Richard had me perform the same ritual on him.

Then Richard began to pray. "Ho Wakan Tanka. Please listen to our prayers. Come and attend…. Ho Takashowa. Please come forward. Attend to us. Listen to our prayers…" Richard turned to the east. "Spirits of the east, you are the guardians of the east. The east that is the birthplace of life. Come forward and lend us your strength for renewal and a new beginning. Come and share with us and Carol."

Richard turned to the south. "Sun Spirit of the south. The south where life begins. Bring us your warmth. You are the Life-Giver. Come forward and share with us and Carol." Then to the north. "Spirits of the

Ten—Through a Glass Darkly

north, the place of renewal ... attend to us, come forward and share." And last the west. "Thunder People, my brothers. Come forward and give us your strength." And after a space Richard concluded, "Thank you, spirits, spirits of the four directions, for attending us, for hearing our prayers, for giving us your strength. Ho."

All this time I was in the role of observer, on alert, hopeful, watching. Carol and Richard stood together, their eyes closed, her hands in his, as they prayed together. A few minutes later, Carol said quietly, to Richard, "I saw a falcon on a ridge." Richard smiled. He let go of one of Carol's hands and pointed upwards. Carol opened her eyes and there was a bird of prey circling high overhead above us. I was watching Carol closely, and her eyes were closed when she had the vision. It seemed too large to me to be a falcon, so in this detail it differed from the specifics of Carol's vision, but why should this large hawk appear at that perfect instant?

The mood was somber three weeks later when we met again at the pain clinic—Carol, Richard, Sandra, and me. We all knew Carol was not doing well.

"Hey, Carol, what color is my aura?" I asked half-heartedly, hoping to break the tension.

"Blue ... still blue."

"Dang, I was hoping by now you would be seeing yellow."

"I have to tell you," Carol said, brightening a bit, "the day before the ceremony I thought I would need to cancel, I was so low. My blood levels were so low they were talking about transfusions. But when we came out of there, there was so much energy, Dave and me, going home it was like wooooo—we were surprised the car wasn't, like, flying down the road."

"I picked up on Dave's energy," Richard said. "Dave and Sandra—big time."

"I felt so good," Carol said. "Sunday, we drove to Steptoe Butte and had a picnic. I had not done anything like that in forever. And Monday, I went up for labs, and they were *normal*, and just two days before that they were really bad. Monday, Tuesday, but then Wednesday was back to chemo, and then I was back in the dumpster again."

Carol looked at Richard and talked about the ceremony. "I remember telling Richard what I was seeing—my vision, and I was just, like, overwhelmed by it. I was there, but I was here too. I was still feeling my body, but my body was out here," Carol opened her arms in front of her, "experiencing this."

"Oh, tell me," I said.

The Spirit Transcendent

"It amazed me that it was as strong as it was. Being on the ridge with the falcon, and then opening my eyes and seeing it right there. But I went into it [Richard's ceremony] praying that I could be open to it."

"It opened a door," Richard said, "from a different perspective than you have ever experienced."

"The fact that is was so clear to me, I've been trying to understand: is this from God? Well, yes, it's got to be from God, but it's interesting that it has taken this path, I think."

"It's *structurally spiritual*,"[1] Richard replied. "It's taking any church or religious belief out of the picture. It's between you and God. That direct."

"Yeah," Carol agreed.

"That's why, deep down, God meant it to be simple," Richard said.

"And it's been happening a lot. It happened several times during the week after Wednesday, when I was really down. I kept on experiencing that. The other thing that I experience, which I told Richard, is I've had people come to me in dreams. There have been different people coming to me in dreams and I don't know if they are spirit guides."

Richard asked, "Are they bringing anything to you?"

"Nothing that I'm picking up on."

"Sounds to me like your spirit family is gathering around."

"That's not good, I think," Carol replied.

"No, no, no," Richard reassured Carol, "not in the way to bring you over, but to help you, to reinforce you—you're not getting a bad feeling? You're not scared?"

"No, no."

"So they're not coming to get you."

"It's like going through a fog," Carol searched for the words, "and trying to see who they are."

"Yeah," Richard said. "You know them, but you don't recognize them."

"I can't place them."

"That's members of your spirit family, I guess. They're out there. All around. Those on the other side can come over and help you, just like your guides. And your guides can ask for help. They can't handle the situation, but they can ask for help [from your spirit family] to help you…. It's possible to see through the veil if we are allowed to experience it."

I asked Richard, "These trips Carol is taking, to the falcon on the ridge, you think that's the spirit guide taking her?"

"Yeah," Richard said. And then he continued, knowingly, asking Carol, "It's a really good experience when you have it, isn't it?"

Ten—Through a Glass Darkly

"Oh yeah; you want to stay there. It's like you and I had when we went through near-death. You don't want to come back from that. Because you have the peace and freedom—you feel freedom, you know, I don't feel the illness."

As ever, I was interested in what it would be like to have visions like Carol's. "What is it like when this happens to you?" I asked.

Carol gestured to a picture on the wall of my office, a picture that I chose because it is peaceful, showing a dock leading to a lake. "It's like that. Either there is a ridge I keep going to, or I've been to a lake. Oh, it's so real, vivid. It's like I'm here on the shore and," Carol tapped the table in front of her, "I'm also here."

"Oh," I said, "you mean both places at the same time?"

"Yeah, my mind in me is here, but I can still feel the breeze, see the water, feel the water."

"You can dip your hand in the water," Richard said, "and feel it. Smell the flowers. It's a pure out-of-body experience and all you have to do is think about yourself and you will pop back in safely. When it happens, you should go to energy places. You could gather that energy, bring it back with you. You could put that energy to work to help you back here."

"I still get hung up on thinking about what, if anything, is traveling," I said.

"It's your spirit," Richard replied. "It is not confined to the body. We are trapped in the body. But the released spirit is free. To move around or whatever. That death experience [that we had]—you don't have any control. At least I didn't other than asking to come back; that worked, but that was it. We were on the fast train to wherever."

"This is different than my near-death experience," Carol said. "That sense of love, for example. I have not had that as much as the peace, the tranquility. You just feel kind of free."

"Yeah, in that near-death experience, it's all encompassing," Richard said. "It's like every hair on your body stands up. It's like—I think I've said this to you a dozen times—there is not a word to describe it. It's that profound. Take every good word in the dictionary and put them all together and it don't even come close."

"And there is the knowledge," Carol added. "You just *know*. You know why there's no pain. You know why there's love."

"Knowledge? How do you mean?" I asked.

"When I was moving forward, each realm I went to had more knowledge of where I was going. You know, because when you're traveling

The Spirit Transcendent

through this light, you're feeling this love. As I kept going, it was more knowledge of where I was going and what was happening around me."

"Not head knowledge," Richard said.

"No, not head knowledge—you know, you are overcome by your feelings."

"Times about 50 billion," Richard added, laughing.

"I can safely say whenever it's time for me to go, I'm ready. That's what I've told God: 'I'm ready.'"

"You have no regrets." Richard echoed Carol's feelings.

"Wednesday when I go to the oncologist we have to decide whether to go to a different chemo. I've tried three different ones, and they're all too much. What that chemo does, it sucks the life out of you to the point where you go to stand up and you feel the blood drain and then you're just sitting down. It's like you have no energy. If you take a two-week period, say, I'm not even going out of my house. And that's not living to me."

Richard personally knew about chemotherapy because he lost his wife to terminal cancer. "Chemo is just basically poisoning our body. Taking you to the tipping point and trying to bring you back. That's how I see it, anyway."

"I've kinda come to the place in my life where I have to make some decision points. And I have my little sister who is connected to me, saying, 'No, no, you can't give up,' and my kids who say, 'Don't talk about it,' and my husband who is not dealing with it at all. So that leaves me by myself, you know, to do what I think is right."

"Ask for that light," Richard offered. "Gather that energy when your soul travels. Gather all of it that you can. Try that first before doing anything drastic. It *can* help you. See if it does."

In the end, Carol decided to forgo treatment. We had another meeting at the pain clinic about five weeks later. This time Dave was with us, together with Richard, Sandra, and me. To look at her, Carol did seem less frail, maybe because she was no longer subject to the chemo. But the downside, Carol told us, was that the cancer was free to advance more quickly. There were more developments on the spiritual dimension.

"I've been having the weirdest experiences—people keep visiting me." Carol laughed. "Dave will tell you."

"She talks to them," Dave said.

"Talks to them?"

"At night when she is asleep, I'll hear her talk to them. This goes on for 40 minutes at a time."

Ten—Through a Glass Darkly

"You see them just when you are asleep?" I asked.

"No, during the day too. And they are becoming more distinct. Now I can almost make out their faces; before it was mostly in spirit form, where all I could tell is maybe male or female."

"When I saw my grandmother," Sandra said, "when I was in that red snow, I saw this fuzzy silhouette for just one second. I was close to death, but I wasn't crossing over. So I wonder if that's why I couldn't make out the features. You truly are getting close to crossing over. You know, I've been with people when they died, playing for them, in the room with them. The hardest thing about death to me is the actual process of it. But all that is, is a transition place. We talk abut hospitals as transition places. It's a place of birth and a place of death."

Sandra was sitting next to Carol across the table from me. "I feel I can see something like—like an outline of a person behind you," Richard said to Sandra. "I think it may be your grandmother."

"No," Carol said, "I think it [the spirit] was one of mine."

After our meeting, when we alone, Richard confided in me that he thought this sense of a spirit, right there in the room with us, was yet another sign that the spirits were beginning to gather around Carol. That had to mean, he feared, that her time was getting close.

Two months later, I got a call from Dave to tell me that Carol had passed away. It was one of those calls. He told me, still shaken, she had died the day before. Friday there was to be a viewing for the family, one for the public on Saturday, and then a service at 10:30 a.m. at the Methodist church in Colfax on Monday. This was no time for my spiritual questioning, but without my asking, Dave told me he was with Carol at the moment of her death. He had tried, and failed, to revive her by CPR. "And then," he said, "I just felt like there was someone over my shoulder, watching."

I made plans to attend the funeral. Richard and his wife would be there as well. Sandra was going to play harp, and we made plans that I would pick up Sandra—and her seven-foot concert harp—on the way to the service. It was still early in the week, and I had plans to meet with Monica in my office at the University of Idaho a few days later.

When I met with Monica, it was now about nine months since her trip to Hell, and the visit Carol and I had made to her house was roughly a month after that. Despite the intervening span of time, and despite Carol's help, Monica was still plagued by the belief that she actually had been in Hell. I was back to my old, ineffectual methods: I argued that, rationally speaking, Hell was not real; that she had a hallucination while in a coma;

that therefore there was no real reason to be afraid; and that the Devil could not be real either. As I might have predicted, my attempts at reason had zero impact. I decided to change tactics.

"Well, what about when I went over to your place with Carol? She had some good advice, don't you think? To put your faith in God."

"Oh, that was so helpful. And I'm worried about her. I talked with her on the phone once, but I really mean to have her visit again."

"I hate to tell you, Monica, Carol passed away from her cancer—I think it's now been two days ago. Dave called me."

"Oh, no, I'm so sorry."

After a respectful pause, I took up the therapy again. "Carol's gone, okay. But wouldn't she have said that your problem with the bad spirits is because you are so negative and down on yourself that it creates a weakness—"

"She *is here* though…. I can feel her spirit over there…. She is just standing there, smiling."

"You can feel her spirit just now? Really?"

"I didn't know her very well, but she is here."

"Well, when did she appear?"

"About an hour ago."

"Really?"

"She's been talking to me."

"Well, now I'm super-curious. How do you know it's her?"

"It's her. It's her soul."

Apparently, Carol's soul was not just in the room with us, but she even had a place—right there in a space between Monica's chair and the door! Of course, at the moment I assumed that Carol's presence in the office was fiction, or let us say fantasy, on Monica's part. I had never before conducted psychotherapy with a spirit in the room—that I knew of, anyway—and despite the strangeness of it, I found the situation pretty amusing. Well, if Carol was here, why not make her a co-therapist? I decided to play along. A few moments before I was asking Monica questions like, "Well, what would Carol *have said*?" Now I decided to up the ante.

"OK, Carol is here with us. In fact, she is right there next to you. Well, what does *she say* about your problem?"

Monica paused; she cocked her head to one side as if listening intently. After a moment, Monica relayed: "Carol said to always trust the Lord."

Ten—Through a Glass Darkly

Now I was definitely humored. Talk about the "empty chair" technique! "Monica, since Carol is here, does she have anything to say *to me*?"

Another pause; again, Monica turned her head to the side, another look of concentration. "She says not to be disappointed that she has not appeared to you, because she just got here and she has to get adjusted. But every time you see that—something she gave to you ... a vase, or was it a flower?—you should know that she is there."

Sounded pretty made-up to me. What if I were to ask something only Carol would know? "Monica, ask Carol for me, 'What color is my aura?'"

Another pause, then "Blue; it's blue—she says it's blue right now."

It was not just Monica's words—and the wording—that made me think of Carol. There was an indefinable sense to the way it was said, something like how you recognize a friend from long ago as much by posture, or how they hold themselves, or their expression, rather than by the exact look of the features on their face. It was as if, for an instant, I was looking through a window. Could it really be her? Later Richard reminded me, in that last meeting of ours at the pain clinic, that Carol promised us all that she would "come back." I had forgotten, but it was in my recording when I went back and listened.

Three days later, Richard and his wife, Sandra and I were at Carol's funeral service. I have not had space to tell it properly here, but Carol was extremely close to her younger sister Michelle. When Michelle saw me, she came over to give me a hug. She told me how important I was to Carol, how if the illness had seemed too much to handle, she could come see me and come away recharged. As we parted, Michelle said to me, with tears in her eyes, "She squeezed my hand."

Then there was the service during which Sandra played. After it was over, finally, I got a chance to take Michelle aside.

"You say she squeezed your hand. How do you mean?"

"I mean *she squeezed* my hand."

At the private viewing of the body the Friday before, members of the family went up to Carol to give their last goodbyes. Carol was in the casket, with her hands folded in the typical way. Michelle was the last to come forward. She prayed: "I was telling her how I felt, how I loved her, and how I was trying to hold the family together through all of this." At last, Michelle reached over to squeeze Carol's hand goodbye, grasping it on the side. It was then that Carol squeezed back. "It so startled me that I jumped backwards."

The Spirit Transcendent

I was filled with questions. "You should talk to the funeral director, Daryl," Michelle said. "He's around here somewhere." And I did. I spoke with him briefly during the service, and what I heard was enough for me to make a trip back to Colfax, recorder in hand, to get his story.

Because of Carol's floral business, Daryl had known Carol for many years. "I knew her more professionally," he said, "so it was more of a working relationship that way. I knew they went to church, that she was a believer and a Christian and all that. I knew nothing of her really spiritual self." I already knew that Daryl had donated all of his services to the family, and perhaps because I didn't grow up in a small town, this rather blew me away. Daryl explained, "Well, she fought so hard and so long, and was just a huge inspiration to everybody, including me. And I just felt like that was something we could do to give back."

"It was very difficult for me to sit with Carol in the weeks leading up to her death, because she wanted to be involved in all her planning."

"I was talking to her about it too," I said. "In fact, we were on the phone just the day before she died, and she was telling me about all the arrangements."

"She was very organized, and I wanted to be there for her, but it was really tough for me to hug her and say goodbye, knowing that probably the next time I saw her—that might be—that might be it."

"I get asked all the time, about how can I do this job, and the creepiness of it and kinda the dark side, and there really isn't that for me. There aren't spooky things and all that. So years ago when I first started, I had one experience where I felt that I wasn't alone, and it was kinda eerie—not in the sense that it scared me, but just a presence. I sensed a presence. I walked through the funeral home—this was in Kellogg, where I started—I walked toward the back of the chapel and a light was on in the chapel, and this time of night it shouldn't have been on. And so I walked over and shut the light off and then continued on. When I came out of the back, and went back through, the light was on again. Well, we had this gentleman in the chapel, he was in his casket there ready for the service, and I stopped and had that feeling of presence. When I came back the next morning, the light was on again. In talking with that gentleman's family, it came up in conversation that he was always afraid of the dark. And immediately the hair stood up on my neck. Immediately I just thought, 'That's why the light was on.' That was my first experience."

"That was when?"

"Twenty-five years ago."

Ten—Through a Glass Darkly

"And you had nothing like that happen to you until the experience with Carol?"

"No. And it didn't scare me either. It kinda gave me the feeling that, well, there's something else out there, you know? Because I get asked that all the time, you know. 'Cause we actually go and pick people up and they're in the back of the car with us. Ninety-nine point nine percent of the time, it doesn't feel like anything. You know, it's just part of what we do. It's just part of taking care of them. With Carol, it was kinda the same sensation again of the feeling of that presence. She was in this room right here, in the casket, embalmed and all that. I had been working with her for most of the day—this was again in the evening—and I came around the hallway and just started up the hall, and I immediately felt her presence. I knew it was her. I didn't see her, but I just felt the presence of her. Immediately I knew it was her."

"Why did she appear, do you think?" I asked.

"What would be the purpose of her being there? I don't have an answer for that. I just felt like she wanted me to know that I had done a good job. 'I'm okay' is kinda the message I felt. Like she was letting me know she was okay."

I told Daryl about the meetings Richard, Sandra, and I had with Carol up to a few months prior to her death. "You know, in the very last meeting she said something to us like 'I'm going to come back and let you know I'm okay.'"

"She predicted it! And now that you mention it, I kinda recall her saying something about coming back. Yeah, we sat in here," Daryl gestured at the nearby table, "Michelle was at the far end, and Dave was here, and Carol was on that side of the table, and I was across from her."

"Oh, so she said in that meeting something about coming back?" I asked.

"I think I recall her saying something about coming back. I didn't feel she was talking to me—I think she was talking to Dave and Michelle, but here she came back to me!"

My next meeting with Monica was in my office in Moscow, about four months after Carol's death. About a week before our meeting she had a terrible headache. Monica fell asleep, but when she woke she didn't know where she was, and she didn't recognize her husband. It was back to Spokane for tests: "I had an MRI the next day," Monica explained, "you know I have that parasite in my brain, and now it's all surrounded by a bag of fluid. Dark fluid. They thought it might be causing pressure … and I

The Spirit Transcendent

probably saw nine, 10 different doctors, and they all had something different to say. Basically, they just released me, and they didn't know."

Who knows what effects a parasite in the brain and a lesion in the frontal lobe might have psychologically? The talk of the MRI and the dark fluid in the brain brought out the traditional psychologist in me, grounded in all of the usual materialistic assumptions. Perhaps this was the true source of Monica's conviction that she had been in Hell. Maybe, I thought, it could also explain her experience with the demons. It made sense for me to check in with her about the level of her symptoms. "Monica," I asked, "you remember how we talked about the demons you kept seeing around the house?"

"They've been gradually leaving. I keep telling them, I rebuke them in the name of the Lord. I've been doing that all over the windows and the doors, and they stopped coming all of a sudden."

"That is tremendous, and I am so glad to hear it." Parasite or not, in this meeting, Monica could express herself pretty well. Her thoughts did not wander, and she seemed clear-minded. I wondered how she would now view her perception of Carol, the spirit, from our meeting four months ago. Would she now recognize that as a delusion? "Monica, I can't help but ask you about some of the spiritual stuff."

"Such as what?"

"Do you remember, when you were here last, and you were talking to me about Carol being present? Do you remember that?"

"She is with me all the time."

"All the time?" I was surprised.

"Yeah. It's like she's my spirit guide. I can't get rid of her! And I didn't even know her that well, but now I know her. She's there *all the time.*"

"Do you want to get rid of her?" I asked.

"No!" And with a laugh, Monica said, "She's great! She's helping me, I think. She's helping me through a lot of this…. And I only met her that one time."

"Well, how do you know it's her that is with you?"

"*I see her.* She's standing right there."

"You can actually see her right there?"

"Yeah! Just right here, standing right here. She's always right by my side."

I was curious. "When you see her, is it just like a real person? Is it like she is actually, totally, physically here?"

"It's different. It's hard to describe. I see her as I last saw her, you

Ten—Through a Glass Darkly

know, with the scarf on her head. And how happy she was. I see more of an outline, with a face. You know, it's like real faint—you can see through it. She's standing. She doesn't take up space, but she's with me and she's in my head all the time, and I can't quit thinking about her. It's almost like I have become like her. I don't know why she has picked me, because I hardly know her."

"It's interesting to me that you say she *picked* you."

"It's like I have become a different person, the way I see things. The way I have come out of my depression—I'm happier. She is very outgoing. What a wonderful person she is, and even in her darkest hour, she helped me and came over to my house. And I know she was in pain and not feeling well. She told me that [the *spirit* told Monica that]."

"So you are a different person?"

"Because she has kinda taken over me."

On the psychiatric level, this was sounding to me like multiple personality. Perhaps this was another diagnosis to add to the list, except I had the worried thought it might be a condition that I myself had unwittingly created. I asked, "Has anything like that happened to you before?" I wanted to know if there were other possession experiences.

"No, no. I do see spirits and stuff. Like, more and more. When I look at you I see, like, five spirits with you right now. They are kinda lights right now."

"Wait, there are *more* spirits in the room with us?"

"Yeah. They are not showing their faces, you know, [to tell] who they are. But they are bright lights. Four over here and one over there."

"Really? You see five?"

"Each one stands for a different person. That is, your spirit guides, that are watching out for you. Say you are going to run off the road, and you almost do. They are the ones that pull you back and protect you."

"You've had these perceptions before? How far back? Is this before you were sick and went to Hell?"

"It started with the first near-death experience when I went to Heaven. It started after that. And it seems it is getting more and more all the time."[2]

"Why didn't you tell me about it before?"

"I didn't want to talk about it because I didn't want you to think I was crazy."

On one level, it seemed to me that all Monica's experiences could be nothing more than a set of symptoms: hallucinations, delusions, and now a disturbance of her very identity was to be added to the list. Goodness

The Spirit Transcendent

knows, there was enough going on with her on a physical level to explain it. But it was not long since Carol's funeral, and what about everyone I spoke to who seemed to have experienced Carol in the spirit? Carol's husband, her sister, the funeral director—*none of them* had mental illness. Could it be that beneath the symptoms, Monica *really was* in touch with Carol? I decided to put it to Monica directly: "Do you remember last time when we asked Carol some questions? Are you in communication with her?"

"Yes."

Again, like in our last session, I was in the position of trying to communicate with the deceased. My first test was to try to ask Carol about a gift she had given me. Only Carol could know what it was.

"She's not telling me," was Monica's answer to my questions.

I tried a different tact. I was reminded of something Sandra had asked me. "Monica, I've been talking with Sandra. You know she almost died and that would mean leaving her son behind. Sandra wanted to know, if someone actually does die, can they stay connected to their kids?"

"To Sandra's kids?"

"No, to *Carol's kids.* Carol as a mom was connected to her kids and felt bad about leaving them. Does she connect with her children afterwards?"

"Yeah! She does things like move things. She'll turn lights on. She'll ring the phone and there's nobody there. But that's her."

"How about Dave? Has she done anything with Dave?"

"Um, she did something special for him. He didn't recognize it—she changed the sheets on the bed. She washed the old ones and put new ones on there. They were clean."

"She washed the sheets?" Seemed pretty unlikely to me. "You mean she washed the sheets, put new ones on, and he hasn't discovered it yet?"

"And then she opens the shades in the house because he forgets to."

"Would that mean he would come into the house and all of a sudden the shades are open?" Apparently, Carol—the *spirit Carol*—was acting just like a wife would.

"Yeah, or just one [curtain]. She likes lots of light. That's just her personality. Very bright, she wants him to not be sad and get out more, and not just sit around. Because he is having a hard time. She does stuff like that. And when the daffodils were growing she would pick one and lay it on the counter."

"So that would mean she would lay a daffodil down—it wasn't there before—and he would discover it?"

Ten—Through a Glass Darkly

"He should have. Anyway, she told me, and I saw her do it in my head. It's really weird.... She talks to me all the time. Just about stuff, oh you know, 'You should have done the dishes today but didn't.'"

"She's getting on you about doing your dishes?"

"No, Dave," Monica laughed, "because he lets them go."

Monica seemed positively intimate with Carol's husband Dave, just as if I had been talking with Carol herself. "Have you ever met Dave?" I asked Monica.

"No, but I'd like to."

"What does Dave *look like*?" Another test.

Monica paused for a moment and listened. "I don't know. Is he shorter?"

"I'm not going to say anything. I want to see what she tells you."

Another pause. "I think he is shorter and heavier set. Balding or bald. Maybe, I don't know. That's all I have. This is kinda guessing because she won't tell me."

Dave, in actual fact, is shorter, portly, and nearly bald. But, of course, it could be a lucky guess. I decided to call Dave later that day. Dave did not know I had been seeing Monica, and I decided I would try my best not to give him any cues about the supposed messages from Carol. This meant not asking a direct question, for example, "Someone I ran into says Carol left you a flower. Did you see one?" I had not spoken with Dave since the funeral. I simply asked, "Dave, has anything been happening since Carol's death to make you think she was still around?"

"Lots of things."

"Such as what?"

"The lights would go on and off. Like I'm in the bedroom, and all of a sudden the light goes on in the kitchen. So I get out of the bedroom to turn the light off. Then I get back to the bedroom and the light goes on again ... and the TV would go on, once twice, all by itself ... and after [the funeral] I came in the house and Carol's cell phone started playing. And it was the three songs from the funeral. And I know the last one—we put that one on her phone—but not the other two. I don't know where they came from."

Dave had recently been staying with his daughter who lives near Mountain Home, Idaho. Without any prompting on my part, he told me, "I believe Carol came to me twice, night before last, and two nights before."

"Why? Did you have some sense of her?"

"I came home twice and the curtains were open. About two feet open. My daughter tried to explain it as being pushed open from the air from the vent. I told her, 'No way—they're way too heavy.' And that happened *twice*. Plus, when I came home I had the strong feeling that she was there ... and before, she left me a flower."

I tried not to reveal my surprise. "A flower?"

"I found a red carnation set next to my nightstand, next to my CPAP machine. It was not like it had been just picked. It was cut, as if someone took the time to do it. I *know* it was Carol. See, when she was 19, I gave her 19 carnations for her birthday, because carnations was her favorite flower. You know, I asked her to marry me back then, but she said no, she didn't want to be married to a Navy man."

About a week later I was able to meet with Monica again. I was so taken with the story of the flower I had to ask again: "Monica, you remember Carol told you she left a flower for Dave. Could you ask Carol—just what kind of flower was it? And what color?"

Monica paused, cocked her head to the side, for all the world as if she were receiving a message, and then answered, "It was ... red, red ... a rose?"

Was this test a success or a failure? To my mind, Monica was a window to spiritual world, but as a human, she was an imperfect instrument. Getting the wrong type of flower, or getting the color right but not the type of flower, seemed trivial in this context. Speaking with Monica about Carol was like "seeing through a mirror darkly," to quote Corinthians from the Bible. One day, the passage implies, "we will see face-to-face. Then we will *know*."[3] Even, I might add, if it takes our death to achieve it.

The skeptic in me had no answer to the many phenomena surrounding Carol after her death. The case for survival is so strong that I cannot, honestly, think of a decent counter-explanation. This is true especially when it comes to Monica's statements of what Dave was experiencing after Carol's death. Monica never met Dave, and as for Monica knowing Carol, there was only that one meeting between them. Further, I was present at that meeting, and I know nothing was communicated between the two of them that would explain later events. None of it makes sense without input from Carol, input that could only have come after her death.[4]

What became of Monica? Following up with her months and then two and three years later, the visits from Carol had become less frequent. Carol was no longer the constant internal presence she once was. Monica believed she could still manage to make contact with Carol if she called her or sent out a question. She did, sometimes, put in an appearance spontaneously. In one of our meetings, more than a year after Carol's actual

Ten—Through a Glass Darkly

death, Monica told me she was enjoying herself on vacation, staying in a rented house, and then Carol appeared, seated at a table on the deck, for all the world as if she were an invited guest. Monica acted in the same way that you would if an old friend, whom you had not seen for some time, had dropped by. And there was another session of ours when Monica interrupted what we were doing to announce that Carol was sitting at my desk: "You can't see her? She's right there." It was a visit, I suppose, to check up on how things were going.

As time went on Monica's visions seemed more confused, as if the rational part of her was being submerged by delusions. Now, rather than there being five spirit entities present with us in the room, there were as many as 17. Many months later, Monica talked about not just one personality she believed was the presence of someone who had died, but now there were four or five. All of them were the spirits of deceased persons. She could have a good day, or a bad day, she told me, depending upon whether these internal presences themselves were in good or bad moods. She believed they really were present, and she told me that they ate food from her table and left their dirty dishes behind. My feeling at the time was that I was gradually losing the rational part of Monica, the personality and presence that I had enjoyed so thoroughly. It seemed to me that it was all related to her physical problems, her advanced liver disease or the infection in her brain, which seemed to be affecting her more and more.

I'm glad to report that Monica surprised me yet again. After a gap of about two years she called me to resume psychotherapy. When we visited she was off of most of her medications and was much healthier emotionally as well as physically. I found her thinking to be very clear. I asked her, again, about her visions from the past. Monica remembered very clearly everything she had told me—from the paranormal events from her childhood through her positive near-death experience, her trip to Hell and her experience with the demons, and the appearances of Carol as a spirit guide and onwards. It all fit exactly what she had told me before in all of its particulars, and, further, Monica was adamant that it was all true.

So here I am, a practicing psychologist, and the consciousness of one of my clients seemed to possess the other and did so in a way that gave evidence for survival. It really was as if the soul were real, that it could transcend the body, and that it could even inhabit others. When I considered what it all implied, I thought to myself that I could not possibly be the sole witness to phenomena that were at the same time so eerie and marvelous.

I was reminded of Betty's reaction when she had her vision of Palora.

The Spirit Transcendent

Surely, Betty thought, for something so important, "somebody, some scholar or other, would have written about this before." She searched for more than a decade until she stumbled upon what she was looking for among the Gnostic scriptures. In my case, thinking of my experience with Carol, I could say the same—*someone* must have written about this before—events like those I witnessed seem hard to ignore. The answers to Betty's questions were found buried in the sands of Egypt. In a way, the answers to my questions were buried too. Not physically, but beneath the tide of scientific opinion that refuses to take the paranormal seriously.

In fact, and to my amazement, I found that I was treading upon very old ground. It had all been discovered before, at the turn of the century, in the days when the survival hypothesis was investigated seriously and where the subjects of those investigations were mediums who produced all kinds of phenomena during séances. I was simply ignorant of the older literature, perhaps because, like my skeptical colleagues, I was too disdainful of anything that deviated from materialism to consider the literature seriously. In retrospect, my ignorance was embarrassing, really.

Had my eyes been opened back then, I might have seen the similarity between my observations and the famous medium Mrs. Piper, who was discovered by William James more than a century ago.[5] True, most mediums from that time were found out to be frauds, but Mrs. Piper of Boston was the exception. She was probably more thoroughly investigated than any medium before and since and was never caught in any fraudulent activity.

In 1885, William James first visited Mrs. Piper after the death of his four-year-old son. James was impressed, so impressed that as a test he brought in 25 strangers, all disguised under various pseudonyms. About half of the sittings produced nothing remarkable, but the others, like James himself, were amazed at the details that were revealed. In an 1886 paper James wrote, "I am persuaded of the medium's honesty, and of the genuiness of the trance.... I now believe her to be in the possession of a power as yet unexplained."[6]

The investigation of Mrs. Piper was handed over to Richard Hodgson, a great debunker of mediumistic claims. The testing began in Boston. Whereas James had earlier sent 25 individuals to Mrs. Piper, Hodgson sent 50 more, all strangers, and the results continued to impress. Hodgson took extreme measures to reduce the chance of fraud. Piper was followed by private investigators to rule out any collusion with others. And even these steps were not enough: Piper was taken to England where she was secluded and knew no one. She was assigned servants to whom she had no relation; her luggage was inspected; her mail was read.

The case took a fascinating turn in 1892. Hodgson had a casual friend, George Pellew, with whom he debated the possibility of the afterlife. Pellew did not believe it possible, but said, if he passed before Hodgson, he would make efforts to communicate from beyond the grave. Pellew did pass away, from a fall from a horse, at age 32. Four or five weeks later he appeared in Piper's trance. Soon *he* became a new control.

Hodgson arranged yet another test. He introduced 150 sitters to the Pellew control, 30 of which were known to the living George Pellew. Piper/Pellew identified 29 of the 30 immediately, talking to many as if old acquaintances, just as if he was the spirit he claimed himself to be. Data for this experiment were collected over a period of about two years. Never, ever did Piper/Pellew mistake one of the other 120 sitters for someone known to the living Pellew. Hodgson, the main skeptic among psychic investigators, became convinced that Mrs. Piper's claim was basically correct, that what was revealed in a trance did come from the afterlife. James was more conservative. He did not doubt the genuineness of the medium but was not convinced that survival was the only explanation of the facts.

The remarkable case of Mrs. Piper is debated even today. The skeptical viewpoint is that, although she was never caught, she was a very clever fraud—we just don't know how she did it but can only surmise.[7] Everything in my training and background would have had me accept this interpretation. Not based on observed facts, but because, if one accepts materialism, how could it be otherwise?

That is why my work with Monica is so interesting and important. It is a replication of the old study of Mrs. Piper, leading to the same conclusions about the afterlife, and with a subject that was not a paid medium! Some have argued that Mrs. Piper had the motivation, and ability, to deceive and not be caught at it. But Monica? Further, I worked with Monica for a good 15 years, off and on, and it is obvious to me, regardless of what one might ultimately make of the truth of her visions, that she is genuine.

There are so many parallels between Mrs. Piper and my client Monica. In both cases everything came out of a dissociative state. For the medium it was a trance. Monica possessed a dissociative state of mind which today would be labeled as dissociative identity disorder. Both Monica and Mrs. Piper felt they were in contact with spirits. Both were like a transmission line connecting our world with another. In both cases information was provided that could not possibly be known to the patient/medium.

The Spirit Transcendent

And finally, and most radically, some of this information would seem to be available only to the deceased and to no one else.

William James called Mrs. Piper his "white crow." He famously said, "If you wish to upset the law that all crows are black, you mustn't seek to show that no crows are; it is enough if you prove one single crow to be white,"[8] meaning a single example like Mrs. Piper is enough to challenge all of materialism.

Monica was to me what Mrs. Piper was to William James. A single case, impossible to ignore, that is enough to challenge the entire framework of what we think we know.

Eleven

Science and Spirituality

> I do not see why a critical Science of Religions ... might not eventually command as general a public adhesion as is commanded by a physical science. Even the personally non-religious might accept its conclusions on trust, much as blind persons now accept the facts of optics—it might appear as foolish to refuse them. Yet as the science of optics has to be fed in the first instance, and continually verified later, by facts experienced by seeing persons; so the science of religions would depend for its original material on facts of personal experience, and would have to square itself with personal experience through all its critical reconstructions.
> —William James, *Varieties of Religious Experience*, p. 497

When I met Betty I never would have believed that our association would mark the beginning of a personal journey, or that she, a modern-day mystic, would have started me, a skeptic through and through, on a path where I ended up believing in a spiritual reality. Just like a real footpath, there were many forks in the road, points where a direction was chosen. It always seemed I was fated to reject the more comfortable of two alternatives in preference to the more difficult one. At the beginning I could have just assumed Betty was an eccentric old woman with crazy ideas. But I chose to listen and tried to understand her instead. A little further down the path I could have fallen back on my clinical training, assumed her visions were only symptoms, and our association would have ended then and there. But still I listened, and eccentric as she seemed, Betty and I became friends. Last, I could have thought of Betty as simply someone with deep religious convictions to be respected but not necessarily believed. Instead, I took what Betty presented to me seriously and as *possibly true*, even when the laws of logic meant a challenge to my views of reality itself.

The Spirit Transcendent

Thinking back on it, it seems an unlikely story: I came to Betty without any particularly firm religious convictions. I was not a believer, but it did not matter and to my amazement I had a spiritual experience of my own. Some form of ultimate goodness, some immense power, shook me to the roots. For a few moments I was in the grip of something that was not like ordinary experience at all. It truly was "other," and at the same time it seemed real in an ultimate sense.

And then the next unlikely turn of events—there were spiritual stories all around me, waiting to be discovered. I did not solicit them, and rarely did I bring the topic up myself. But there they were, sometimes even more than one in a day.

When Betty passed away from cancer I was saddened. Selfishly, I felt I had lost my potential key to understanding what the spirit was all about. But only months later I met Carol, and when I think back on it, it seems to me that she finished what Betty had started. This, too, in retrospect, seems to defy chance. Carol was every bit as accomplished as Betty in the spiritual realm. And who would have thought that she would continue to provide me lessons about the nature of the spirit that would continue *after* her death? Yet it does seem that Carol left me with evidence of survival, and powerful evidence at that.

Everyone I have spoken with about their experience was convinced that the spirit is real. But how can we be sure? So much is based on private visions, and as for the evidence outside of personal perception—actual events that happen to people—almost always they seem impossible given what we know about the physical world.

Yet there is reason to believe something real lies behind these experiences and events. I first got a glimmer of this with my own spiritual experience. I found myself, while observing my surroundings—in this case, a man walking in front of an altar in a church—in touch with pure being, a kind of "isness" that seemed, if it were possible, realer than real. A few weeks later I happened to read Aldous Huxley's *Doors of Perception*.[1] Huxley experimented with mescaline, and an hour and a half after ingesting the drug, Huxley looked at a vase of flowers. To him the vase became the "miracle, moment by moment, of naked existence." Huxley connected it with the fundamental "ground of being" that had been talked about by mystics, among them Meister Eckhart.[2]

This is precisely what I experienced, and without peyote. And I too found (before I read Huxley) a resonance with Meister Eckhart's writings. Huxley made a connection with the interior experience of those who

170

Eleven—Science and Spirituality

meditate within Eastern religious traditions. Why are these experiences (Huxley's with mescaline, mine without, and those of individuals deep in meditation) so similar? On one level, we could all share similar brain states, but at another level of description it could be, just as William Blake famously said, "if the doors of perception were cleansed everything would appear to man as it is: Infinite."[3]

There is another universality, easy to see, and exactly what you would expect if the spirit is real: universality throughout time or era. In my work with Betty, I often thought her visions and revelations could have come straight out of the Bible, if only she had been at the right place at the right moment in time. The Old Testament Book of Ezekiel comes to mind: In Ezekiel's vision, God is seen on a throne supported by four angels, beside which were wheels within wheels, with rims of eyes all around. Betty's vision of God's parents, joined at the hip, was just as bizarre. Ezekiel's vision was connected with Jewish mystical tradition. Betty's vision had connections too, in her case with Gnostic myth and imagery. Ezekiel was a prophet that proclaimed events in the future, one of which was the destruction of the temple at Jerusalem, which he foresaw (Ezekiel 11: 1–13). Betty too thought she could see into the future, and many of her predictions came true.

The difference between the two, besides the fact that Betty is in our present and Ezekiel goes back 2,500 years, is that Ezekiel was educated, from the upper class, and a priest. He was in a position to be heard and to have a following. Betty, in contrast, was in our era, lived at the margin of society, and had no followers. Had the circumstances been different, and had she lived in a different time, could she too have found a place in some future scripture?

If Betty's place could have been in the Old Testament, then I feel Carol deserves to be placed in the New. I honestly believe she could have had a gospel of her own. Think about her life: not only could Carol cast out spirits, at least once she healed the sick. After she died, a few days after, when her sister felt her squeeze her hand back, it was—to her sister, at least—a resurrection. And then there are all the experiences that involve Carol after her death: both her husband and the funeral director felt her presence, and it was if her spirit had returned *inside* the mind of client Monica. There are many comparisons with Jesus, during his life and even after his death. It really is the New Testament told over again.

The skeptic will say that Carol produced effects like Jesus because of human expectations, mostly unconscious, that are part of our culture.

The Spirit Transcendent

The alternative is that there really is a spirit that is a constant, operating throughout time. Then Carol, and the visions of her after her death, would be a product of the spirit, the same spirit manifest in Christ 2,000 years ago.

Then there are my clients with all of their near-death experiences. *They* believed they were in direct touch with the spirit. They felt the spirit was real. The main skeptical objection to their belief is that you cannot take a private vision as real, even if seems that way. But even if I cannot say the spirit as perceived by Carol, Richard, Sandra, was direct evidence of its reality, I still can claim a reality based on the lasting *effects* of their spiritual experiences. This is sometimes missed in studies of near-death experience because data usually are collected on the basis of one-time interviews. Rarely are patients followed over time. I had a different perspective because I had the fortune of getting to know my clients very well, and sometimes our association lasted for years.

Those effects were apparent: for Richard, his near-death experience was only the beginning of a process. His spirituality solidified and deepened with his practice in the sweat lodge. When Carol came back from her near-death experience, it was with "gifts," and it was in the form of these gifts that her spiritual experiences continued. One of these was seeing auras, and they were so pronounced that, at first, she thought "there was something wrong with my eyes." After Sandra's brush with death, when she came back her senses and intelligence were enhanced. She had a power of memory she did not have before, and she was so intuitive that people around her thought she was clairvoyant.

Betty might have said it best of all: Many times she told me she felt she was no longer human, but, perhaps as an accumulation of her near-death and other spiritual experiences, she had turned into a "spirit person": "The human is like water before it freezes," she told me, "or like a crude ore before it is made into gold, or like a potato, before it is peeled, washed, cooked, and mashed." She was changed by her spiritual experiences, and the change was permanent.

And there were the many other examples, events that seemed impossible to explain without the influence of an active agency. The young man who was warned of the attack of the pit bull; Raymond's vision of his godfather who insisted he save himself by climbing the cliff; Betty's message from God that allowed her to avoid the tornado. The experiences in these examples are very different, perhaps because the spiritual message can only be understood through the equipment of the human, through his or her

Eleven—Science and Spirituality

powers of perception, conception and imagery. But the fact that all of these visions had a purpose suggests there is a reality behind the diverse forms and shapes of experience. Only something real can exert real effects.

Many of the experiences and events told to me were not much different from those reported to William James and his fellow investigators of spirituality more than a hundred years ago. James felt there was enough of substance to begin, as he says in the opening quote of this chapter, "*a science of religions.*" James thought the time had come, but obviously it had not, and even a hundred years later his science of spirituality has yet to get off the ground.

I think I know the reason James' program never progressed. It is an issue that troubled me from the beginning when I first met with Betty, and one that has haunted me ever since: it is the duality between the spirit and nature.

I have been given by my clients example after example of events that defy the natural order. They *cannot be true* given what we know about the physical world. Take just one example—Betty's ability to see the future. There is absolutely no physical basis for it! In the material world, effects always follow causes. You cannot have an effect (for example, Betty's perception of Mount St. Helens exploding) before it is caused.

I am convinced that Betty could see into the future, at least at times. I feel equally certain that seeing into the future is physically impossible. This kind of conflict—the conflict between reported facts and what we know about the world—is what has prevented James' dream of a science of religions from realization.

Maybe there is some yet undiscovered physical process that allows seeing into the future. This would give us a materialistic explanation and resolve the problem of duality. But if the past is any guide, a solution within science may not be forthcoming. Physical solutions to paranormal events have been proposed before, but they always seem to lead to pseudoscientific nonsense.

I think there is a third alternative. Once again, Betty helped me understand the problem. It was toward the end of our second session that she explained to me how she felt she was different from everyone else: "It is like I am standing on the head of a nickel," she said. "One side is human, and the other side is spirit." Later, she wrote to me: "I am a Combo-Person ... not human, not spirit, but something new." At first, I thought Betty was merely saying there were two sides to her personality or perhaps you could think about the world in two different ways. Later, I found out that she seriously

The Spirit Transcendent

believed there were two separate actual *realities*. Betty directly felt the gap between the material and spiritual worlds. She saw what many mystics have tried to describe, a fundamental incompatibility between the spirit and the everyday world. As Betty tried to tell me, her insights were not just novel or unique, they were *"unearthly."*

Suppose Betty's internal experience—her *perception* of duality—holds a truth about the fundamental *nature* of the world—that the world, and not just its perception, holds a dualism within itself? It makes sense given everything that has been told to me. There are many examples: a client is unconscious in the operating room, yet she floats to the ceiling and remembers events during the surgery; Richard seemed to control nature in his ceremonies, but there is no conceivable way this could happen; Carol could see spirits who turned out to be actual persons she never had met, although this is physically impossible; Carol dies, yet she appears as the alternative personality of my client Monica, and that personality knows things only Carol could know.

Giving up the assumption that there is a single reality, that of the material world, could hardly be more radical. But at least it is, and maybe in an odd way, parsimonious. The principle of Ockham's razor, named after William of Ockham, a theologian and philosopher of the 14th century, sometimes has been invoked as a model of good scientific reasoning. His principle has been formulated to state that "one should not multiply entities beyond necessity."

Ockham's razor has been used to argue for atheism, the idea being that God or spirit are unnecessary additional entities and that natural law is enough to explain all events. I come to the exact opposite conclusion: when I look at all of the experiences described in this book and try to explain them, it seems if I try to without the unifying notion of spirit or God, I have to multiply my entities endlessly—I literally have to invent an explanation with little or no independent support that is different in each and every case. In the end, I suppose you will have to pick your poison: a convoluted explanation that uses post-hoc reasoning and that is guilty of entity multiplication, or a simpler explanation that only works if materialism is not the overarching framework it appears to be.

Duality does defy logic, I will admit. But that may not be cause enough for its rejection. There is already an example in the "hard" sciences where dualism seems inescapable—quantum mechanics, the properties of matter on very small scales. Quantum physicists have often spoke of the "weirdness" of the quantum world and of "quantum reality," a reality that

Eleven—Science and Spirituality

is clearly in conflict with logical reason. Nobody seems to know what to make of it, and the illogic is simply accepted—much in the way I feel we may have to accept the contradiction between the facts my patients have presented and what everyone assumes is possible.

Seeing as it was Betty who started me on this pathway, I think it is only fair to let my final words come from her. My personal nature is such that I try to explain and understand, and in writing this book I have used my human equipment to try to bridge the very same duality that I have been talking about. My attempts to reason my way to an understanding of the spirit spilled over into my many conversations with Betty. I even gave her an early draft of some of my writing to read.

Gently, Betty told me I was missing the point. "You are missing the mark," she said. "You have the gravy, but not the potatoes that's underneath. If you really want to enjoy, you need the potatoes that's underneath. You're not getting down to bedrock." Betty let it sink in. "There is this ... spirit-level is what I'm trying to say. There's the human level, and that's great. Hopefully you can reach humans on the human level, but down here is the spirit level, the bedrock."

Well, Betty was right in that my book was written for humans, trying to understand the spirit from the human level—how could it be otherwise? Yet, from the human level, it is so difficult to express what Betty knew, that there is something more.

"You are like a blind person," Betty told me, "You are sitting at this table and you got this great big feast in front of you—you are blind; you can't see a darn thing. And somebody has to come along and put the fork in the hand and tell 'em where the potatoes are and the knife. And get in there and start digging. And then tell 'em, 'Well, hey, you put it in your mouth,' you see." Betty was trying to get across to me that the spirit is at hand, but we do not see it—all this power and goodness is ours, but we don't know it.

Betty continued with an important lesson: "But the human himself does not have the power [to produce the spirit]. And this is where it is so difficult for people to understand. They think that the human can do it. The human doesn't do it.... The human has to make the decision to *allow* the spirit. And the human has to be subdued ... so you can mentally, as a human, enter into the spirit realm." And Betty continued by saying she had to throw away all of her church teaching about how to be close to God. In the end, "what brought God to me was my heart's desire. You see, I really wanted with my whole heart and I didn't want nothin' else.

The Spirit Transcendent

"It's like eating fried chicken, you see. You hear about fried chicken, or somebody tells you about it, but you've never tasted it, you think, 'Oh no.' But if you taste it, you eat it, you see, 'Ah ha, I *know* what it is.'" With this, Betty laughed, and, peering at me with her one good eye, continued, "And it's the same way about spirit things. Until you experience it, it's still just a figment of your imagination ... then it becomes a reality to you because you are experiencing it."

"But Betty," I asked, "if you cannot understand it or grasp it, how do you get to have it?"

"I was thinking," she responded, "if you, a human, wanted this experience you would have to follow God's rules: it has to be when a person really and truly wants God in their lives. It won't happen unless you really want it. And God *knows*, in your mind or in your heart, whether you want it or not. You have to be perfectly and completely honest with yourself and with Him. And when that time comes, when you're honest, when your desire is to experience, *then* it will happen. And you have to go back to that same kind of plane, day after day after day after day, because you have to continue to be honest, you have to continue to be desirous or it don't happen. Just like going after the chicken.... You have to really desire the chicken and go after it. And of course, I had the desire, since I was eight years old, to know God and know Jesus, so it happened.... It is not a figment of my imagination.... You have to go after it. Like the Bible says, 'Seek and ye shall find.'"

Many times, and across the more than two years I was with her, Betty told me she wanted a science of the spirit. In the end, I believe that it is possible to grant her wish, but only by changing the accepted definition of science. In contrast with science, this project would have to make the critical assumption that materialism does not have a monopoly on reality. Only in this way would there be a freedom to explore the implications of a wider view of nature. Yet whatever this new form of inquiry is to be—call it *metascience*, perhaps—it would not be a branch of philosophy either. Unlike most of philosophy it would seek its truths not from careful reasoning alone, but by checking ideas and theories against results, including the data of personal experience. I suppose I would say, echoing James, that perhaps the time has come for an *experimentally-based* metaphysics. Perhaps, based on everything revealed to me by my clients, there really is room for an entirely new field of inquiry. Perhaps. Perhaps not. But I am certain, at least, that it would be the only way to grant Betty's wish.

Chapter Notes

Introduction

1. The Society for Psychic Research (SPR) was established in 1882 for the purpose of the scientific investigation of the paranormal. William James himself was president in 1894. One of the first important works of the Society was *Phantasms of the Living* by E. Gurney, F.W.H. Myers, and Frank Podmore (Cambridge: Cambridge University Press, 1886). It included dramatic accounts involving apparitions and telepathy. Later the Society put these observations on a more objective footing with its "Report on the Census of Hallucinations" by H. Sidgwick et al., *Proceedings for the Society for Psychical Research* 10 (1894): 25–422. A sample of some 17,000 individuals were questioned and about 10 percent responded in the positive. On the hypothesis that the hallucinations were actual spirits, strict criteria were used to determine if the hallucination was associated with a death, unknown to the percipient, within 12 hours of the actual death. Even with these strict criteria, 43 positive cases were documented. Equally notable is the fact that of the 1078 visual hallucinations reported by the "Census," fully 95 were seen by at least *two* persons.

2. Perhaps it is not surprising that views on the evidence for survival based on the early research of the Society for Psychic Research are very polarized, some investigators writing in support, others writing from the skeptic's viewpoint. For an unbiased and wonderfully readable treatment of those early investigations, see *Ghost Hunters: William James and the Search for Scientific Proof of Life After Death* by Deborah Blum (New York: Penguin Books, 2006).

3. A reader with interest in this topic can do no better than to begin with James' *The Varieties of Religious Experience* (New York: Modern Library, 1994) based on the Gifford Lectures on Natural Religion delivered at the University of Edinburg in 1901–1902.

4. There is a comparison here with phenomenological psychology which takes its inspiration from Husserl. There is also much in common between my work and David J. Hufford's development of his "experience-centered approach to the study of supernatural belief" (cf. David Hufford, *The Terror That Comes in the Night: An Experience-Centered Study of Supernatural Assault Traditions* [Philadelphia: University of Pennsylvania Press, 1982]).

Chapter One

1. Most of my clinical work was performed at Interventional Pain Consultants, which at the time was in Lewiston, Idaho. The reader will see that I was exposed to many, many stories of spiritual experience. It possible that the particular demographics of patients at the clinic—a rural population, mostly white, but with some Native Americans, and from the West—could somehow be related to the number of these occurrences. On the other hand, my patients were not preselected for spiritual concerns: none of them knew of my spiritual interests before I met them, and in fact those interests were

Chapter Notes—One

unknown to the anesthesiologists who ran the clinic and who were the source of my referrals.

2. Orofino is a town with a population of about 3,100 which sits on the bank of the Clearwater River, about 40 miles east of Lewiston. The name itself derives from the Spanish for "fine gold," which is descriptive because Orofino has its origins in gold mining camps that sprung up in that area in the late 1800s.

3. This seems to be a reference to Exodus 3:14 (*Holy Bible: New International Version* [Grand Rapids: Zondervan, 2017]). Just prior to the quoted passage God had called Moses from the burning bush. Moses argues with God that he is being given an impossible task: "Who am I that I should go to Pharaoh and bring the Israelites out of Egypt?" Then Moses asks God what he would tell the Israelites is the name of the God who sent him. God answers, "I am who I am. This is what you are to say to the Israelites. *I AM* has sent me to you" (emphasis mine). Likewise, Betty was told that she would not have to worry about how to fulfill her life's mission—"*you* won't have to do it; the *I AM* will do it."

4. A classic history of mysticism is provided by Evelyn Underhill, *Mysticism: A Study in the Nature and Development of Man's Spiritual Consciousness* (London: Methuen, 1911). Walter Stace provides a very accessible summary of the various mystical traditions: *Teachings of the Mystics* (New York City: New American Library, 1960).

5. Gregory McNamee, "The Explosion of Mount St. Helens," http://blogs.britannica.com/2007/05/the-explosion-of-mount-st-helens/ (accessed April 17, 2019).

6. The actual evidence for precognition is of two kinds: anecdotal reports and the result of controlled laboratory studies. To my mind, these sources of information are complementary. Anecdotal reports are uncontrolled, but they most often concern situations of great personal import, e.g., Sally Rhine Feather and Michael Schmicker, *The Gift* (New York: St. Martin's, 2007). In fact, Betty's own comment "For it to happen it has to be something that *matters* to me" suggests that it would not be easy to confirm precognition in the laboratory. Nevertheless, there are tightly controlled studies that show evidence of precognition, most notably the recent studies of Daryl Bem: "Feeling the Future: Experimental Evidence for Anomalous Retroactive Influences on Cognition and Affect," *Journal of Personality and Social Psychology* 100, no. 3 (2011): 407–25. Bem's results have been challenged, Jeff Galak et al., "Correcting the Past: Failures to Replicate Psi," *SSRN Electronic Journal*, 2012, https://doi.org/10.2139/ssrn.2001721, but also supported by metaanalysis, Daryl Bem et al., "Feeling the Future: A Meta-Analysis of 90 Experiments on the Anomalous Anticipation of Random Future Events," *F1000Research* 4 (2016): 1188, https://doi.org/10.12688/f1000research.7177.2.

7. Dan Simmons, *Ilium* (New York: HarperCollins, 2005).

8. Sermon 13b in Meister Eckhart and Maurice O'C Walshe, *The Complete Mystical Works of Meister Eckhart* (New York: Crossroad, 2009), 109.

9. *Ibid.*, Sermon 57, 298.

10. Rudolf Otto speaks of the phenomenology of direct religious experience as a "Mysterium Tremendum," of which one defining feature is being in contact with the "wholly other." See Sumner B. Twiss and Walter H. Conser, *Experience of the Sacred: Readings in the Phenomenology of Religion* (Hanover, NH: University Press of New England, 1998), 83.

11. It might be described as a direct perception of Paul Tillich's definition of God as the "ground of being." That is, a god that precedes "being itself," and is so basic that it cannot be thought of as being created by any person or thing. See Paul Tillich, *Dynamics of Faith* (New York: Perennial, 2001).

12. A description of "intellectual visions" is found in Chapter 27 of St. Teresa's autobiography: Teresa and John Joseph Burke, *St. Teresa of Jesus of the Order of Our Lady of Carmel; Embracing the Life, Relations, Maxims and Foundations Written by the Saint, Also, a History of St. Teresa's Journeys and Foundations* (New York: Columbus Press, 1911), 189–91.

Chapter Two

1. Hallucinations occur in individuals who are psychotic about 70 percent of the time: J. Landmark et al., "The Positive Triad of Schizophrenic Symptoms," *British Journal of Psychiatry* 156, no. 03 (1990): 388–94. Because of this, it is natural to assume the converse: that having hallucinations is an indicator of mental illness. Actually, it is a *poor* indicator: hallucinations are common among persons in general, a fact that was first demonstrated in the classic "Census of Hallucinations" published in 1894: H. Sidgwick et al., "Report on the Census of Hallucinations," *Proceedings for the Society for Psychical Research* 10 (1894): 25–422. It was found that about 10 percent of people in the general population have experienced apparitions. Later research has shown similarly high rates of hallucinatory experience. See, for example, Vanessa Beavan, John Read, and Claire Cartwright, "The Prevalence of Voice-Hearers in the General Population: A Literature Review," *Journal of Mental Health* 20, no. 3 (2011): 281–92, in which data from 17 surveys collected in nine countries were summarized showing that 13 percent of individuals, on the average, have heard voices.

Related research suggests that hallucinations among the non-clinical population should not be labeled pathological. For that population, voices are more often seen as positive and enriching rather than, as in the clinical case, dominant and intrusive. See Kirstin Daalman and Kelly M. Diederen, "A Final Common Pathway to Hearing Voices: Examining Differences and Similarities in Clinical and Non-Clinical Individuals," *Psychosis* 5, no. 3 (2013): 236–46. A study by Barrett and Etheridge is relevant: Terry R. Barrett and Jane B. Etheridge, "Verbal Hallucinations in Normals, I: People Who Hear 'Voices,'" *Applied Cognitive Psychology* 6, no. 5 (1992): pp. 379–87. They found, in sample of college students, that fully 37 percent sometimes heard their own thoughts out loud, and 9 percent stated they had heard God's voice. Yet there were no differences in pathology (using the MMPI) when those who frequently heard voices were compared to those who did not. Then, of course, there are many historical figures, by definition high-functioning individuals, who have had auditory hallucinations/heard voices: Socrates (who called his voice his *daimon*, the divine), Winston Churchill, Martin Luther King, Jr., George Washington Carver, St. Thomas Aquinas, Martin Luther, Robert Louis Stevenson, among them. See Michell B. Liester, "Inner Voices: Distinguishing Transcendent and Pathological Characteristics," *The Journal of Transpersonal Psychology* 28, no. 1 (1996): 1–30 and Daniel B. Smith, *Muses, Madmen, and Prophets Rethinking the History, Science, and Meaning of Auditory Hallucination* (New York: Penguin Press, 2007).

2. See Joseph M. Pierre, "Hallucinations in Nonpsychotic Disorders," *Harvard Review of Psychiatry* 18, no. 1 (2010): 22–35. The analogy between coughs and hallucinations is Pierre's.

3. See I. O. Azuonye, "A Difficult Case: Diagnosis Made by Hallucinatory Voices," *British Medical Journal* 315, no. 7123 (1997): 1685–86 for a case in the medical literature that is challenging in ways similar to all of the cases presented in this chapter. Azuonye, a psychiatrist, documented voices in a patient that were insistent and seemed bent on helping, just as seemed true for Damon. By Auonye's description, his patient "AB," who had no prior history of pathology, began to hear voices that introduced themselves as individuals "who used to work at the Children's Hospital, Great Ormond Street," and they further stated, "we would like to help you." The voices provided information they implied the patient could check out as proof of their reality. The presented evidence was correct, but by this time, AB had decided she had gone insane and began to see a psychiatrist (the author of the article) who prescribed an antipsychotic. At first, the voices remitted but they later returned and insisted she visit a specific address which turned out to correspond to the tomography department of a London hospital. The voices demanded that she go in and ask to have a brain scan because she possessed a tumor. AB's psychiatrist spoke with her, pointing out that she had absolutely no

Chapter Notes—Two

symptoms of a brain tumor. Eventually, to reassure her that she had nothing to worry about, a brain scan was performed, which did in fact show a meningioma. The tumor was removed, and when AB recovered consciousness, her voices spoke once again: "We are pleased to have helped you—goodbye." The voices never returned.

4. In all of these cases I am suggesting that to fully appreciate the cause of these hallucinations/visions, one needs to understand their purpose. Students of philosophy may recognize a connection to what Aristotle terms "final causes," which he felt were essential to explanation in general. Therefore (but in the good company of Aristotle) I am offering a *teleological* explanation of why Damon, and others in this chapter, have hallucinations. A summary of Aristotle's philosophy of causation is given by Andrea Falcon: "Aristotle on Causality," March 7, 2019, https://plato.stanford.edu/entries/aristotle-causality/.

5. William James, in his *Varieties*, was the first and most eloquent critic of this view which he calls "medical materialism." For example, he quotes Maudsley (*Varieties*, pp. 23): "What right have we to believe Nature under any obligation to do her work by means of complete minds only? She may find an incomplete mind a more suitable instrument for a particular purpose..."

6. See Carney Landis, *Varieties of Psychopathological Experience* (New York, 1964) for the phenomenology of hallucinations.

7. Mike Jackson and K.W.M. Fulford describe three cases which involve clear symptoms of psychosis but which, at the same time, were seen as fundamentally spiritual by the persons involved: "Spiritual Experience and Psychopathology," *Philosophy, Psychiatry, & Psychology* 4, no. 1 (1997): 41–65. Traditional psychiatry would define these cases in terms of psychopathology, but Jackson and Fulford point out that in each case the symptoms involved a positive outcome involving growth and greater adaptation. Therefore, those same symptoms may alternatively and perhaps more validly be viewed as spiritual phenomena.

St. Teresa preceded some of Jackson and Fulford's thinking by about five centuries. She was concerned with the distinction between visions from God and visions that were the product of the Devil. (The latter category corresponds to what we today would call hallucinations as a symptom of mental illness.) St. Teresa was convinced that a vision could be known as spiritual (e.g., of God) because of its *fruits*: tranquility, growth of the personality, and strength of purpose. See Teresa and John Joseph Burke, *St. Teresa of Jesus of the Order of Our Lady of Carmel; Embracing the Life, Relations, Maxims and Foundations Written by the Saint, Also, a History of St. Teresa's Journeys and Foundations* (New York: Columbus Press, 1911), 141, and also Chapter Three in Teresa and E. Allison Peers, *Interior Castle* (Bottom of the Hill, 2010), written as a guide to the spiritual life for her fellow nuns.

8. See, for example, Sidney Zisook et al., "Command Hallucinations in Outpatients with Schizophrenia," *Command Hallucinations in Outpatients with Schizophrenia* 56, no. 10 (1995): 462–65.

9. This was a good example of selective listening. At that time I would not have taken the notion of spirits seriously and therefore paid no attention to the fact that Grandpa Johansson was recently deceased.

10. Of all the cases that I present, Melissa's is most similar to those that were selected by Jackson and Fulford to illustrate the difficulty of distinguishing between psychopathology and spiritual events.

11. Cases like Melissa's blur the distinction between spirituality and psychopathology. But often the separation is clear. See Andrew Sims, "Commentary on 'Spiritual Experience and Psychopathology,'" *Philosophy, Psychiatry, & Psychology* 4, no. 1 (1997): 79–81. Sims points out that in cases of mental illness there would be symptoms in other aspects of the patient's life, delusions and hallucinations and so forth, separate from the person's religious interests. Also, in mental illness there is compromised functioning in many areas. In contrast, a person who describes religious experience typically has the insight to understand that others might be incredulous about their own experience. In addi-

tion, and in contrast to psychopathology, religious experience often results in personal growth, increased resilience, and the feeling of freedom (cf., St. Teresa's writings cited above).

12. *The Varieties*, lectures XVI and XVII, 413–69.

13. *Ibid.*, 422.

14. Raymond A. Moody, *Life After Life: The Investigation of a Phenomenon—Survival of Bodily Death* (New York: HarperCollins, 2001). For reviews of research on near-death experience, see Emily Williams Kelly, Bruce Greyson, and Edward F. Kelly, "Unusual Experiences Near-Death and Related Phenomena," in *Irreducible Mind: Toward a Psychology for the 21st Century*, ed. Edward F. Kelly et al. (Lanham, MD: Rowman & Littlefield, 2010), 367–421 and Bruce Greyson, "Near-Death Experience," in *Varieties of Anomalous Experience: Examining the Scientific Evidence*, ed. Etzel Cardeña (Washington, D.C.: American Psychological Association, 2014), 333–68.

15. There are three prospective studies with fairly large sample sizes. All found rates of near-death experience among resuscitated patients of 9 percent or more: Sam Parnia et al., "AWARE—AWAreness during REsuscitation—A Prospective Study," *Resuscitation* 85, no. 12 (2014): 1799–1805, found a rate of 9 percent; Bruce Greyson, "Incidence and Correlates of Near-Death Experiences in a Cardiac Care Unit," *General Hospital Psychiatry* 25, no. 4 (2003): 269–76, found a rate of 18 percent; and Pim Van Lommel et al., "Near-Death Experience in Survivors of Cardiac Arrest: a Prospective Study in the Netherlands," *The Lancet* 358, no. 9298 (2001): 2039–2045, found a rate of 10 percent.

Chapter Three

1. As a clinician who has worked with individuals who have faced trauma, I began with the assumption that a brush with death would lead to increases in fearfulness and anxiety afterwards. It was surprising to observe the actual opposite in every patient that I interviewed. My observations were representative, and in fact many others have commented on the phenomenon. It is mentioned, for example, by Cherie Sutherland in *Transformed by the Light: Life After Near-Death Experiences* (Sydney: Bantam, 1992) and by Kenneth Ring in *Heading Toward Omega* (New York: Wm. Morrow, 1984). Empirical work confirms what seems apparent from self-reports. See for example, Pim van Lommel et al., "Near-Death Experience in Survivors of Cardiac Arrest: A Prospective Study in the Netherlands," *The Lancet* 358, no. 9298 (2001): 2039–2045.

2. Many of the cases presented by Kenneth Ring in his book *Heading Toward Omega* (New York: Wm. Morrow, 1984) capture this feeling particularly well.

3. For a review of the many difficulties with attempts to explain the near-death experience as a product of disordered physiology, see Emily Williams Kelly, Bruce Greyson, and Edward F. Kelly, "Unusual Experiences Near-Death and Related Phenomena," in *Irreducible Mind: Toward a Psychology for the 21st Century*, ed. Edward F. Kelly et al. (Lanham, MD: Rowman & Littlefield, 2010), 367–421, and Robert G. Mays and Suzanne B. Mays, "Explaining Near-Death Experiences: Physical or Non-Physical Causation?" *Journal of Near-Death Studies* 33, no. 3 (2015): 125–49. For a general summary of problems with materialist explanations, see Bruce Greyson, "Implications of Near-Death Experiences for a Postmaterialist Psychology," *Psychology of Religion and Spirituality* 2, no. 1 (2010): 37–45.

4. It seems we can cut through all of the debate surrounding possible physiological explanations for near-death experience with the observation that similar phenomena are found in individuals who are *not dying*: cf. Vanessa Charland-Verville et al., "Near-Death Experiences in Non-Life-Threatening Events and Coma of Different Etiologies," *Frontiers in Human Neuroscience* 8 (2014): 1–8. Even more dramatic are cases similar to the one presented in this chapter where the near-death experience is shared by others. They show, I believe, that the near-death experience is fundamentally a *spiritual* product. Glennys Howarth and

Allan Kellehear describe several such cases that they culled from the literature: "Shared Near-Death and Related Illness Experiences: Steps on an Unscheduled Journey," *Journal of Near-Death Studies* 20, no. 2 (2001): 71–85.

5. St. Teresa in Chapter V of the *Interior Castle* writes: "When the soul ... returns to itself, it finds it has reaped very great advantages and it has such contempt for earthly things that, in comparison with those it has seen, they seem like dirt to it. Thenceforward to live on earth is a great affliction to it, and, if it sees any of the things which used to give it pleasure, it no longer cares for them" ("The Sixth Mansion," 128).

6. Changes in personality are very well described in the cases presented by Kenneth Ring in his *Heading Toward Omega* (New York: Wm. Morrow, 1984). See also Cherie Sutherland's *Transformed by the Light: Life After Near-Death Experiences* (Sydney: Bantam, 1992). Empirical research on the aftereffects of positive NDEs is reviewed by Russell Noyes et al., "Aftereffects of Pleasurable Western Adult Near-Death Experiences," in *The Handbook of Near-Death Experiences: Thirty Years of Investigation*, ed. Janice Miner Holden, Bruce Grayson, and Debbie James (Santa Barbara, CA: Praeger, 2009), pp. 41–107.

7. Betty expressed the same feeling, using her own colorful terminology. In one of her letters to me, she called herself a "combo-person," not quite human, not completely spirit: "I am like petrified wood," she wrote, "wood that's been turned, bit by bit, into beautiful stone." Later she said to me, "The human is like water before it changes form when it freezes, or like a crude ore before it is made into gold, or like a potato, before it is peeled, washed, cooked, and mashed." In this way the spirit uses the human as a raw material, but then gradually transforms him or her, turning them into something else, into something or someone who is no longer human.

8. Donald Treffert devotes a chapter to acquired savant syndrome in his book *Islands of Genius* (London: Jessica Kingsley, 2010).

9. Increases in psychic sensitivity and paranormal experience after the near-death experience has been reported by many. See particularly Cherie Sutherland, "Psychic Phenomena Following Near-Death Experiences: An Australian Study," *Journal of Near-Death Studies* 8, no. 2 (1989), and Bruce Greyson, "Increase in Psychic Phenomena Following Near-Death Experiences," *Theta* 11, no. 2 (1983): 26–29.

Chapter Four

1. In Loretta's case her symptoms—especially in light of later developments—might best be explained as a "spiritual emergency," the notion that writers in transpersonal psychology have advanced as an alternative to psychopathology: Stanislav Grof and Christina Grof, *Spiritual Emergency: When Personal Transformation Becomes a Crisis* (Los Angeles: TarcherPerigree, 1989).

2. William James writes eloquently on the transformative nature of this process. Many similar examples are provided within his two lectures on conversion in the *Varieties of Religious Experience*. The scholar and mystic Evelyn Underhill considered conversion experiences such as Loretta's as the beginning of a process of spiritual development (which she called "the Mystic Way"). See especially the chapter "The Awakening of the Self" in Part II of her book *Mysticism: A Study in the Nature and Development of Man's Spiritual Consciousness* (London: Methuen, 1911).

3. There are many accounts of addiction suddenly being healed as part of the conversion process. William James relates one (*Varieties*, 223–25). I personally, in the course of my practice, have heard a half-dozen or more, besides the one related here.

4. For examples of faith healing within the Christian tradition, see William P. Wilson and J. Harold Ellens, "How Religious or Spiritual Miracle Events Happen Today," in *Miracles: God, Science, and Psychology in the Paranormal*, vol. 1, ed. J Harold Ellens (Westport, CT: Praeger, 2008), 264–79. Emily Williams Kelly reviews faith healing along with related phenomena: "Psychophysiological Influence," in

Irreducible Mind: Toward a Psychology for the 21st Century, ed. Edward F. Kelly et al. (Lanham, MD: Rowman & Littlefield, 2010), 132–48.

5. Evelyn Underhill (in *Mysticism*) describes how, as part of "The Mystic Way," the personal ego is supplanted by something larger. Personal interests become less important and, as if she possesses an internal compass, the mystic is impelled by something higher.

6. Then there is the fact—which begs for explanation—that individuals who have had direct spiritual experience also are involved in paranormal events: see Ralph W. Hood, "Mysticism and the Paranormal," in *Miracles: God, Science, and Psychology in the Paranormal*, vol. 3, ed. J. Harold Ellens (Westport, CT: Praeger, 2008), 16–37. One way to account for the association is the old idea, proposed by F.W.H. Myers in *Human Personality and Its Survival of Bodily Death* (New York: Longmans, Green, 1903), that that the boundary between the subliminal and the liminal (e.g., ordinary consciousness) is more permeable in certain individuals. Therefore, spiritual sensitivity is a matter of individual differences, and both phenomena (the paranormal and the mystic) should occur together in individuals made sensitive because of their more permeable boundaries. M.A. Thalbourne provides a more recent version of this thesis in which he proposes that the correlation is the product of an underlying condition he called "transliminality": see "Psychiatry, the Mystical, and the Paranormal," *Journal of Parapsychology* 70 (2006): 143–65. Also relevant is an article by Paul Marshall, "The Psychical and the Mystical: Boundaries, Connections, Common Origins," *Journal for the Society for Psychical Research* 75, no. 1 (2011): 1–13, wherein he reviews the need for a theory that joins the fields of mysticism and parapsychology.

Among accounts of answered prayer I would like to cite one lesser-known work: C.G. Bevinton's *Remarkable Miracles* (South Plainfield, NJ: Bridge, 1992). It is an account by an itinerant preacher and faith healer, working in the Midwest around the second decade of the century. I mention it because Betty herself was fond of the book and owned a number of copies that she liked to lend out. Clearly, she believed Bevington's writings mirrored her own personal experience.

7. Reminiscent of Jesus's words to his disciples, e.g., John 1:43: "The next day Jesus decided to leave for Galilee. Finding Philip, he said to him, 'follow me.'"

Chapter Five

1. See Stewart Goetz and Charles Taliaferro, *A Brief History of the Soul* (Malden, MA: Wiley-Blackwell, 2011), 66–80, for an accessible summary of Descartes' thought.

2. The prevailing opinion among philosophers who consider the relation between mind and body hold that materialism is correct. (I vastly simplify the issue.) To most, duality and the reality of the soul are unpalpable for many reasons. A review of the arguments, and a summary of the counterargument that the reality of the soul is a viable alternative, is provided by Stewart Goetz and Charles Taliaferro in *A Brief History of the Soul* (Malden, MA: Wiley-Blackwell, 2011) and by Mark C. Baker and Stewart Goetz in *The Soul Hypothesis: Investigations into the Existence of the Soul* (New York: Continuum International, 2011).

My approach, in this chapter and elsewhere, is more empirical than it is strictly philosophical. I believe my strategy is parallel to the kind of thinking that separated psychology from its parent, philosophy, in the late 1800s. Thus, going back to those earlier times, individuals like Fechner, Wundt, and Wundt's many students, were interested in questions concerning the mind and consciousness, but rather than taking a philosophical approach, they sought their answers in careful observation and the methods of experimental psychology: see, for example, Thomas Hardy Leahey, *A History of Psychology: Main Currents in Psychological Thought* (Upper Saddle River, NJ: Prentice Hall, 2010). Modern philosophy has a great number of carefully crafted objections to the concept of the soul and the possibility of dualism. But my interest, as a psychologist, is more centered on actual observations that can shed light on the issue.

3. Interestingly enough, this seemed to be a direct observation bearing on the philosophers' "zombie problem." The main debate about zombies concerns whether there is something "special" about consciousness, or whether consciousness is the inevitable outcome of our biological equipment: See, for brief and clear discussion, Susan J. Blackmore, *Consciousness: A Very Short Introduction* (Oxford: Oxford University Press, 2005).

When James looked down and observed his machine-self he was testifying that his consciousness was "something more" than his biological endowment, e.g., the mechanism of the body alone cannot produce consciousness; without consciousness, despite all of the machinery of the body, we would be zombies.

4. The study of out-of-body experiences (OBEs) tends to be dominated by the assumption that they are the product of psychological processes that produce illusion or hallucination: cf. Etzel Cardeña et al., "Anomalous Self and Identity Experiences," *Varieties of Anomalous Experience: Examining the Scientific Evidence* (Washington, D.C.: American Psychological Association, 2014), 175–212. This explanation cannot account for those cases where there is *veridical* perception during the OBE—like my patient Beth, who saw and knew things that ought to be impossible to see or know, especially while unconscious. The literature on veridical OBEs is reviewed by David Ray Griffin in *Parapsychology, Philosophy, and Spirituality: A Postmodern Exploration* (Albany: State University of New York Press, 1997) and also by Janice Miner Holden in "Veridical Perception in Near-Death Experiences," in *The Handbook of Near-Death Experiences: Thirty Years of Investigation*, ed. Janice Miner Holden, Bruce Greyson, and Debbie James (Santa Barbara, CA: Praeger, 2009), 185–211.

There are several famous cases of veridical perception where there is good evidence that the brain could not support conscious experience at the time of the OBE, for example, the famous case of Pam Reynolds: Michael B. Sabom, *Light & Death: One Doctor's Fascinating Account of Near-Death Experiences* (Grand Rapids: Zondervan, 1998). Understandably, given the implication that conscious experience can go on without the support of a functioning brain, there are critiques. See, for example, G.M. Woerlee, "Could Pam Reynolds Hear? A New Investigation into the Possibility of Hearing During This Famous Near-Death Experience," *Journal of Near-Death Studies* 30, no. 1 (2011): 3–25. But, while any single case might be suspect, there are a great *many* such cases where an argument for veridical perception may be made. More than 100 of them have been collected together and presented by Titus Rivas et al., *The Self Does Not Die: Verified Paranormal Phenomena from Near-Death Experiences* (Durham: IANDS, 2016).

5. My first idea was that perhaps Beth was conscious, even though under anesthesia. In fact, it seems that consciousness under anesthesia is possible, but happens rarely, at a rate of one or two patients per 1,000: Peter S. Sebel et al., "The Incidence of Awareness During Anesthesia: A Multicenter United States Study," *Anesthesia & Analgesia* 99, no. 3 (2004): 833–39. But even if she were conscious in the traditional sense, that still does not explain Beth's knowledge of her allergy to morphine. Also, whereas consciousness during anesthesia might account for some of the reports of OBEs, it certainly cannot account for all veridical near-death experiences: see Janice Miner Holden, "Veridical Perception in Near-Death Experiences," *The Handbook of near-Death Experiences: Thirty Years of Investigation*, 185–211. The mystery remains: how do patients, during times when brain function must surely be compromised, show such great lucidity?

6. Putting aside the religious focus, one might say that Betty had learned the technique of voluntary OBEs. (A talented individual such as Tart's "Miss Z"—who likewise could control her OBEs—comes to mind. See C.T. Tart, "A Psychophysiological Study of Out-of-the-Body Experiences in a Selected Subject," *Journal for the American Society for Psychical Research* 62 [1968]: 3–27.) Betty conceived of her talent differently: she felt it was just one

of many spiritual gifts that had evolved within her over time and that her spiritual growth was shaped and guided by the Spirit.

7. There are anecdotal reports of shared OBEs, much like that involving Lisa and her sister. Hornell Hart provides a number of examples, discussed under the title "ESP projection": "ESP Projection: Spontaneous Cases and the Experimental Method," *The Journal of the American Society for Psychical Research* 48, no. 4 (1954): 121–46.

8. For accounts from percipients who were directly involved in the Star Gate project, see Paul H. Smith, *Reading the Enemy's Mind: Inside Star Gate, America's Psychic Espionage Program* (New York: Forge Books, 2005), and Joseph McMoneagle, *The Stargate Chronicles: Memoirs of a Psychic Spy* (Newburyport, MA: Hampton Roads, 2002).

9. Stephan A. Schwartz provides an interesting history of the large-scale efforts to investigate remote viewing: "Through Time and Space: The Evidence for Remote Viewing," in *Evidence for Psi: Thirteen Empirical Research Reports*, ed. Damien Broderick and Ben Goertzel (Jefferson, NC: McFarland, 2015), 168–212. A review of the evidence is provided by Johann Baptista, Max Derakhshani, and Patrizio E. Tressoldi, "Explicit Anomalous Cognition," in *Parapsychology: A Handbook for the 21st Century*, ed. Etzel Cardeña, John Palmer, and David Marcusson-Clavertz (Jefferson, NC: McFarland, 2015), 192–214.

Chapter Six

1. Betty's spiritual evolution, and her movement toward union with God, seems to illustrate what Underhill believed to be a general pattern, what she called "The Mystic Way" (see Mysticism).

2. H. F. Ellenberger, in his wonderful *The Discovery of the Unconscious: The History and Evolution of Dynamic Psychiatry* (New York: Basic Books, 1970), would call this "the mythopoetic function of the unconscious." But this obscures an important fact, at least from Mary's—or a mystic's—perspective, that her experience is *sacred*.

3. The book in question was Werner Foerster's *Gnosis: A Selection of Gnostic Texts, Vol. 2: Coptic and Mandean Sources* (Oxford: Clarendon Press, 1974).

4. Marvin W. Meyer et al., *The Nag Hammadi Scriptures: The Revised and Updated Translation of Sacred Gnostic Texts Complete in One Volume* (New York: HarperOne, 2009).

5. Elaine Pagels, *The Gnostic Gospels* (New York: Random House, 1979).

6. See Chapter Six, "Confrontation with the Unconscious," in Jung's autobiography: C.G Jung, Jaffé Aniela, and Richard Winston, *Memories, Dreams, Reflections* (New York: Vintage, 1963).

7. An excellent treatment of Jung is provided by H. F. Ellenberger in his book *The Discovery of the Unconscious*.

Chapter Seven

1. Russell Noyes found the loss of the fear of death to be the most frequently reported changing attitudes after a near-death experience: "The Human Experience of Death or, What Can We Learn from Near-Death Experiences?" *OMEGA—Journal of Death and Dying* 13, no. 3 (1983): 251–59. Among the 50 NDErs in her study, Cherie Sutherland found a marked absence of the fear of death. In fact, many now found the concept "laughable": see "Psychic Phenomena Following Near-Death Experiences: An Australian Study," *Journal of Near-Death Studies* 8, no. 2 (1989). Freedom from the fear of death is likewise emphasized by Kenneth Ring in his *Life at Death* (New York: Coward, McCann & Geoghegan, 1980) and in his *Heading Toward Omega* (New York: Wm. Morrow, 1984) as well as by Michael B. Sabom in *Recollections of Death: A Medical Investigation* (New York: Simon & Schuster, 1982) and in *Light & Death: One Doctor's Fascinating Account of Near-Death Experiences* (Grand Rapids: Zondervan, 1998).

2. Cf. Raymond Moody's classic work, *Life After Life*.

3. The theory of ideal forms is devel-

Chapter Notes—Seven

oped in Plato's Republic: Plato and Desmond Lee, The Republic (New York: Penguin, 1987). This work contains the famous analogy of the cave, where our human perception is understood to be only a shadow, projected on the cave wall, of a deeper reality.

4. As James says in the *Varieties*, the central aspect of mystic experience is its noetic quality: "Mystical states seem to those who experience them to be also states of knowledge" (414).

5. Cf. the changes in personality and ability described in Kenneth Ring's *Heading Toward Omega*.

6. Auras are specifically mentioned by Bruce Greyson in "Increase in Psychic Phenomena Following Near-Death Experiences," *Theta* 11, no. 2 (1983): 26–29, by Cherie Sutherland in "Psychic Phenomena Following Near-Death Experiences: An Australian Study," *Journal of Near-Death Studies* 8, no. 2 (1989), and by R. L. Kohr, "Near-Death Experience and Its Relationship to Psi and Various Altered States," *Theta* 10 (1982): 50–53. The experience also seems surprisingly frequent: in Grayson's study about one-third NDErs experienced auras, and in Sutherland's the proportion was about one-half. Bruce Greyson and R.L. Kohr each compared the frequency of seeing auras before and after the NDE and found the difference to be highly significant.

7. After the NDE an increase in spiritual sensitivity has been widely reported (see, for example, the studies by Bruce Greyson, Cherie Sutherland, and R. L. Kohr, cited above in note 6). Also relevant are reports of "spontaneous mediumship experience" after a NDE: Janice Miner Holden, Ryan D. Foster, and Lee Kinsey, "Spontaneous Mediumship Experiences: A Neglected Aftereffect of Near-Death Experiences," *Journal of Near-Death Studies* 33, no. 2 (2014): 67–84 and Ryan D. Foster, Deborah Lee, and Ann Grau Duvall, "Two Cases of Spontaneous Mediumship Experiences of Near-Death Experiencers," *Journal of Near-Death Studies* 34, no. 1 (2015): 44–54.

8. As surprising as it was to her, Carol's apparition of her grandfather appears typical: William Roll indicates that typically apparitions are either "local" (tied to a particular location) or "personal" (associated with a person). "On Apparitions and Mediumship: An Examination of the Evidence That Personal Consciousness Persists After Death," in *The Survival of Human Consciousness: Essays on the Possibility of Life after Death*, ed. Lance Storm and Michael A. Thalbourne (Jefferson, NC: McFarland, 2006), 142–73. This observation was first made by Edmund Gurney and F. W. H. Myers: "On Apparitions Occurring Soon after Death," *Proceedings of the Society for Psychical Research* 5 (1888): 403–85.

9. One source of comparsion is William Fletcher Barrett's classic work, *Death-Bed Visions* (London: Methuen, 1926).

10. The question goes back to the origins of the Society for Psychical Research and to Frederic W. H. Myers' classic *Human Personality and Its Survival of Bodily Death* (New York: Longmans, Green, 1903). Exactly a century later, Stephen E. Braude reviewed the evidence in his book *Immortal Remains: The Evidence for Life After Death* (Lanham, MD: Rowman & Littlefield, 2003). Other excellent reviews are provided by David Fontana, *Is There an Afterlife?* (Ropley: O Books, 2010) and by David Ray Griffin, *Parapsychology, Philosophy, and Spirituality: A Postmodern Exploration* (Albany: State University of New York Press, 1997).

11. Poltergeist phenomena are reviewed by A. Gauld and A.D. Cornell in *Poltergeists* (London: Routledge & Kegan Paul, 1979). For a very well documented and interesting case see two studies by David Fontana: "A Responsive Poltergeist: A Case from South Wales," *Journal of the Society for Psychical Research* 57 (1991): 385–403 and "The Responsive South Wales Poltergeist: A Follow-Up," *Journal of the Society for Psychical Research* 58 (1992): 225–31.

12. For a treatment of the interrelations between dissociative phenomena and possession, see Adam Crabtree's *Multiple Man: Explorations in Possession and Multiple Personality* (New York: Praeger, 1985).

13. For further examples supporting the reality of evil spirits and their effects, see the first chapter in Phillip H. Wiebe's *God*

and Other Spirits: Intimations of Transcendence in Christian Experience* (New York: Oxford University Press, 2004).

Chapter Eight

1. Gary's direct experience that everything is connected and everything is part of God is an example of the unity that Stace felt to be the common feature of mystic experience: W. T. Stace, *Mysticism and Philosophy* (London: Macmillan, 1961). According to Stace, Gary's experience of unity reflected in the many forms of the external world is an example of "extrovertive" mysticism.

2. William James recognized that the core of mystic experience transcends systems of belief. He wrote, "This overcoming of all the usual barriers between the individual and the Absolute is the great mystic achievement. In mystic states we both become one with the Absolute and we become aware of our oneness. This is the everlasting and triumphant mystical tradition, hardly altered by differences of clime or creed" (*Varieties* 457).

3. See Raymond A. Bucko, *The Lakota Ritual of the Sweat Lodge: History and Contemporary Practice* (Lincoln: University of Nebraska Press, 1998), for firsthand accounts of the important sweat lodge ritual.

4. A Lakota elder who was a pipe-bearing descendent of Nicholas Black Elk (the author of the famous "Black Elk Speaks"). Wallace H. Black Elk, together with William S. Lyon, are the authors of *Black Elk: The Sacred Ways of a Lakota* (New York: HarperOne, 1990), a book that gives a good feel for Gary's conviction that spirits are as real, and as active, as anything we might find in the material world. It would be accurate to say that Gary was a student of the students of Nicholas Black Elk.

5. We are fortunate to have accounts of these other sacred traditions of the Oglala Sioux from the mouth of Nicholas Black Elk himself, a few years before his death: Black Elk and Joseph Epes Brown, *The Sacred Pipe* (Norman: University of Oklahoma Press, 1953).

6. Naturally, there is the question "How can this be?" Setting aside simple coincidence, C.G. Jung suggested that there can be meaningful connections that are acausal: "I have picked on the term 'synchronicity' to designate a hypothetical factor that is equal in rank in rank to causality as a principle of explanation." C.G. Jung and W. Pauli, *The Interpretation of Nature and the Psyche* (New York: Pantheon Books, 1955), 27–28. This is a different approach, compared to some of the recent thinking in parapsychology, which assumes that there is a causal explanation for psi phenomena (e.g., telepathy or precognition), perhaps lying in the realm of physics, that has yet to be fully understood.

7. Cf. Mike Jackson and K.W.M. Fulford, "Spiritual Experience and Psychopathology," *Philosophy, Psychiatry, & Psychology* 4, no. 1 (1997): 41–65.

8. See Adam Crabtree for examples, both historical and current: *Multiple Man: Explorations in Possession and Multiple Personality* (New York: Praeger, 1985).

9. The problem is in parallel to the one considered in Chapter Two: "Hallucinations of the Angelic Variety." There the difficulty for the standard psychiatric view was that it had no way to account for *purpose* in a hallucination and, further, that that purpose provided an anchor in reality. Similarly, the psychiatric view of dissociation (as an explanation for the experience of the medium) has no way to take into account shared aspects of visionary experience (Richard and others seeing Akalian walking down the street; seeing a picture of Akalian drawn by an artist above the door; Akalian introducing himself through the mouth of the medium; etc.).

10. Fontana (*Is There an Afterlife?* 134–36) mentions a very similar phenomena which he personally witnessed. He was working with a medium, Dorothy, who was sitting a few feet away: "I watched Dorothy closely and to my complete surprise became aware of another face building up just beside her own ... simultaneously I could see Dorothy's face, looking as normal, and the new face partially superimposed over it.... The new face was male, and unmistakably Chinese and sage-like in

appearance." After the event (called transfiguration in psychic terminology) a second sitter independently gave an accurate description of Fontana's own perception. Fontana remarks that observations of this kind give doubt to the hypothesis that controls (in this case the "control" would be Akalian) can be written off as secondary personalities, e.g., as simple phenomena of dissociation.

11. The gift of extreme spiritual sensitivity, coming after a near-death experience, has been commented on my many others (see Chapter Seven, notes 6 and 7).

Chapter Nine

1. This entire set of events was a near-death experience, but of the negative variety. Greyson and Bush detail the phenomenon, and describe three types of negative NDE: Bruce Greyson and Nancy Evans Bush, "Distressing Near-Death Experiences," *Psychiatry* 55, no. 1 (1992): 95–110. Monica's experience was of the third type, the hellish experience. Nancy Evans Bush also provides a review and commentary on the negative near-death experience: "Distressing Western Near-Death Experiences: Finding a Way through the Abyss," in *The Handbook of Near-Death Experiences: Thirty Years of Investigation*, ed. Janice Miner Holden, Bruce Greyson, and Debbie James (Santa Barbara: Praeger, 2009), 63–86.

2. Thomas of Celano's *The First Life of St. Francis*, written in 1228. Leah Shopkow, "The First Life of St. Francis," accessed June 18, 2019, http://www.indiana.edu/~dmdhist/francis.htm. The direct witness was the fellow monk Brother Leo; see Herbert Thurston and J. H. Crehan, *The Physical Phenomena of Mysticism* (Chicago: Henry Regnery, 1952).

3. See C. J. Simpson, "The Stigmata: Pathology or Miracle?" *British Medical Journal* 289, no. 6460 (1984): 1746–48 and Marco Margnelli, "An Unusual Case of Stigmatization," *Journal of Scientific Exploration* 13, no. 3 (1999): 461–82. Emily Williams Kelly provides an excellent review, "Psychophysiological Influence," in *Irreducible Mind: Toward a Psychology for the 21st Century*, ed. Edward F. Kelly et al. (Lanham, MD: Rowman & Littlefield, 2010), 152–67.

4. The case study by Marco Margnelli, cited above in note 3, is very well controlled and very convincing.

5. See F.A. Pattie, Jr., "The Production of Blisters by Hypnotic Suggestion: A Review," *The Journal of Abnormal and Social Psychology* 36, no. 1 (1941): 62–72 and Gordon L. Paul, "The Production of Blisters by Hypnotic Suggestion: Another Look," *Psychosomatic Medicine* 25, no. 3 (1963): 233–44.

6. See Robert L. Moody, "Bodily Changes During Abreaction," *The Lancet* 248, no. 6435 (1946): 934–35 and Robert L. Moody, "Bodily Changes During Abreaction," *The Lancet* 251, no. 6512 (1948): 964.

7. For examples of poltergeist activity in all their splendid variety, see A. Gauld and A.D. Cornell, *Poltergeists* (London: Routledge & Kegan Paul, 1979).

Chapter Ten

1. I don't think there could be a better phrase for capturing the universality of the spirit and also the fundamental difference between religious experience and religious belief.

2. Again, wholly in keeping with the observation of greatly increased spiritual sensitivity after a near-death experience, for example, as discussed in Ring's *Heading Toward Omega* or by Cherie Sutherland in "Psychic Phenomena Following Near-Death Experiences: An Australian Study," *Journal of Near-Death Studies* 8, no. 2 (1989).

3. I am quoting 1 Corinthians 13:12.

4. My experience with Caroline and Monica bears on the long-standing counter explanation for survival: the so-called "super-psi hypothesis." (For treatments see Griffin's *Parapsychology, Philosophy, and Spirituality: A Postmodern Exploration* and Braude's *Immortal Remains: The Evidence for Life After Death.*) According to "super-psi," a medium who receives messages ostensibly from a discarnate entity might have access to information

through the minds of others (i.e., the sitters in a séance) through paranormal means. Researchers interested in survival have gone to great lengths, to say the least, in their attempts to exclude the actions of psi. Again, the case described here would argue for survival in favor of super-psi because Monica's messages from Caroline concern knowledge that would only be available to her (that is to *her spirit*) *after* her death. A dedicated advocate of super-psi might have us consider that even events occurring after death might be knowable, through paranormal means, to the living through some form of precognition, but it seems that extensions of this sort to super-psi would place it in the category of hypotheses that can never be refuted.

5. Much has been written about Mrs. Piper. I feel one of the best sources is Deborah Blum's wonderfully written *Ghost Hunters: William James and the Search for Scientific Proof of Life After Death* (2006). I have also made use of David Fontana's *Is There an Afterlife?* and David Ray Griffin's *Parapsychology, Philosophy, and Spirituality: A Postmodern Exploration*.

6. William James, "A Record of Observations of Certain Phenomena of Trance," in *Essays in Psychical Research* (Cambridge: Harvard University Press, 1986), 79–88 (originally published in 1890).

7. Martin Gardner, based on his experience with psychics and showmen maintained that Mrs. Piper was a fraud and that she was simply very good at "cold reading." As to the objection that she was never caught in fraudulent activity despite great efforts to do so, Gardner confidently asserts that it was because she was so good at it! See Martin Gardner, "William James and Mrs. Piper," in *The Night Is Large: Collected Essays, 1938–1995* (New York: St. Martin's Griffin, 1997).

8. William James, "Address of the President before the Society for Psychical Research," essay, in *Essays in Psychical Research* (Cambridge MA: Harvard University Press, 1986), pp. 127–37 (originally published in 1896).

Chapter Eleven

1. Aldous Huxley, *The Doors of Perception* (New York: Harper Perennial, 2009).

2. See notes 8 and 9 from Chapter One: The Witch of Orofino

3. The quote is from Blake's *The Marriage of Heaven and Hell*, published in 1794 and reproduced by Dover Publications (New York: Dover Publications, 2012).

References

Azuonye, I. O. "A Difficult Case: Diagnosis Made by Hallucinatory Voices." *British Medical Journal* 315, no. 7123 (1997): 1685–86.
Bacon, Francis. *Bacon's Essays*. Cambridge: Cambridge University Press, 2015.
Baker, Mark C., and Stewart Goetz. *The Soul Hypothesis: Investigations into the Existence of the Soul*. New York: Continuum International, 2011.
Barrett, Terry R., and Jane B. Etheridge. "Verbal Hallucinations in Normals I: People Who Hear 'Voices.'" *Applied Cognitive Psychology* 6, no. 5 (1992): 379–87.
Barrett, William Fletcher. *Death-Bed Visions*. London: Methuen, 1926.
Beavan, Vanessa, John Read, and Claire Cartwright. "The Prevalence of Voice-Hearers in the General Population: A Literature Review." *Journal of Mental Health* 20, no. 3 (2011): 281–92.
Bem, Daryl J. "Feeling the Future: Experimental Evidence for Anomalous Retroactive Influences on Cognition and Affect." *Journal of Personality and Social Psychology* 100, no. 3 (2011): 407–25.
Bem, Daryl, Patrizio E. Tressoldi, Thomas Rabeyron, and Michael Duggan. "Feeling the Future: A Meta-Analysis of 90 Experiments on the Anomalous Anticipation of Random Future Events." *F1000Research* 4 (2016): 1188. https://doi.org/10.12688/f1000research.7177.2.
Bevington, G. C. *Remarkable Miracles*. South Plainfield, NJ: Bridge, 1992.
Black Elk, and Joseph Epes Brown. *The Sacred Pipe*. Norman: University of Oklahoma Press, 1953.
Black Elk, Wallace H., and William S. Lyon. *Black Elk: The Sacred Ways of a Lakota*. New York: HarperOne, 1990.
Blackmore, Susan J. *Consciousness: A Very Short Introduction*. Oxford: Oxford University Press, 2005.
Blake, William. *The Marriage of Heaven and Hell: A Facsimile in Full Color*. New York: Dover, 2012.
Blum, Deborah. *Ghost Hunters: William James and the Search for Scientific Proof of Life After Death*. New York: Penguin, 2007.
Braude, Stephen E. *Immortal Remains: The Evidence for Life after Death*. Lanham, MD: Rowman & Littlefield, 2003.
Bucko, Raymond A. *The Lakota Ritual of the Sweat Lodge: History and Contemporary Practice*. Lincoln: University of Nebraska Press, 1998.
Bush, Nancy Evans. "Distressing Western Near-Death Experiences: Finding a Way through the Abyss." In *The Handbook of Near-Death Experiences: Thirty Years of Investigation*, edited by Janice Miner Holden, Bruce Greyson, and Debbie James, 63–86. Santa Barbara, CA: Praeger, 2009.
Cardeña, Etzel, and Carlos S. Alvarado. "Anomalous Self and Identity Experiences." In *Varieties of Anomalous Experience: Examining the Scientific Evidence*, edited by Etzel Cardeña, Steven Jay Lynn, and Stanley Krippner, 175–212. Washington, D.C: American Psychological Association, 2014.

References

Charland-Verville, Vanessa, Jean-Pierre Jourdan, Marie Thonnard, Didier Ledoux, Anne-Francoise Donneau, Etienne Quertemont, and Steven Laureys. "Near-Death Experiences in Non-Life-Threatening Events and Coma of Different Etiologies." *Frontiers in Human Neuroscience* 8 (2014): 1–8.
Crabtree, Adam. *Multiple Man: Explorations in Possession and Multiple Personality.* New York: Praeger, 1985.
Daalman, Kirstin, and Kelly M. Diederen. "A Final Common Pathway to Hearing Voices: Examining Differences and Similarities in Clinical and Non-Clinical Individuals." *Psychosis* 5, no. 3 (2013): 236–46.
Eckhart, Meister, and Maurice O'C Walshe. *The Complete Mystical Works of Meister Eckhart.* New York: Crossroad, 2009.
Ellenberger, H.F. *The Discovery of the Unconscious: The History and Evolution of Dynamic Psychiatry.* New York: Basic Books, 1970.
Falcon, Andrea. "Aristotle on Causality," March 7, 2019. https://plato.stanford.edu/entries/aristotle-causality/.
Feather, Sally Rhine, and Michael Schmicker. *The Gift.* New York: St. Martin's, 2006.
Fink, David Harold. *Release from Nervous Tension.* New York: Simon & Schuster, 1953.
Foerster, Werner. *Gnosis: A Selection of Gnostic Texts, Vol. 2: Coptic and Mandean Sources.* Oxford: Clarendon Press, 1974.
Fontana, David. *Is There an Afterlife?* Ropley: O Books, 2010.
Fontana, David. "A Responsive Poltergeist: A Case from South Wales." *Journal of the Society for Psychical Research* 57 (1991): 385–403.
Fontana, David. "The Responsive South Wales Poltergeist: A Follow-Up Report." *Journal of the Society for Psychical Research* 58 (1992): 225–31.
Foster, Ryan D., Deborah Lee, and Ann Grau Duvall. "Two Cases of Spontaneous Mediumship Experiences of near-Death Experiencers." *Journal of Near-Death Studies* 34, no. 1 (2015): 44–54.
Galak, Jeff, Robyn A. Leboeuf, Leif D. Nelson, and Joseph P. Simmons. "Correcting the Past: Failures to Replicate Psi." *SSRN Electronic Journal*, 2012. https://doi.org/10.2139/ssrn.2001721.
Gauld, A., and A D Cornell. *Poltergeists.* London: Routledge & Kegan Paul, 1979.
Goetz, Stewart, and Charles Taliaferro. *A Brief History of the Soul.* Malden, MA: Wiley-Blackwell, 2011.
Greyson, Bruce. "Implications of Near-Death Experiences for a Postmaterialist Psychology." *Psychology of Religion and Spirituality* 2, no. 1 (2010): 37–45.
Greyson, Bruce. "Incidence and Correlates of Near-Death Experiences in a Cardiac Care Unit." *General Hospital Psychiatry* 25, no. 4 (2003): 269–76.
Greyson, Bruce. "Increase in Psychic Phenomena Following Near-Death Experiences." *Theta* 11, no. 2 (1983): 26–29.
Greyson, Bruce. "Near-Death Experience." In *Varieties of Anomalous Experience: Examining the Scientific Evidence*, edited by Etzel Cardeña, 333–68. Washington, D.C.: American Psychological Association, 2014.
Greyson, Bruce. "Near-Death Experience." In *Varieties of Anomalous Experience: Examining the Scientific Evidence*, second edition, edited by Etzel Cardeña, Steven Jay Lynn, and Stanley Krippner, 333–68. Washington, D.C.: American Psychological Association, 2014.
Greyson, Bruce, and Nancy Evans Bush. "Distressing Near-Death Experiences." *Psychiatry* 55, no. 1 (1992): 95–110.
Griffin, David Ray. *Parapsychology, Philosophy, and Spirituality: A Postmodern Exploration.* Albany: State University of New York Press, 1997.
Grof, Stanislav, and Christina Grof. *Spiritual Emergency: When Personal Transformation Becomes a Crisis.* Los Angeles: TarcherPerigree, 1989.
Gurney, E., and F.W.H. Myers. "On Apparitions Occurring Soon After Death." *Proceedings of the Society for Psychical Research* 5 (1888): 403–85.

References

Gurney, Edmund, F.W.H. Myers, and Frank Podmore. *Phantasms of the Living.* Cambridge: Cambridge University Press, 1886.

Holden, Janice Miner. "Veridical Perception in Near-Death Experiences." In *The Handbook of Near-Death Experiences: Thirty Years of Investigation*, edited by Janice Miner Holden, Bruce Greyson, and Debbie James, 185–211. Santa Barbara, CA: Praeger, 2009.

Holden, Janice Miner, Ryan D. Foster, and Lee Kinsey. "Spontaneous Mediumship Experiences: A Neglected Aftereffect of Near-Death Experiences." *Journal of Near-Death Studies* 33, no. 2 (2014): 67–84.

Holy Bible: New International Version. Grand Rapids: Zondervan, 2017.

Hood, Ralph W. "Mysticism and the Paranormal." In *Miracles: God, Science, and Psychology in the Paranormal*, edited by J. Harold Ellens, Vol. 3:16–37. Westport, CT: Praeger, 2008.

Howarth, Glennys, and Allan Kellehear. "Shared Near-Death and Related Illness Experiences: Steps on an Unscheduled Journey." *Journal of Near-Death Studies* 20, no. 2 (2001): 71–85.

Hufford, David. *The Terror That Comes in the Night: An Experience-Centered Study of Supernatural Assault Traditions.* Philadelphia: University of Pennsylvania Press, 1982.

Huxley, Aldous. *The Doors of Perception.* New York: Harper Perennial, 2009.

Jackson, Mike, and K.W.M. Fulford. "Spiritual Experience and Psychopathology." *Philosophy, Psychiatry, & Psychology* 4, no. 1 (1997): 41–65.

James, William. "Address of the President Before the Society for Psychical Research." In *Essays in Psychical Research*, 127–37. Cambridge: Harvard University Press, 1986.

James, William. "A Record of Observations of Certain Phenomena of Trance." In *Essays in Psychical Research*, 79–88. Cambridge: Harvard University Press, 1986.

James, William. *The Varieties of Religious Experience: A Study in Human Nature.* New York: Modern Library, 1994.

Jung, C.G., and W. Pauli. *The Interpretation of Nature and the Psyche.* New York: Pantheon Books, 1955.

Jung, C.G., Jaffé Aniela, and Richard Winston. *Memories, Dreams, Reflections.* New York: Vintage, 1963.

Kelly, Emily Williams. "Psychophysiological Influence." In *Irreducible Mind: Toward a Psychology for the 21st Century*, edited by Edward F. Kelly et. al., 132–48. Lanham, MD: Rowman & Littlefield, 2010.

Kelly, Emily Williams, Bruce Greyson, and Edward F. Kelly. "Unusual Experiences Near Death and Related Phenomena." In *Irreducible Mind: Toward a Psychology for the 21st Century*, edited by Edward F. Kelly et. al., 367–421. Lanham, MD: Rowman & Littlefield, 2010.

Kohr, R. L. "Near-Death Experience and Its Relationship to Psi and Various Altered States." *Theta* 10 (1982): 50–53.

Landis, Carney. *Varieties of Psychopathological Experience.* New York, 1964.

Landmark, J., H. Merskey, Z. Cernovsky, and E. Helmes. "The Positive Triad of Schizophrenic Symptoms." *British Journal of Psychiatry* 156, no. 3 (1990): 388–94.

Leahey, Thomas Hardy. *A History of Psychology: Main Currents in Psychological Thought.* Upper Saddle River, NJ: Prentice Hall, 2010.

Liester, Michell B. "Inner Voices: Distinguishing Transcendent and Pathological Characteristics." *The Journal of Transpersonal Psychology* 28, no. 1 (1996): 1–30.

Margnelli, Marco. "An Unusual Case of Stigmatization." *Journal of Scientific Exploration* 13, no. 3 (1999): 461–82.

Marshall, Paul. "The Psychical and the Mystical: Boundaries, Connections, Common Origins." *Journal for the Society for Psychical Research* 75, no. 1 (2011): 1–13.

Mays, Robert G., and Suzanne B. Mays. "Explaining Near-Death Experiences: Physical or Non-Physical Causation?" *Journal of Near-Death Studies* 33, no. 3 (2015): 125–49.

References

McMoneagle, Joseph. *The Stargate Chronicles: Memoirs of a Psychic Spy.* Newburyport, MA: Hampton Roads, 2002.
McNamee, Gregory. "The Explosion of Mount St. Helens," 2007. http://blogs.britannica.com/2007/05/the-explosion-of-mount-st-helens/.
Meyer, Marvin W., James M. Robinson, Elaine H. Pagels, Wolf-Peter Funk, and Paul-Hubert Poirier. *The Nag Hammadi Scriptures: The Revised and Updated Translation of Sacred Gnostic Texts Complete in One Volume.* New York: HarperOne, 2009.
Moody, Raymond A. *Life After Life: The Investigation of a Phenomenon—Survival of Bodily Death.* New York: HarperCollins, 2001.
Moody, Robert L. "Bodily Changes During Abreaction." *The Lancet* 248, no. 6435 (1946): 934–35.
Moody, Robert L. "Bodily Changes During Abreaction." *The Lancet* 251, no. 6512 (1948): 964.
Myers, Frederic W. H. *Human Personality and Its Survival of Bodily Death.* New York: Longmans, Green, 1903.
Noyes, Russell. "The Human Experience of Death or, What Can We Learn from Near-Death Experiences?" *OMEGA—Journal of Death and Dying* 13, no. 3 (1983): 251–59.
Pagels, Elaine. *The Gnostic Gospels.* New York: Random House, 1979.
Parnia, Sam, Ken Spearpoint, Gabriele De Vos, Peter Fenwick, Diana Goldberg, Jie Yang, Jiawen Zhu, et al. "AWARE—AWAreness During REsuscitation—A Prospective Study." *Resuscitation* 85, no. 12 (2014): 1799–1805.
Pattie, F.A., Jr. "The Production of Blisters by Hypnotic Suggestion: a Review." *The Journal of Abnormal and Social Psychology* 36, no. 1 (1941): 62–72.
Paul, Gordon L. "The Production of Blisters by Hypnotic Suggestion: Another Look." *Psychosomatic Medicine* 25, no. 3 (1963): 233–44.
Pierre, Joseph M. "Hallucinations in Nonpsychotic Disorders." *Harvard Review of Psychiatry* 18, no. 1 (2010): 22–35.
Plato, and Desmond Lee. *Plato the Republic.* New York: Penguin, 1987.
Ring, Kenneth. *Heading Toward Omega.* New York: Wm. Morrow, 1984.
Ring, Kenneth. *Life at Death.* New York: Coward, McCann & Geoghegan, 1980.
Rivas, Titus, Anny Dirven, Rudolf Smit, Stan Michielsens, Janice Miner. Holden, and Wanda Boeke. *The Self Does Not Die: Verified Paranormal Phenomena from Near-Death Experiences.* Durham: IANDS, 2016.
Roll, William. "On Apparitions and Mediumship: an Examination of the Evidence That Personal Consciousness Persists After Death." In *The Survival of Human Consciousness*, edited by Lance Storm and Michael A. Thalbourne, 142–73. Jefferson, NC: McFarland, 2006
Sabom, Michael B. *Light & Death: One Doctor's Fascinating Account of near-Death Experiences.* Grand Rapids, MI: Zondervan, 1998.
Sabom, Michael B. *Recollections of Death: A Medical Investigation.* New York: Simon & Schuster, 1982.
Schwartz, Stephan A. "Through Time and Space: The Evidence for Remote Viewing." In *Evidence for Psi: Thirteen Empirical Research Reports*, edited by Damien Broderick and Ben Goertzel, 332–426. Jefferson, NC: McFarland, 2015.
Schwartz, Stephan A. "Through Time and Space: The Evidence for Remote Viewing." In *Evidence for Psi: Thirteen Empirical Research Reports*, edited by Damien Broderick and Ben Goertzel, 168–212. Jefferson, NC: McFarland, 2015.
Sebel, Peter S., T. Andrew Bowdle, Mohamed M. Ghoneim, Ira J. Rampil, Roger E. Padilla, Tong Joo Gan, and Karen B. Domino. "The Incidence of Awareness During Anesthesia: A Multicenter United States Study." *Anesthesia & Analgesia* 99, no. 3 (2004): 833–39.
Shopkow, Leah. "The First Life of St. Francis." Accessed June 18, 2019. http://www.indiana.edu/~dmdhist/francis.htm.
Sidgwick, H., A. Johnson, F.W.H. Myers, F Podmore, and E.M. Sidgwick. "Report on the

References

"Census of Hallucinations." *Proceedings for the Society for Psychical Research* 10 (1894): 25–422.
Simmons, Dan. *Ilium*. New York: HarperCollins, 2005.
Simpson, C J. "The Stigmata: Pathology or Miracle?" *British Medical Journal* 289, no. 6460 (1984): 1746–48.
Sims, Andrew. "Commentary on 'Spiritual Experience and Psychopathology.'" *Philosophy, Psychiatry, & Psychology* 4, no. 1 (1997): 79–81.
Smith, Daniel B. *Muses, Madmen, and Prophets Rethinking the History, Science, and Meaning of Auditory Hallucination*. New York: Penguin, 2007.
Smith, Paul H. *Reading the Enemy's Mind: Inside Star Gate, America's Psychic Espionage Program*. New York: Forge Books, 2005.
Stace, W.T. *Mysticism and Philosophy*. London: Macmillan, 1961.
Stace, W.T. *Teachings of the Mystics*. New York: New American Library, 1960.
Stevenson, Ian. *Reincarnation and Biology: A Contribution to the Etiology of Birthmarks and Birth Defects*. Westport, CT: Praeger, 1997.
Sutherland, Cherie. "Psychic Phenomena Following Near-Death Experiences: An Australian Study." *Journal of Near-Death Studies* 8, no. 2 (1989).
Sutherland, Cherie. *Transformed by the Light: Life After Near-Death Experiences*. Sydney: Bantam, 1992.
Tart, C.T. "A Psychophysiological Study of out-of-the-Body Experiences in a Selected Subject." *Journal for the American Society for Psychical Research* 62 (1968): 3–27.
Teresa, St., and E. Allison Peers. *Interior Castle*. Bottom of the Hill, 2010.
Thalbourne, M.A. "Psychiatry, the Mystical, and the Paranormal." *Journal of Parapsychology* 70 (2006): 143–65.
Thurston, Herbert, and J.H. Crehan. *The Physical Phenomena of Mysticism*. Chicago: Henry Regnery, 1952.
Tillich, Paul. *Dynamics of Faith*. New York: Perennial, 2001.
Treffert, Darold A. *Islands of Genius: The Bountiful Mind of the Autistic, Acquired, and Sudden Savant*. London: Jessica Kingsley, 2010.
Twiss, Sumner B., and Walter H. Conser. *Experience of the Sacred: Readings in the Phenomenology of Religion*. Hanover, NH: University Press of New England, 1998.
Underhill, Evelyn. *Mysticism: A Study in the Nature and Development of Man's Spiritual Consciousness*. London: Methuen, 1911.
van Lommel, Pim, Ruud Van Wees, Vincent Meyers, and Ingrid Elfferich. "Near-Death Experience in Survivors of Cardiac Arrest: A Prospective Study in the Netherlands." *The Lancet* 358, no. 9298 (2001): 2039–45.
Wiebe, Phillip H. *God and Other Spirits: Intimations of Transcendence in Christian Experience*. New York: Oxford University Press, 2004.
Wilson, William P. "How Religious or Spiritual Miracle Events Happen Today." In *Miracles: God, Science, and Psychology in the Paranormal*, edited by J Harold Ellens, Vol. 1: 264–79. Westport, CT: Praeger, 2008.
Woerlee, G.M. "Could Pam Reynolds Hear? A New Investigation into the Possibility of Hearing During This Famous Near-Death Experience." *Journal of Near-Death Studies* 30, no. 1 (2011): 3–25.
Zisook, Sidney, Desiree Byrd, and Dilip V. Jeste. "Command Hallucinations in Outpatients with Schizophrenia." *Journal of Clinical Psychiatry* 56, no. 10 (1995): 462–65.

Index

Adam, alternate story of creation 85-87; see also Betty
agrace 47
Akalian 116-117, 120, 124
angels 29-30, 35, 36-37, 103, 141
answered prayer 64, 106
Ari 34-35
Auras 99-100, 124-125, 151, 157

benign hallucination 23
Beth 71-72
Betty 5-17, 24-25, 64-87, 172-176
biofeedback 75
Black Elk, Wallace 113

Carol 93-111, 121-125, 147-154
Challenger disaster 15-17
collective unconscious 81, 90
command hallucination 27-29
The Creation of Man 87
cured of cancer 8-10; see also Betty

Damascus Way 59
Damon 20-23
Daryl 158-159
deathbed visions 103-104
Debra 46-48
demons 107-108, 137-140, 142-146
Descartes, Rene 69
Doors of Perception 170
the dove 62-63

Eckhart, Meister 18, 170
evil spirits *see* demons
Ezekiel 171

faith healing 61-62
Fink, David Harold *see* *Release from Nervous Tension*
four horseman ceremony 114

ghosts (of the deceased) 25-28, 101-102, 131-134, 156-157, 164-165
The Gnostic Gospels 88, 89
The Gnostics 87
God Allie 84-85, 87, 88
God Jehovah 83, 88

Hodgson, Richard 166-167
Huxley, Aldous see *Doors of Perception*

I Am (Biblical reference) 12, 18
Illium 17

James 70-71
James, William 2, 3, 39-40, 168-169
Jean 33-34
Jesus, vision of 11-12, 66-68; see also Betty
Jung, C.G. 90

Karen (and Judy) 35-37
Kennedy, John F. 15

"Dr. L" 23-24
Leah 38-39
Linda 60-61
Lisa 76-79
Loretta 57-64

manna from heaven 18, 87
Melissa 35-38
Monica 44-46, 127-146, 155-157, 159-163
Mount St. Helens 13-15

Nag Hammadi 88
NDE *see* near death experience
near death experience 40-56, 74-76, 93-98, 110-112, 134-136
9/11 15

Index

OBE *see* Out of body experience
Ockham's razor 174
out of body experience 46-48, 51-53 70-72, 74-76, 83-85; *see also* near death experience

Pagels, Elaine 89
Palora, trip to 82-85; *see also* Betty
Paul (the medium) 117-119, 120
Piper, Leonora 166-168
Plain Error (the god) 85, 89
Plato's ideal realm 97
possession 107, 160-161
powwow 112
precognition *see* visions of the future

quantum reality 174

Raymond (and Grandpa Johansson) 29-32
Red Fox, Ralph 114, 121
Release from Nervous Tension 72
remote viewing 79-80
Revelation 22:13 59
Richard 41-44, 110-126, 147-154

St. Teresa 19
Sandra 50-56, 125-126

science of religions 169, 173
Sean 39
The Secret Book of John 88
Shannon 48-50
Simmons, Dan *see Illium*
The Society for Psychical Research 2, 3
Sophia (the god) 84, 88
soul travel 77-79, 151-153
spirit guides 105, 115-116, 118, 120, 126, 148, 152
spirit of the stone 113
spirit procedures 68; *see also* Betty
spirit sister 116
spiritual presence 158-159
stigmata 136-138
sweat lodge 112-113

The Varieties of Religious Experience 3, 169
visions of the future 10, 14-17, 24-25, 27-29, 123

Wakan Tanka (the great mystery) 112
White Buffalo Calf Woman 113-114
White Cloud (Richard's spirit guide) 115-116, 120

Yaldabaoth 89

www.ingramcontent.com/pod-product-compliance
Ingram Content Group UK Ltd.
Pitfield, Milton Keynes, MK11 3LW, UK
UKHW042008140426
5217IPUK00015B/1051